Social Science

Class 06

Social Science

Class 06

Authors
Shruti Sharma
Saumya Aggarwal

ARIHANT PRAKASHAN

(School Division Series)

ADMINISTRATIVE & PRODUCTION OFFICES

Regd. Office

'Ramchhaya' 4577/15, Agarwal Road, Darya Ganj, New Delhi -110002
Tele: 011- 47630600, 43518550; Fax: 011- 23280316

Head Office

Kalindi, TP Nagar, Meerut (UP) - 250002, Tel: 0121-7156203, 7156204

SALES & SUPPORT OFFICES

Agra, Ahmedabad, Bengaluru, Bareilly, Chennai, Delhi, Guwahati, Hyderabad, Jaipur, Jhansi, Kolkata, Lucknow, Nagpur & Pune.

PO No. : TXT-59-T071508-6-26

Published By Arihant Publications (India) Ltd.

For further information about the books published by Arihant, log on to www.arihantbooks.com or e-mail at info@arihantbooks.com

Follow us on    

PRICE ₹250.00

PRODUCTION TEAM

Publishing Managers
Mahendra Singh Rawat & Keshav Mohan

Project Coordinator
Shivam Gupta

Cover Designer
Bilal Hashmi

Inner Designer
Ankit Prajapati

Page Layouting
Sundar Bisht

Proof Reader
Sundip

Inside the Book

Key Features

Social Science Class 6

Chapter Intro

A quick information about the coverage of the chapter to explain students about what they are going to study.

CHAPTER 1

Locating Places on the Earth

Maps are graphical representations of various geographical areas, essential for understanding natural features, political boundaries and thematic information. Components of the map include distance, direction and symbols, along with latitude and longitude, to provide accurate and detailed insights into the Earth's surface and time zones.

Must Know

Additional but informational matter related to given concept. It helps & motivate students to explore more beyond their books.

Must Know !

The boundaries of the Indian Ocean are around Asia to the North, Africa to the West and Australia to the East, apart from the Southern Ocean in the South.

Boxed Matter

Information given in the boxes cover some important facts related to the concept given.

Indian Prime Meridian

- The Greenwich Meridian is not the first prime meridian.
- Many centuries ago India had a prime meridian of its own. It was called **Madhya rekha** (or 'middle line'). It passed through the city of **Ujjayini.** (today Ujjain). It was a reputed centre for astronomy for many centuries. A famous astronomer, **Varahamihira** lived and worked there some 1,500 years ago.

Try These

1. What kind of map would you use to identify the location of rivers and mountains?
2. If you need to understand the political boundaries of different states in India, which type of map would you look for?
3. When looking at a map, how could one determine the real-world distance between two points?

Try These

A set of 3-5 Questions given in between the text, helps students to remain connected with the text while studying. They can instantly assess themselves for their understanding.

Key Features

NCERT Folder

To make students completely understand NCERT books, answers of all the NCERT Exercises have been given in each chapter in NCERT Folder. Accuracy, Detailing and Simplicity of Answers are the major features of this section.

NCERT FOLDER

Detailed Answers of All NCERT Questions

Let's Explore (Page 9)

Q.1 On the map given below

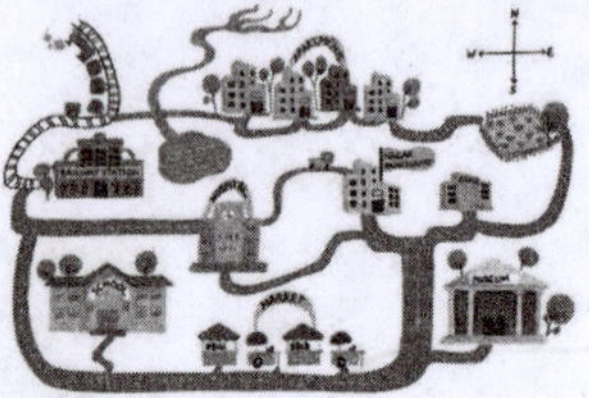

(a) Mark the hospital.

Ans. Do it yourself.

(b) What is the meaning of the blue-coloured areas?

Ans. The blue-coloured areas on the map show the water bodies like rivers and ponds.

(c) Which is farther away from the railway station, the school, the Nagar Panchayat or the public garden?

Ans. The public garden is farthest away from the railway station.

Let's Explore (Page 11)

Q.4 Consider the map of the small city again. Identify the correct and incorrect statements in the list below.

(a) The market is North of the hospital.

Ans. Incorrect

(b) The museum is South-East of the bank.

Ans. Incorrect

(c) The railway station is North-West of the hospital.

Ans. Correct

(d) The lake is North-West of the apartment blocks.

Ans. Correct

Don't Miss Out (Page 17)

Q.5 If the globe or atlas in your class has well-marked latitudes and longitudes, try to note down approximate values for the latitude and longitude of (1) Mumbai, (2) Kolkata, (3) Singapore, (4) Paris.

Ans. (1) Mumbai: 19° N latitude and 72° E longitude

(2) Kolkata: 23° N latitude and 88° E longitude

(3) Singapore: 1° N latitude and 104° E longitude

(4) Paris: 49° N latitude and 2° E longitude

Let's Explore (Page 21)

Q.6 Return to the two friends sitting in Gujarat and Assam. Use this example to explain the difference between local time and standard time.

Glossary

Meaning or definition of important words/terms given on the pages.

Glossary

Axis The Earth's axis is an imaginary line that runs from the North Pole to the South Pole, around which the Earth rotates.

Equator The Equator is an imaginary line around the middle of the Earth, at an equal distance from the North and South Poles, dividing the Earth into the Northern and Southern Hemispheres.

Globe A globe is a spherical model of Earth that accurately represents its continents, oceans and geographical features.

Grid lines Grid lines are the network of intersecting horizontal and vertical lines on maps and globes used to locate a particular place.

Mind Map

A quick revision visual tool for the complete chapter.

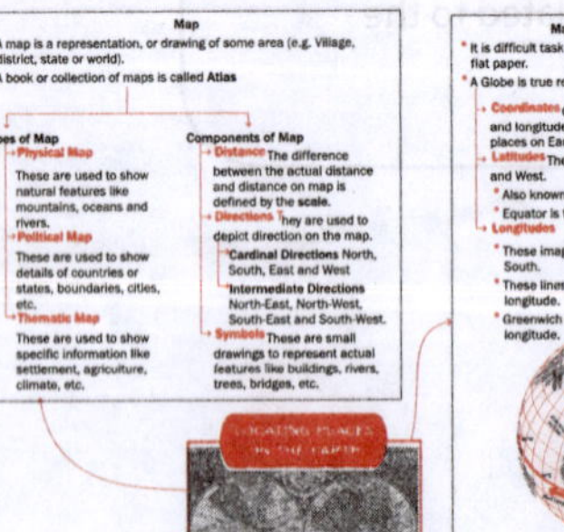

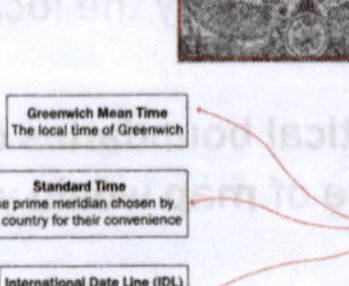

Locating Places on the Earth

CHAPTER 1

Maps are graphical representations of various geographical areas, essential for understanding natural features, political boundaries and thematic information. Components of the map include distance, direction and symbols, along with latitude and longitude, to provide accurate and detailed insights into the Earth's surface and time zones.

1.1 Map

- A **map** is a representation, or a drawing, of an area. A map can be drawn for a small area (a village, a town, etc.), a bigger area (district or state), or a vast area like India or even the whole world.
- An **Atlas** is a book or collection of maps.
- There are several kinds of maps. These are as follows
  (i) **Physical Maps** Physical maps are used to show natural features such as mountains, oceans and rivers.
  (ii) **Political Maps** Such maps show details of countries or states, boundaries, cities, etc. For example, a map of India with all its States, Union Territories and their capitals.
  (iii) **Thematic Maps** These maps are used to show specific kind of information. For example, settlements and transportation.

Components of Map

There are three important components of maps i.e. distance, direction and symbols.

(i) Distance

- The actual distance between two points on the map depends on the **scale**. The scale is represented in the bottom left corner of the map.
- Each centimetre on the map represents a certain distance on the ground. For example; we say that the scale is 1 cm = 500 m. This means every 1 cm on the map is equal to 500 m on the ground.

(ii) Direction

- The arrow at the top right of the map is used to point the direction. Most maps simply have an arrow marked with the letter 'N', which points to the North direction.
- By moving the map in a clockwise direction one can locate, the East, South and West directions. These are called the **cardinal directions** or **cardinal points**. Other than these, **intermediate directions** are also used. These are North-East (NE), South-East (SE), South-West (SW) and North-West (NW).

(iii) Symbols

- Symbols are small drawings and representations on the map of large physical structures on the ground. All the elements like building cannot be drawn on the map of a large city or a country, thus, symbols are used for representing these elements on the map.
- The symbols are used to represent features such as railways, roads, police stations, hospitals, trees, lakes, ponds, etc. In this way, numerous details can be shown in the limited space available on a map.

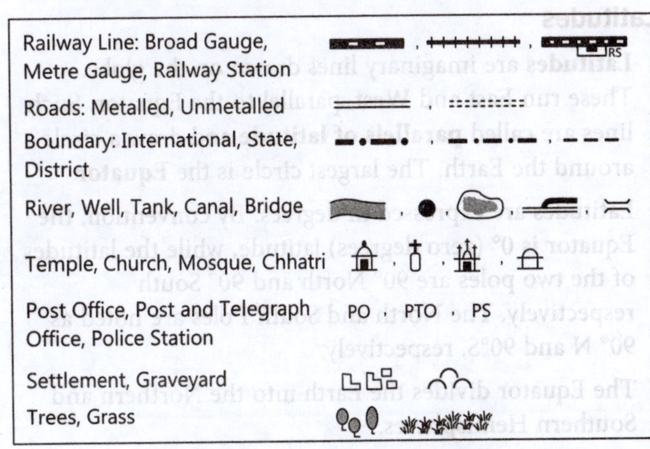

Some Common Symbols used on Map

- Different countries use different sets of symbols. Specific symbols are used by mapmakers to make maps more easily understood by different users. You can notice several symbols in the map given below that show trees, roads, railway tracks and houses.
- The **Survey of India** has fixed a set of symbols for maps of India (or parts of India).

Try These

1. **What kind of map would you use to identify the location of rivers and mountains?**
2. **If you need to understand the political boundaries of different states in India, which type of map would you look for?**
3. **When looking at a map, how could one determine the real-world distance between two points?**

1.2 Mapping the Earth

- A **globe** is used for actual representation of the Earth, then a flat map.
- Mapping the Earth is difficult because our planet is not a flat surface. It nearly has the shape of a sphere or it is not a perfect sphere. Representing a sphere accurately on a flat sheet of paper is not possible.
- When a spherical surface is flattened, distortions occur in the size, shape, distance and direction of landmasses. In this, the actual representation of the Earth and its features gets disrupted. Thus, the globe is used for mapping the Earth because both the Earth and the globe have the same spherical shape.

Understanding Coordinates

A system of **coordinates** is used in the world of maps to determine the location of any place on a map. This includes **latitudes** and **longitudes**.

Latitudes

- **Latitudes** are imaginary lines drawn on the globe. These run East and West, parallel to the Equator. Such lines are called **parallels of latitude** and draw a circle around the Earth. The largest circle is the **Equator**.
- Latitudes are expressed in degrees. By convention, the Equator is 0° (zero degrees) latitude, while the latitudes of the two poles are 90° North and 90° South respectively. The North and South Poles are noted as 90° N and 90°S, respectively.
- The Equator divides the Earth into the Northern and Southern Hemispheres.
- It is easy to identify the **North Pole** and the **South Pole** on the globe. The fixed points at the top and bottom are the two poles.
- The North Pole and South Pole are at an equal distance from the **Equator**. As we move towards the pole, the distance between us and the Equator increases.
- There is a relationship between latitude and climate. Near the Equator, the climate is generally **hot** (also called **torrid**).
- As we move away from the Equator towards one of the two poles, the climate becomes more **moderate** (or **temperate**). As we move closer to the North or South Pole, the climate becomes **colder** (or 'frigid').

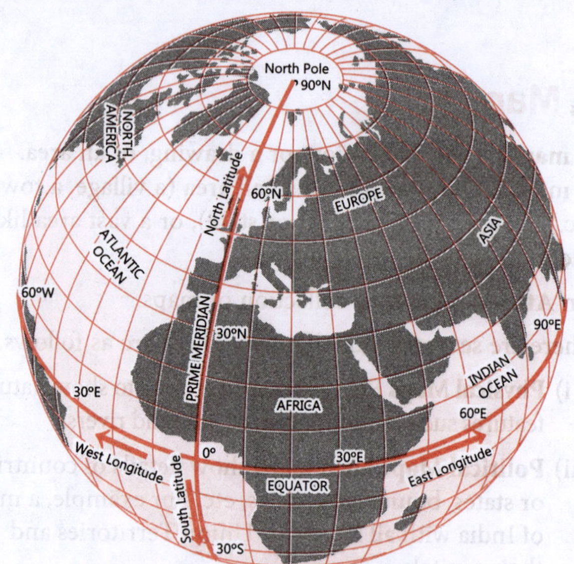

This globe shows both parallels of latitude and meridians of longitudes

Longitudes

- The imaginary lines of half-circles running from one pole to the other are called **meridians of longitude.**
- To measure longitudes, we need to define a reference point called the **Prime Meridian**. It is also called **Greenwich Meridian** because, in the year 1884, some nations decided that the meridian passing through Greenwich, an area of London in England, would become the international standard for the Prime Meridian. It is marked as 0° longitude.
- The Prime Meridian divides the Earth into the Western and Eastern Hemispheres.
- While latitude is a measure of the distance from the Equator if you travel towards one of the poles, longitude is a measure of the distance from the Prime Meridian.

- Longitude is also measured in degrees. Longitudes are measured in the East and West directions. The values of longitudes are between 0° to 180°. For example, New York is located on 74°W longitude, while Delhis is 77°E and Tokyo is 140°E.
- By measuring the longitude of a place, we can also measure the time at that place.
- By slowly rotating the globe Eastward, we can note that for some places on the Earth, it is morning, while for others it is midday, evening or night.

Grid Lines

- Latitude and longitude together are the two coordinates of a place. With the help of these co-ordinates, we can locate any place on Earth.
- To locate a place on the Earth all the lines of latitudes and longitudes together constitute a grid for the globe. They are also called **grid lines**.
- 180°W and 180°E are the same longitude on the globe. Hence, this longitude is noted as 180°, without the letter W or E.

Indian Prime Meridian

- The Greenwich Meridian is not the first prime meridian.
- Many centuries ago India had a prime meridian of its own. It was called **Madhya rekha** (or 'middle line'). It passed through the city of **Ujjayini** (today Ujjain). It was a reputed centre for astronomy for many centuries. A famous astronomer, **Varahamihira** lived and worked there some 1,500 years ago.
- Indian astronomers were aware of concepts of latitude and longitude, including the need for a zero or prime meridian.
- The Ujjayini meridian became a reference for calculations in all Indian astronomical texts.

1.3 Understanding Time Zones

- The Earth rotates in a West to East direction around its **axis**. This one rotation takes 24 hours.
- Since a full rotation is 360 degrees, the earth turns 15 degrees each hour (15 degrees multiplied by 24 hours equals 360 degrees).
- Let's mark the meridians of longitude every 15 degrees. Starting from the Prime Meridian, we have 0°, 15°E, 30°E, 45°E and so on, up to 180°E. Each meridian represents one hour of local time. For example, if it is 12 pm (noon) at Greenwich (0°), it will be 1 pm at 15°E, 2 pm at 30°E and so on.

When moving Westward from the Prime Meridian, the time decreases. For example, it will be 11 am at 15°W and 10 am at 30°W. The same method can be used to calculate the local time of any place on the Earth.

- All these standard times are organised in time zones, which broadly follow the zones of 15°. The lines dividing the time zones are not straight. This is because they have to respect each country's standard time and, therefore, tend to follow international borders.
- Most countries adopt a standard time based on a meridian passing through them.
- As we move farther from the Greenwich Prime Meridian towards the East we are required to add hours to the Greenwich Mean Time (GMT). On the other hand, if we move towards the West we are supposed to subtract hours from the Greenwich Mean Time (GMT).
- **Indian Standard Time** (IST) is 5 hours 30 minutes (also noted as 5.5 hours) ahead of the local time at Greenwich (called Greenwich Mean Time or GMT).
- While the Prime Meridian was fixed at Greenwich, the opposite line at approximately 180° longitude is called the **International Date Line**. The +12 and the –12 time zones touch each other at this line.
- If we cross the International Date Line travelling Eastward, we have to subtract a day (say, from Monday to Sunday). On the other hand, if we cross it travelling Westward, we have to add a day (from Sunday to Monday).

Try These

1. **What is the significance of the Prime Meridian in determining global time zones?**
2. **If you cross the International Date Line from East to West, what changes will happen to the calendar date change?**
3. **What are grid lines?**

Glossary

Axis The Earth's axis is an imaginary line that runs from the North Pole to the South Pole, around which the Earth rotates.

Equator The Equator is an imaginary line around the middle of the Earth, at an equal distance from the North and South Poles, dividing the Earth into the Northern and Southern Hemispheres.

Globe A globe is a spherical model of Earth that accurately represents its continents, oceans and geographical features.

Grid lines Grid lines are the network of intersecting horizontal and vertical lines on maps and globes used to locate a particular place.

LOCATING PLACES ON THE EARTH

Map

- A map is a representation, or drawing of some area (e.g. Village, district, state or world).
- A book or collection of maps is called **Atlas**

Types of Map

- **Physical Map** These are used to show natural features like mountains, oceans and rivers.
- **Political Map** These are used to show details of countries or states, boundaries, cities, etc.
- **Thematic Map** These are used to show specific information like settlement, agriculture, climate, etc.

Components of Map

- **Distance** The difference between the actual distance and distance on map is defined by the **scale.**
- **Directions** They are used to depict direction on the map.
  - **Cardinal Directions** North, South, East and West
  - **Intermediate Directions** North-East, North-West, South-East and South-West.
- **Symbols** These are small drawings to represent actual features like buildings, rivers, trees, bridges, etc.

Mapping the Earth

- It is difficult task to map the spherical Earth on a flat paper.
- A Globe is true representation of Earth.
  - **Coordinates** Coordinates are set of latitudes and longitudes used precisely for locating places on Earth.
  - **Latitudes** These imaginary lines runs East and West.
    - Also known as parallels of latitudes.
    - Equator is the largest and 0° latitude.
  - **Longitudes**
    - These imaginary lines run from North to South.
    - These lines are also called meridians of longitude.
    - Greenwich meridian is marked as 0° longitude.

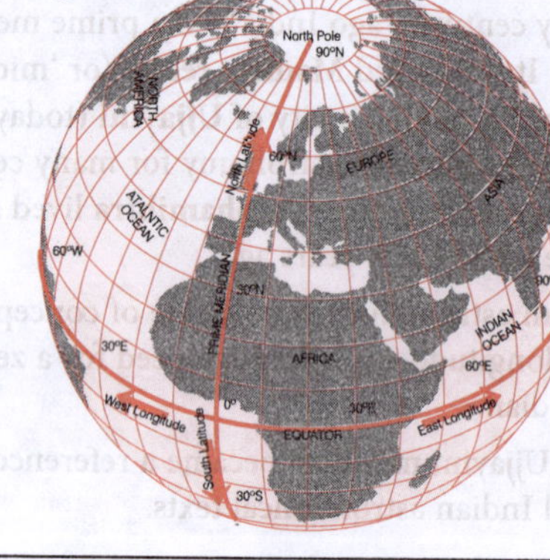

Understanding Time Zones

- Earth rotates on axis from East to West in 24 hours.
- A full turn is 360° hence, 15° per hour rotation is observed.
- Moving Eastward from prime meridian add one hour to local time with each meridian.
- Moving Westward from prime meridian subtracts one hour to local time on each meridian.

Greenwich Mean Time
The local time of Greenwich

Standard Time
The prime meridian chosen by the country for their convenience

International Date Line (IDL)
180° longitude is the International date line.

NCERT FOLDER

Detailed Answers of All NCERT Questions

Let's Explore (Page 9)

Q.1 On the map given below

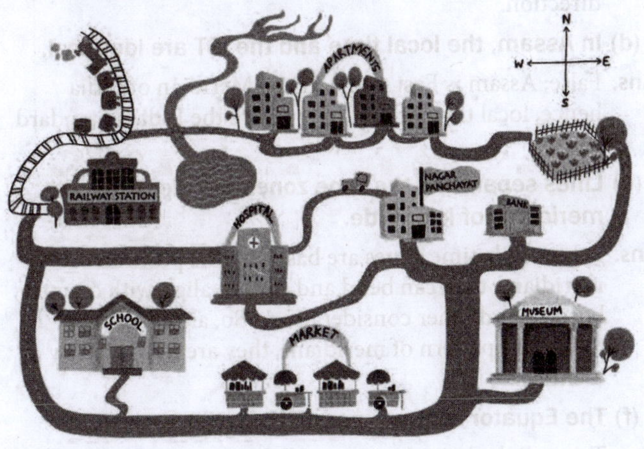

(a) Mark the hospital.

Ans. Do it yourself

(b) What is the meaning of the blue-coloured areas?

Ans. The blue-coloured areas on the map show the water bodies like rivers and ponds.

(c) Which is farther away from the railway station- the school, the Nagar Panchayat or the public garden?

Ans. The public garden is farthest away from the railway station.

Let's Explore (Page 10)

Q.2 Draw a simple map of a school's playground. Let us assume it is a rectangle, 40 m in length and 30 m in width. Draw it precisely with your ruler on a scale of 1 cm = 10 m.

Ans. When the scale is 1 cm =10 m, it means every 1 cm on the map is 10 m on the ground.

Q.3 Now measure the diagonal of the rectangle. How many centimetres do you get? Using the scale, calculate the real length of the playground's diagonal, in metres.

Ans. The diagonal of the rectangle measures 5 cm. With the given scale of 1 cm= 10 m, the real length of the playground's diagonal will be 50 m.

Let's Explore (Page 11)

Q.4 Consider the map of the small city again. Identify the correct and incorrect statements in the list below.

(a) The market is North of the hospital.

Ans. Incorrect

(b) The museum is South-East of the bank.

Ans. Incorrect

(c) The railway station is North-West of the hospital.

Ans. Correct

(d) The lake is North-West of the apartment blocks.

Ans. Correct

Don't Miss Out (Page 17)

Q.5 If the globe or atlas in your class has well-marked latitudes and longitudes, try to note down approximate values for the latitude and longitude of (1) Mumbai, (2) Kolkata, (3) Singapore, (4) Paris.

Ans. (1) Mumbai: 19° N latitude and 72° E longitude

(2) Kolkata: 23° N latitude and 88° E longitude

(3) Singapore: 1° N latitude and 104° E longitude

(4) Paris: 49° N latitude and 2° E longitude

Let's Explore (Page 21)

Q.6 Return to the two friends sitting in Gujarat and Assam. Use this example to explain the difference between local time and standard time.

Ans. One of the two friends is sitting in Porbandar (Gujarat) and the other in Tinsukia (Assam).

There is a difference in local time between both the two cities. Local time is the time based on the position of the Sun at a specific longitude or place. For example, since Assam is in the East of Gujarat, the Sun rises and sets earlier in Assam as compared to Gujarat.

Standard time on the other hand, is the official time set for a region or country, used to maintain uniformity. It is based on the standard meridian of the country. In India, both Gujarat and Assam follow Indian Standard Time (IST), which is the same across the country.

Questions, Activities and Projects

Q.1 Returning to page 10 and to Fig. 5.2 in Chapter 5 of this textbook, taking the scale to be 2.5 cm = 500 km, calculate the real distance from the estuary of the Narmada River to the estuary of the Ganga River. (Hint: round off your measurement on the map to an easy number.)

Ans. 1,000 km

Q.2 Why is it 5:30 pm in India when it is 12 pm or noon in London?

Ans. India is 5 hours and 30 minutes ahead of London because of the difference in time zones. The Earth is divided into 24 time zones and each time zone is 1 hour apart from its neighbouring time zones. Since India is to the East of London, it is ahead of time.

So, when it is 12:00 PM (noon) in London, it is already 5:30 PM in India.

Q.3 Why do we need symbols and colours in the map?

Ans. We need symbols and colours on a map to make it easier to represent the real features of the Earth. Symbols represent different features like cities, rivers, police stations and temples while colours help show different areas like countries, forests and oceans.

Q.4 Find out what you have in the eight directions from your home or school.

Ans. Do it yourself

Q.5 Draw a simple map showing the location of the Ujjayini meridian and its significance in ancient Indian astronomy.

Ans. Do it yourself

Q.6 Delhi's and Bengaluru's latitudes are 29°N and 13°N; their longitudes are almost the same, 77°E. How much will be the difference in local time between the two cities?

Ans. There will be no difference in the local times of the two cities. The difference in time depends on the difference in longitudes. If Delhi and Bengaluru are almost on the same longitude there will be no difference in local time between the two cities.

Q.7 Mark the following statements as true or false; explain your answers in a sentence or two.

(a) All parallels of latitude have the same length.

Ans. False; the size of latitude reduces as we move away from the Equator. This happens because of the Earth's spherical shape.

(b) The length of a meridian of longitude is half of that of the Equator.

Ans. True; since each meridian runs from pole to pole, they are all half the circumference of the Earth, while the Equator circles the entire Earth. Therefore, the length of a meridian of longitude is half of the length of the Equator.

(c) The South Pole has a latitude of 90°S.

Ans. True; the poles are marked as 90° and S shows the South direction.

(d) In Assam, the local time and the IST are identical.

Ans. False; Assam is East to the Prime Meridian of India hence, local time of Assam is before the Indian Standard Time.

(e) Lines separating the time zones are identical with meridians of longitude.

Ans. False; while time zones are based on the position of meridians, they can bend and shift to align with country borders and other considerations. So, although they follow the pattern of meridians, they are not perfectly identical.

(f) The Equator is also a parallel of latitude.

Ans. True; all the latitudes are parallel in nature.

Q.8 Solve the crossword below.

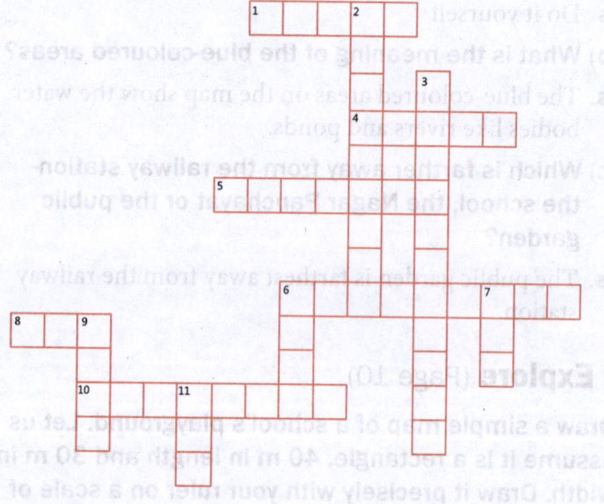

Across

1. Lets you squeeze a huge area into your map
4. A convenient sphere
5. The longest parallel of latitude
6. The place the Prime Meridian is attached to
8. So convenient to find your way
10. A measure of the distance from the Equator

Down

2. A measure of the distance from the Prime Meridian
3. These two together allow us to locate a place
6. What latitudes and longitudes together create
7. The time we all follow in India
9. These two are poles apart

11. An abbreviation for a line across which the day and date change

Ans. 1. Scale 2. Longitudes 3. Coordinates 4. Globe 5. Equator 6. Across- Greenwich, Down- Grid 7. IST 8. Map 9. Pole 10. Latitudes 11. IDL

REVIEW EXERCISE

Including Competency Based Questions

Part I

Very Short Answer Type Questions

1. What kind of representation might you use to see the layout of a country or even the whole world?

Ans. A map can be used to see the layout of a country or even the whole world.

2. Which term describes a book that contains multiple maps?

Ans. A book that contains multiple maps is called an Atlas.

3. Which type of map would detail political boundaries, cities and states?

Ans. The political map gives details of political boundaries, cities and states.

4. In a map, what component helps you understand how distances on the map relate to real world distances?

Ans. In a map, scale helps us to understand distance on the map and in the real world.

5. On a map, what term describes the four main directions as North, South, East and West?

Ans. The Cardinal direction is the term that is used to describe the four main directions.

6. If you wanted to locate a position using a grid system on a map, what system would you be using?

Ans. The system of coordinates is used to locate a position on a map.

7. What imaginary lines on the globe measure distance North or South of the Equator?

Ans. The latitudes on the globe measure the distance to the North or South of the Equator.

8. Which lines on the globe measure distances East or West from the Prime Meridian?

Ans. The longitudes measure the distances from East or West on the Prime Meridian.

9. What happens to the date when crossing the International Date Line from West to East?

Ans. When crossing the International Date Line from West to East, a day gets reduced.

Short Answer Type Questions

1. Explain how a map serves as a representation of different areas and what features it might include.

Ans. A map is a visual representation of a geographic area, made to depict various features of that region. It might include natural elements such as mountains, rivers and forests, and human-made structures like roads, cities, and boundaries. Maps often use symbols and colours to differentiate between types of information and may include a scale to represent distances accurately.

2. What distinguishes physical maps from political maps, and how does each type provide different types of information about a region?

Ans. Physical maps focus on natural features like mountains, rivers and plains, using colour and shading to highlight elevation and terrain. They give useful information for understanding the landscape. On the other hand, political maps focus on human-made boundaries such as countries, states and cities and include information about administrative divisions. Political maps are useful for recognising geopolitical boundaries and locations of settlements.

3. **How does the scale of a map impact the representation of distances? Illustrate using an example.**

Ans. The scale of a map defines the relationship between distances on the map and actual distances on the ground. For example, if a map has a scale of 1 cm = 10 m, it means that each centimetre on the map represents 10 meters in reality.

When drawing a playground map with a scale of 1 cm = 10 m, the playground's actual dimensions are represented proportionally, allowing for precise measurement and layout planning.

4. **Discuss how cardinal directions are used in maps and why they are important for navigation. Include an example of how you would use these directions in a practical situation.**

Ans. Cardinal directions (North, East, South and West) are used on maps to indicate orientation and help with navigation. They provide a framework for understanding relative locations and directions. For example, if a map indicates that a school is North of a park, we can use this information to navigate from the park to the school by heading North. These directions help users orient themselves and travel efficiently between locations.

5. **What is the significance of latitude and longitude in locating places on Earth and how do these coordinates work together to specify locations?**

Ans. Latitude and longitude are coordinates used to identify locations on Earth precisely.

Latitude measures the distance North or South of the Equator, while longitude measures the distance East or West of the Prime Meridian. Together, these coordinates provide a unique address for any point on the globe. For example, New York City is located at approximately 40.7°N latitude and 74.0°W longitude.

6. **Describe the role of the International Date Line in this system.**

Ans. The International Date Line, located approximately at 180° longitude, marks where the date changes by one day. It is the opposite line of the Prime Meridian. Crossing this line Eastward subtracts a day, while crossing Westward adds a day to the calendar. It deviates in places to avoid dividing some countries into two different days.

7. **How did historical practices, such as the use of the Ujjayini meridian, contribute to our current understanding of longitude and timekeeping?**

Ans. The Ujjayini meridian, was used in ancient Indian astronomy. It was an early reference for calculating longitude.

Indian astronomers, including Varahamihira, utilised this meridian to develop astronomical texts and timekeeping methods. Their understanding of longitude and the concept of a prime meridian influenced later practices and contributed to the development of modern timekeeping and longitude systems.

Long Answer Type Questions

1. **Discuss different types of maps and their specific uses.**

Ans. Maps are indispensable tools for understanding both geographical and political landscapes. The different types of maps are as follows

- Physical maps depict natural features such as mountains, rivers and forests, helping us comprehend the terrain and environment of a region.
- Political maps focus on human-made boundaries, showcasing countries, states and cities, which are crucial for understanding geopolitical divisions and administrative areas.
- Thematic maps present specific data like population density, climate patterns, or economic activities, providing insights into various aspects of human and natural phenomena.

2. **Analyse the importance of latitude and longitude in navigation and global positioning. Describe how these coordinates are used to locate places on Earth and explain their role in time zone determination.**

Ans. Latitude and longitude are essential for navigation and global positioning, forming a coordinate system that uniquely identifies any location on Earth. Latitude lines run parallel to the Equator, measuring distances North or South, while longitude lines run from the North to the South Pole, measuring distances East or West of the Prime Meridian.

These coordinates enable precise location pinpointing for navigation, aviation and mapping technologies like GPS. For example, the coordinates 40.7128°N (latitude) and 74.0060°W (longitude) identify New York City.

Additionally, longitude plays a key role in time zone determination. The Earth is divided into 24 time zones, each covering 15 degrees of longitude, aligning with the planet's 24-hour rotation cycle. As one travels East or West across these zones, local time changes by one hour for every 15-degree shift, ensuring synchronised time keeping globally.

Part-II

Multiple Choice Questions (MCQs)

1. What is a map?
(a) A projection
(b) A globe on paper
(c) A drawing of the Earth's surface on a flat paper
(d) None of the above

2. Which of the following is not a component of a map?
(a) Distance (b) Direction
(c) Sketch (d) Symbol

3. Scale is compulsory for
(a) a globe (b) a map
(c) a sketch (d) a symbol

4. The arrow with 'N' on the map is used to depict ....
(a) direction of North (b) direction of South
(c) direction of East (d) direction of West

5. Which one of the following is not an intermediate direction?
(a) North-West (b) South-West
(c) West (d) North-East

6. Cardinal points show the .... in the map.
(a) distance (b) area
(c) symbols (d) direction

7. There is an international agreement to use .... .
(a) national symbols (b) conventional symbols
(c) local symbols (d) None of these

8. Green colour in the map is used for showing
(a) mountains (b) rivers
(c) plants (d) plains

9. 'PO' in the map is a symbol of
(a) Post Office (b) Public Office
(c) Private Office (d) Police Office

10. What is the imaginary line that runs on the globe and divides the Earth into two equal parts?
(a) Axis (b) Equator
(c) Tropic of Cancer (d) Prime Meridian

11. What is the latitude of the North Pole?
(a) 23 1/2°N (b) 66 1/2°N
(c) 90°N (d) 0°

12. Rajesh, a geography enthusiast, is studying the Earth's characteristics and geographic features. He is particularly interested in understanding the imaginary lines that help in locating places on the globe. Which of the following statements about latitude is incorrect?
(a) All parallel circles from the equator up to the poles are called parallels of latitudes.
(b) The distance from the equator to either of the poles is one-third of a circle around the Earth.
(c) The equator represents the zero-degree latitude.
(d) The size of the parallels of latitude decreases as we move away from the equator.

13. In which hemisphere is Chandrapur (India) located, if it is at 20°N latitude?
(a) Northern Hemisphere
(b) Southern Hemisphere
(c) Eastern Hemisphere
(d) Western Hemisphere

14. What is the time difference between two locations for every 15° of longitude?
(a) 30 minutes (b) 1 hour
(c) 1 hour and 15 minutes (d) 45 minutes

15. The Earth takes how many minutes to cross a meridian?
(a) 15 (b) 60
(c) 4 (d) 20

16. What is the Indian Standard Time (IST) meridian's longitude?
(a) 0° (b) 45°
(c) 82° 30′ (d) 180°

17. When it is 4 pm in India, what is the time of Greenwich?
(a) 10:30 pm (b) 11:00 am
(c) 10:30 am (d) 11:00 pm

18. India is located in the ...... of Greenwich.
(a) East (b) West
(c) North (d) South

19. How many time zones are there on the Earth?
(a) 12 (b) 24
(c) 36 (d) 48

20. Identify the type of map being discussed below statements and mark the correct answer.
I. It is used to depict the elevation and relief of the land.
II. Rivers, lakes, oceans, seas and other water bodies are displayed.

Codes
(a) Thematic map
(b) Physical map
(c) Political map
(d) None of the above

21. Arrange the following directions from right to left in chronological order supposing a man is standing facing North.
I. NE II. SW III. SE IV. NW

Codes
(a) I, II, III, IV (b) II, III, IV, I
(c) IV, II, I, III (d) III, I, IV, II

22. Which of the following statements is/are correct?

I. A globe is a representation or a drawing of the Earth's surface.

II. Plateaus, plains and rivers are shown in the physical map.

III. Thematic map shows roads, rainfall and forests.

Codes

(a) I, II and III (b) I and II

(c) II and III (d) I and III

23. Which of the following statements is/are correct?

I. The places situated East of Greenwich will be behind Greenwich time.

II. The distance between the meridians is the same everywhere.

III. Both latitudes and longitudes are required to find any location.

Codes

(a) Only I

(b) Both I and II

(b) I, II and III

(d) Both I and III

Answers

1. (c)	2. (c)	3. (b)	4. (a)	5. (c)
6. (d)	7. (b)	8. (d)	9. (a)	10. (b)
11. (c)	12. (b)	13. (a)	14. (b)	15. (c)
16. (c)	17. (c)	18. (a)	19. (b)	20. (b)
21. (d)	22. (c)	23. (d)		

Fill in the Blanks

1. A .... is used to find the main direction.

2. Maps provide more information than a ....

3. The symbol for the Post and Telegraph Office is ......

4. The Northern half of the Earth is known as the ....

5. All parallel circles from the equator up to the poles are called ....

Ans. 1. compass 2. globe 3. PTO 4. Northern Hemisphere 5. parallels of latitudes

True or False

1. The collection of maps is called Atlas.

2. Political maps show the natural features of the Earth.

3. There are five intermediate directions.

4. Brown colour in the map is used to show plains.

5. The Earth's axis is a physical line passing through the planet's centre.

Ans. 1. True 2. False 3. False 4. False 5. False

Match the Following

1.

List I (Symbols)	List II (Representation)
A. PS	1. North-East
B. Red	2. Plateau
C. Yellow	3. Police Station
D. NE	4. Graveyard

Codes

	A	B	C	D		A	B	C	D
(a)	2	1	3	4	(b)	3	4	2	1
(c)	4	1	2	3	(d)	3	1	2	4

2.

List I (Symbols)	List II (Representation)
A. Equator	1. The line that divides the Earth into two halves.
B. Cardinal points	2. Point to four directions (North, East, South and West)
C. Ujjayini	3. Indian Prime Meridian
D. Prime Meridian	4. Accepted by all nations as the International Standard Time.

Codes

	A	B	C	D		A	B	C	D
(a)	4	1	3	2	(b)	2	3	1	4
(c)	1	2	3	4	(d)	4	3	2	1

Ans. 1. (b) 2. (c)

Picture Based Questions

1. What is the 82 1/2°E meridian that is shown in the picture given below also known as?

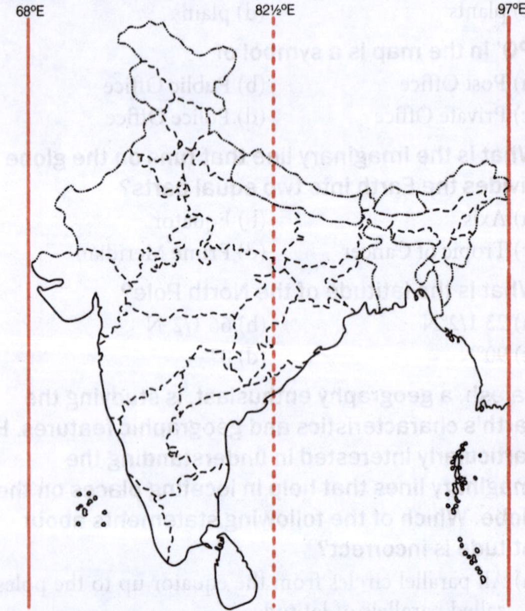

(a) Prime Meridian (b) International Time

(c) International Date Line (d) Indian Standard Time (IST)

Ans. 1. (d) Indian Standard Time (IST)

2. Look at the picture given below and answer the following questions.

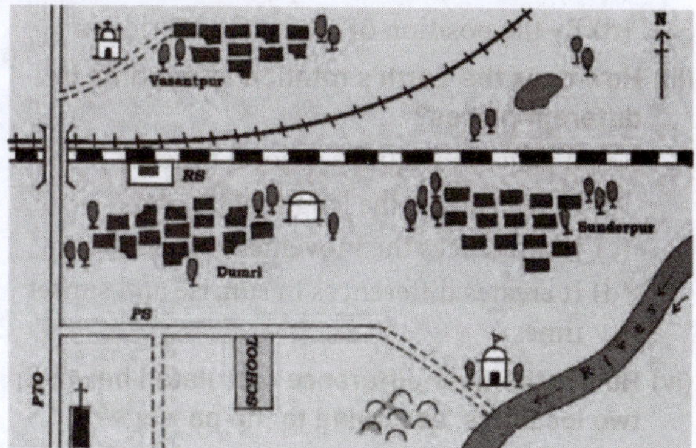

(i) In which direction is the river flowing?

(ii) What kind of road passes by the side of village Dumri?

(iii) On what type of railway line is Sunderpur situated?

(iv) On which side of the railway bridge is the police station situated?

Ans. (i) The river is flowing in the South-West direction.

(ii) Metalled road is passing by the side of village Dumri.

(iii) Sunderpur is situated on a broad gauge railway line.

(iv) Police station is situated on the South side of the railway bridge.

Assertion-Reason

1. Assertion (A) Globe is used when we study Earth as a whole.

Reason (R) Map is used when we study a part of the Earth.

Codes

(a) Both A and R are true and R is the correct explanation of A

(b) Both A and R are true, but R is not the correct explanation of A

(c) A is true, but R is false

(d) A is false, but R is true

2. Assertion (A) The Earth's equator plays a crucial role as a reference point for locating places on the globe.

Reason (R) The equator is an imaginary circular line that divides the Earth into two equal parts, namely the Northern Hemisphere and the Southern Hemisphere.

Codes

(a) Both A and R are true and R is the correct explanation of A

(b) Both A and R are true, but R is not the correct explanation of A

(c) A is true, but R is false

(d) A is false, but R is true

3. Assertion (A) Standard Time is necessary to address variations in local times across different meridians.

Reason (R) Local times on different meridians vary due to the Earth's rotation, making it challenging to create timetables for activities that involve crossing multiple longitudes.

Codes

(a) Both A and R are true and R is the correct explanation of A

(b) Both A and R are true, but R is not the correct explanation of A

(c) A is true, but R is false

(d) A is false, but R is true

4. Assertion (A) The Earth completes one full rotation on its axis every 24 hours.

Reason (R) Each full rotation of the Earth equals 360 degrees.

Codes

(a) Both A and R are true and R is the correct explanation of A

(b) Both A and R are true, but R is not the correct explanation of A

(c) A is true, but R is false

(d) A is false, but R is true

5. Assertion (A) At 30°W, the local time is 10 am, if it is 12 pm at Greenwich.

Reason (R) Moving Westward from the Prime Meridian, local time decreases by one hour for every 15°

Codes

(a) Both A and R are true and R is the correct explanation of A

(b) Both A and R are true, but R is not the correct explanation of A

(c) A is true, but R is false

(d) A is false, but R is true

Ans. 1. (a) 2. (a) 3. (a) 4. (b) 5. (a)

Case Based Questions

1. Read the passage given below and answer the following questions.

It is the third important component of a map. It is not possible to draw on a map the actual shape and size of different features such as buildings, roads, bridges, trees, railway lines or a well. So, they are shown by using certain letters, shades, colours, pictures and lines. These symbols give a lot of information in a limited space. With the use of these symbols, maps can be drawn easily and are simple to read. Even if you don't know the language of an area and therefore cannot ask someone for directions, you can collect information from maps with the help of these symbols.

Maps have a universal language that can be understood by all. There is an international agreement regarding the use of these symbols. These are called conventional symbols.

(i) Which component of the map is useful for representing the features like buildings, roads, bridges, trees or railway lines?

(ii) Mention any one benefit of using the symbols in the map.

(iii) Why are different features shown by symbols on a map?

Ans. (i) The symbols are useful in representing the features like buildings, roads, bridges, trees or railway lines on a map.

(ii) The maps use universal symbols, so even if you don't understand the language of an area you will be able to understand the directions using a map.

(iii) Different features such as buildings, roads, bridges, railway lines, etc. cannot be shown on a map due to their size. That is why, they are shown by symbols.

2. Read the passage given below and answer the following questions.

The best means of measuring time is by the movement of the Earth, the Moon and the planets. The Sun regularly rises and sets every day and naturally, it is the best time-keeper throughout the world. Local time can be reckoned by the shadow cast by the Sun, which is the shortest at noon and longest at sunrise and sunset. When the Prime Meridian of Greenwich has the Sun at the highest point in the sky, all the places along this meridian will have mid-day or noon. As the Earth rotates from West to East, those places East of Greenwich will be ahead of Greenwich time and those to the West will be behind it. The rate of difference can be calculated as follows. The Earth rotates 360° in about 24 hours, which means 15° an hour or 1° in four minutes. Thus, when it is 12 noon at Greenwich, the time at 15° East of Greenwich will be $15 \times 4 = 60$ minutes, i.e., 1 hour ahead of Greenwich time, which means 1 pm but at 15° West of Greenwich, the time will be behind Greenwich time by 1 hour, i.e., it will be 11.00 am Similarly, at 180°, it will be mid-night when it is 12 noon at Greenwich.

(i) How is local time affected in places East of Greenwich?

(a) Local time is behind Greenwich time.

(b) Local time is ahead of Greenwich time.

(c) Local time is the same as Greenwich time.

(d) Local time is not affected.

(ii) How is local time determined according to the passage?

(a) By the movement of the Moon.

(b) By the shadow cast of the Sun.

(c) By the rotation of the planets.

(d) By the position of the Prime Meridian.

(iii) How does the Earth's rotation affect time in different places?

(a) It causes variations in local time.

(b) It determines the length of the day.

(c) It influences the movement of the Moon.

(d) It creates differences in sunrise and sunset times.

(iv) How is the time difference calculated between two locations, according to the passage?

(a) By the length of the day.

(b) By the Earth's revolution around the Sun.

(c) By multiplying the distance by 4 minutes.

(d) By calculating the Moon's position.

Ans. (i) (b) (ii) (b) (iii) (a) (iv) (c)

Competency Based Questions

1. If you were studying different types of maps, which type would primarily show natural features like mountains and rivers?

Ans. Physical maps are primarily used to show natural features like mountains and rivers.

2. How would you describe the system that divides the world into different time zones based on longitudinal lines?

Ans. The system that divides the world into different time zones based on longitudinal lines is known as time zones.

3. How do the concepts of longitudes help in understanding time zones and what is the effect on local time when crossing different longitudinal lines?

Ans. Longitudes are important for understanding time zones because the Earth is divided into 24 time zones, each 15° of longitude apart.

As you move East or West across these zones, local time changes by one hour for each 15° shift. For instance, if it is noon in London (0° longitude), it will be 1 pm in a location 15° East and 11 am in a location 15° West.

4. The grid system of latitudes and longitudes can be used to pinpoint locations on a globe. Explain with an example of how this system can be applied.

Ans. The grid system of latitudes and longitudes divides the Earth into a network of intersecting lines that help locate specific points.

For example, by combining latitude 40° N with longitude 74°W, you can pinpoint New York City on a globe. This grid system provides a precise method for identifying any location on Earth, enabling accurate navigation and mapping.

5. Explore the different elements of a map, such as symbols, scales and legends. How do these elements contribute to the effectiveness of a map as a tool for conveying geographical information?

Ans. A map's effectiveness in conveying geographical information depends on various elements: symbols scales and legends. Symbols are graphical representations of physical and human-made features, such as mountains, rivers, cities and roads.

These symbols provide a visual shorthand, making complex information accessible at a glance. The scale indicates the relationship between distances on the map and actual distances on the ground, allowing users to measure and understand real-world distances accurately.

Legends, or keys, explain the meaning of symbols and colours used on the map, ensuring that users can interpret the information correctly. Together, these elements transform a map into a powerful tool for understanding and navigating the geographic landscape, whether for everyday use, academic study or professional application.

6. Evaluate the role of atlases in modern education and research. What types of information do they typically contain, and how do they help users understand complex geographical data?

Ans. Atlases play a vital role in modern education and research by providing comprehensive collections of maps that cover a wide range of geographical data.

Typically, an atlas contains physical maps showcasing landforms and bodies of water, political maps highlighting boundaries and cities and thematic maps presenting information on climate, population and economic activities.

These diverse maps enable users to explore and analyse complex geographical phenomena from multiple perspectives. In educational settings, atlases help students develop spatial awareness and understand global interconnections. In research, they serve as invaluable references for geographic information, supporting studies in fields such as environmental science, history and urban planning. By offering a wealth of detailed, curated data, atlases facilitate a deeper understanding of the world's physical and human landscapes.

7. How do physical and political maps differ in terms of the information they present and their applications? Provide detailed examples of each type of map and discuss their relevance in various fields.

Ans. Physical and political maps differ fundamentally in the information they present and their applications. These are

Physical Maps	Political Maps
Physical maps focus on natural features, depicting mountains, valleys, rivers and other landforms with colours and shading to indicate elevation and terrain.	Political maps emphasise human-made boundaries, showing countries, states, cities and administrative divisions.
These maps are essential in fields like geology, environmental science and outdoor recreation, where understanding the physical landscape is crucial.	These maps are vital in political science, international relations and education, helping users understand geopolitical structures and governance.
For example, a physical map of the Himalayas highlights the region's peaks, valleys and glaciers, aiding in scientific studies and mountaineering expeditions.	For example, a political map of Europe, delineates national borders and capital cities, providing insights into the continent's political landscape and historical changes.

Skill Based Questions as per NEP 2020

1. Examine the map of a small city given below. If you are at the railway station and need to visit the bank, which direction would you go?

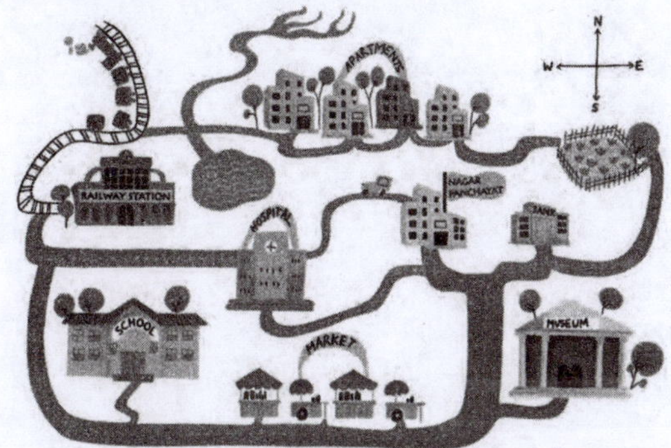

Ans. According to the map if you are at the railway station, you would go North to reach the bank.

2. If a map scale indicates 1 cm = 1 km, how far apart are two cities that are 5 cm apart on the map?

Ans. If the map scale is 1 cm = 1 km, two cities that are 5 cm apart on the map are 5 km apart.

3. What challenges might arise when creating a thematic map of your town? How would you address these challenges?

Ans. Creating a thematic map might be challenging because it requires accurate data collection and deciding which features to emphasise.
I will address these challenges by using reliable data sources and clear criteria for what to include.

4. Imagine you are in charge of planning a new park in your city. Draw a map including all necessary components (scale, symbols, directions) and explain your choices.

Ans. Do it yourself.

HINT Draw a map with a scale (e.g., 1 cm = 100 m), including symbols for trees, playgrounds, walking paths, and benches. Also, explain why you placed these features in certain particular areas.

ASSESSMENT EXERCISE

Objective Type Questions

1. Maps showing mountains, plains, rivers, oceans, etc. are called
   (a) Thematic maps (b) Political maps
   (c) Physical maps (d) All of these
2. The ratio between the actual distance on the ground and the distance on the map is
   (a) distance (b) scale
   (c) direction (d) map
3. Direction is compulsory for
   (a) a symbol (b) a map
   (c) a sketch (d) a globe
4. The area between the Tropic of Cancer and the Tropic of Capricorn receives maximum heat from
   (a) Earth
   (b) Sun
   (c) Stars
   (d) None of the above
5. **Assertion** (A) Moving Eastward from the Prime Meridian, each meridian adds one hour of local time.
   Reason (R) The Prime Meridian is located at 0° longitude.

   Codes
   (a) Both A and R are true and R is the correct explanation of A
   (b) Both A and R are true, but R is not the correct explanation of A
   (c) A is true, but R is false
   (d) A is false, but R is true
6. The Prime Meridian is located at .... degrees longitude.
7. The Earth rotates from East to West. (True/False)

Subjective Questions (VSA, SA & LA)

1. What do political maps show?
2. Why are symbols used on maps instead of actual drawings of buildings?
3. What do you understand by conventional symbols? Explain with examples.
4. Maps play a role in our lives on a daily basis. Discuss.
5. Differentiate between North and South latitudes.
6. Latitudes have a relationship with the climate of the region. Justify with an example.
7. How time zones are divided on the Earth? Explain with an example.

CHAPTER 2

Oceans and Continents

When seen from outer space, the Earth appears mostly blue. This blue colour represents the availability of water on the Earth. Almost 3/4th of the globe is covered with water and hence astronauts often call Earth a **blue planet**. A large body of land is called a **landmass.**

The largest water bodies are called **oceans** and a large continuous expanse of landmass is called a **'continent'**. Both oceans and continents play a vital role in shaping the climate of the Earth.

2.1 The Distribution of Water and Land on the Earth

- Oceans and continents are not distributed equally between the Northern and Southern Hemispheres.
- The oceans together hold most of the water available on the planet. However, seawater is salty and unfit for use by most land animals, including humans.
- Freshwater makes up a very small part of the water resources on the Earth. Fresh water is found in glaciers, rivers, lakes, in the atmosphere and also underground (groundwater).

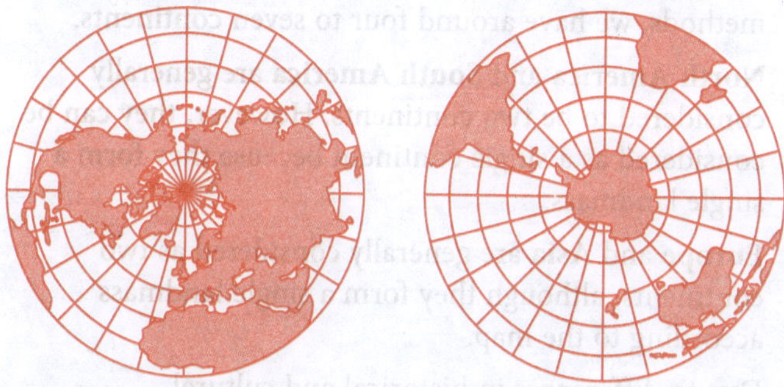

Maps of the Earth as seen from above the North Pole (left) and above the South Pole (right).

2.2 Oceans

- There are five major oceans–the Pacific Ocean, the Atlantic Ocean, the Indian Ocean, the Arctic Ocean and the Southern (or Antarctic) Ocean.
- The Pacific Ocean is the largest among all the oceans, followed by the Atlantic Ocean.
- The Indian Ocean is the third largest ocean. The Indian Ocean is divided in two parts, the Arabian Sea to the West and the Bay of Bengal to the East.
- The Southern Ocean is the fourth largest ocean and the Arctic Ocean is the smallest ocean.
- These oceans are not really separate. The lines which divide the oceans on a map are not more than a convention as they are not followed by the natural world. Thus, there is no natural division among the oceans.
- Seawater constantly flows across different oceans, sustaining a rich diversity of **marine** life. Many plant and animal species can be found across multiple oceans.
- The marine **flora** includes tiny plants called algae and all kinds of seaweeds. The marine **fauna** consists of thousands of species of colourful fish, dolphins, whales, and countless mysterious deep-sea creatures.
- Each part of the ocean, from the Sun-lit surface to the dark depths, has its own diverse life forms.

Must Know !

The boundaries of the Indian Ocean are around Asia to the North, Africa to the West and Australia to the East, apart from the Southern Ocean in the South.

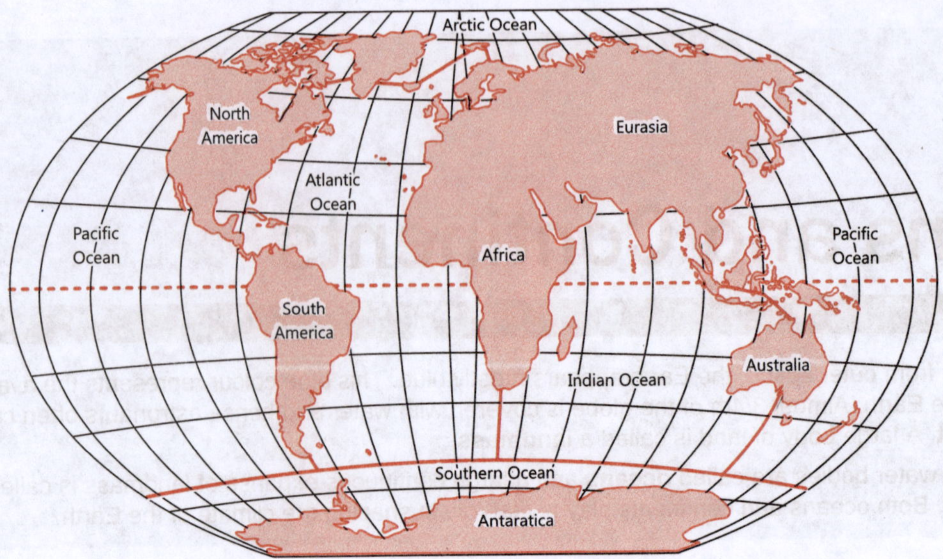

A world map showing the five oceans, their conventional boundaries and the continents.

Oceans and Disasters

- Oceans often give rise to storms. These storms are violent events with extreme rainfall or very strong winds, such as **cyclones**. These cyclones can cause widespread damage to coastal regions of the world.
- A **tsunami** is a natural disaster that originates in the ocean. It is a huge and powerful wave generally caused by a strong earthquake or a volcanic eruption at the bottom of the ocean.
- Tsunamis can travel thousands of kilometers and **submerge** coastal areas, causing widespread damage to life and property.
- Such disasters that lead to loss of life and property are handled under disaster management. India has its own **National Disaster Management Authority** to deal with all kinds of disasters.

The Boxing Day Tsunami

- On **26th December 2004**, India and another 13 countries around the Indian Ocean were struck by a powerful tsunami caused by an earthquake in Indonesia. It was named as **Boxing Day Tsunami**. More than two lakh people lost their lives in the **catastrophe**.
- In India, the Andaman and Nicobar Islands and the coasts of Tamil Nadu and Kerala were severely affected and suffered much damage and loss of life through this tsunami.
- Such tsunamis are rare but very destructive. Tsunamis can be detected before they hit the coast. For example, many countries use **'early warning systems'** for detecting tsunamis.
- There is an **Indian Ocean Tsunami Warning System**, that is developed by the countries and islands that lies within the Indian Ocean. This helps to take measures to protect lives and property.

Try These

1. **What is a large body of land referred to as?**
2. **Name the smallest ocean in the world.**
3. **Which natural disaster is caused by strong earthquakes or volcanic eruptions in the ocean?**
4. **What is the name of the authority in India that deals with disaster management?**

2.3 Continents

- There are seven known continents, but counting the continents is not simple. Hence, based on different methods, we have around four to seven continents.
- **North America** and **South America** are generally considered to be two continents. However, they can be considered as a single continent because they form a single landmass.
- **Europe** and **Asia** are generally considered as two continents, although they form a single landmass according to the map.
- Due to differences in historical and cultural development, Europe and Asia are considered as two different continents. However, geologists often consider it as a single continent named **Eurasia**.
- Eurasia and Africa are usually regarded as two continents, but sometimes as one.
- Since 1981, the **Indian Antarctica Programme** has been exploring Antarctica. It is a continent with a very cold climate and harsh environment. It is located around the Southern pole.

- The following table distributes different numbers or different counts of the continents.

Four continents	Africa-Eurasia, America, Antarctica, Australia
Five continents	Africa, America, Antarctica, Australia, Eurasia
Six continents	Africa, Antarctica, Australia, Eurasia, North America, South America
Seven continents	Africa, Antarctica, Asia, Australia, Europe, North America, South America

Must Know !

- The five Olympic rings, one of the symbols of the Olympic Games, symbolise the gathering of sportspeople from all over the world.
- The rings were chosen to represent five inhabited continents–Africa, America, Asia, Australia and Europe.

2.4 Islands

- **Islands** are pieces of land surrounded by water on all sides. There are many islands on the Earth in various sizes. **Greenland** is considered the largest among all the islands.
- Continents are also surrounded by water, but because of their vast size, they are not called islands.
- There are many islands on the Earth having different sizes. There are more than 1,300 small islands in India. It includes two major groups–Andaman and Nicobar **Islands** in the Bay of Bengal and **Lakshadweep Islands** in the Arabian Sea.
- In 1983, India established its **first scientific base station** in Antarctica, called **Dakshin Gangotri**. Two more stations (Maitri and Bharati) were established later.

2.5 Oceans and Life

- Oceans and continents are vital parts of the environment and affect most aspects of our lives. The oceans play a crucial role in regulating the climate and sustaining life on Earth.
- The oceans play a major role in cloud formation and continuation of the water cycle. Without oceans, there would be no rainfall.
- More than half of the world's oxygen is produced by the oceans' flora, which is why they are called the **planet's lungs**.
- Oceans have deeply impacted humanity in many other ways such as
  - From early times, people have used oceans and seas to migrate to other regions, to trade in all kinds of goods, to conduct military campaigns, and as a source of food through fishing.
  - Oceans have also nourished the cultures of coastal people all over the world.
- The United Nations has designated 8th June as **World Oceans Day**. It is celebrated to 'remind us all of the major role that the ocean plays in everyday life.'

Ocean and Pollution

- Scientific studies have shown how the oceans are polluted by human activities.
- Several million tonnes of plastic waste is thrown into the oceans every year. There are several other forms of pollution. As a result, the marine ecosystem is under threat.
- Overfishing (excessive fishing) is another cause for the decline of marine life.
- It is our collective responsibility to protect oceans for the future of the planet and humanity.

Try These

1. **What term do geologists use to refer to the combined landmass of Europe and Asia?**
2. **What are smaller pieces of land surrounded by water on all sides called?**
3. **Name India's first scientific base station in Antarctica.**
4. **Why are oceans referred to as 'the planet's lungs'?**

Glossary

Marine It means anything related to the ocean or the sea.

Flora All the plant life of a particular region for a period of time.

Fauna All the animal life of a particular region for a period of time.

Cyclone A cyclone is a powerful, rotating storm with strong winds and heavy rain, usually forming over the ocean.

Submerge To move deep inside the Earth.

Catastrophe A huge disaster that caused extensive damage and suffering.

OCEANS AND CONTINENTS

Distribution of Water and Land on Earth

- Oceans are not equally distributed over Northern and Southern Hemisphere.
- Ocean water is available on whole planet but it is saline in nature and not fit for consumption.
- Freshwater is available only in glaciers.

Oceans

- Five major oceans-Pacific, Atlantic, Indian, Arctic and Southern
- No clear boundaries among oceans, seperated based on convention only.
  - Sustain rich marine diversity.
  - Pacific is the largest ocean.
  - Arctic is the smallest ocean.

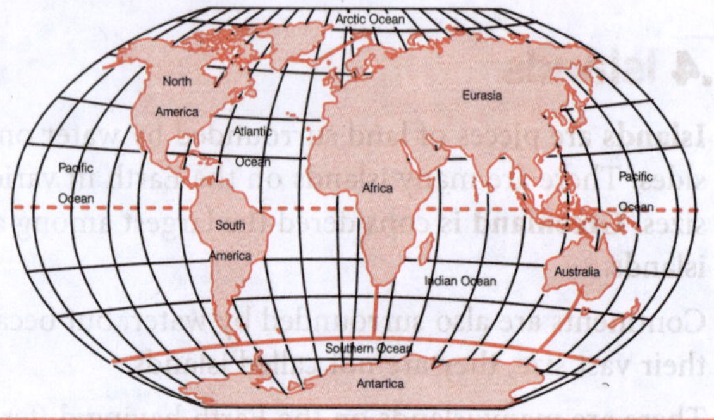

Oceans and Disaster

- Oceans gives rise to storms with extreme rainfall or very strong winds. Such events are called cyclones.
- Tsunami is another natural disaster that originates in the ocean.
- Tsunami is a huge and powerful wave generally caused by a strong earthquake or volcanic eruption below Earth surface.

Continents

- Large continous expanse of land is called continents.
- Seven most common continents are-Asia, Africa, South America, North America, Europe, Australia and Antarctica.
- There are various ways of counting the number of continents.
- When Europe and Asia are counted as single landmass, it is known as 'Eurasia'.

NCERT FOLDER

Answers of All NCERT Questions Detailed

Let's Explore (Page 29)

Q.1 What are the circular lines in each map called? And do you know what the lines radiating out of the two poles are called? (Hint: you studied them in the previous chapter, but here they are presented differently.)

Ans. The circular lines in each map are the latitudes and longitudes. The lines radiating out of the two poles are 90°N and 90°S.

Q.2 Which hemisphere holds more water?

Ans. The Southern Hemisphere contains more water.

Q.3 What do you think could be the approximate proportion of water to land in the Northern Hemisphere and in the Southern Hemisphere? Discuss in groups.

Ans. The approximate proportions of water to land in the Northern and Southern Hemispheres is

Northern Hemisphere

- **Water** About 60% of the surface area.
- **Land** About 40% of the surface area.

Southern Hemisphere

- **Water** About 80% of the surface area.
- **Land** About 20% of the surface area.

Q.4 Are all the oceans connected with one another, or are there separations between them?

Ans. Yes, all the oceans are connected to one another. There is no strict division around the boundaries of the oceans.

Think About It (Page 31)

Q.1 If there is such an abundance of water on the planet, why is there so much talk of 'water scarcity' or a 'water crisis'?

Ans. The water on the planet is in abundance but we often face scarcity of water because only some of the water is useful for human use.

The saline water of oceans cannot be used directly.

Q.2 What ways of saving water are you aware of? Which ones have you seen practised at home, at your school and in your village, town or city?

Ans. The different ways of saving water as follows

(a) **Rainwater harvesting** it is the process of storing rainwater for future use. This rainwater can be stored in the tanks till the next rainfall.

(b) **Recycling waste water** it involves treating and reusing water that has already been used for various purposes.

(c) **Drip irrigation** it is the process of delivering water directly to the roots of plants through small tubes and emitters.

Let's Explore (Page 32)

Q.1 Locate the five oceans in the table below, mark the hemisphere or hemispheres they belong to.

	Northern Hemisphere	Southern Hemisphere
Pacific Ocean		
Atlantic Ocean		
Indian Ocean		
Southern Ocean		
Arctic Ocean		

Ans.

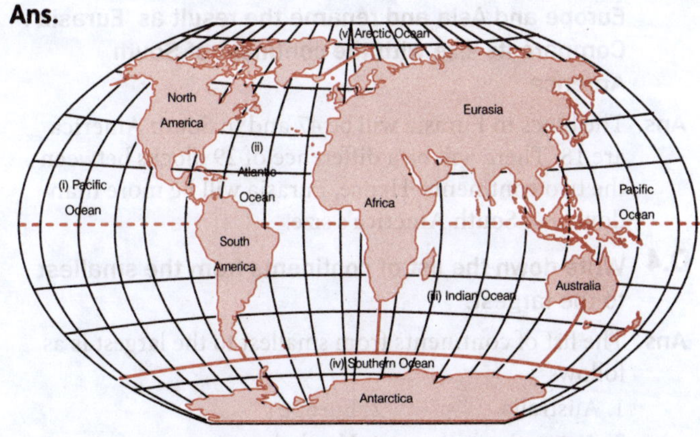

	Northern Hemisphere	Southern Hemisphere
Pacific Ocean	Yes	Yes
Atlantic Ocean	Yes	Yes
Indian Ocean		Yes
Southern Ocean		Yes
Arctic Ocean	Yes	

Let's Explore (Page 36)

Q.1 Counting the number of squares, name the largest continent and the smallest.

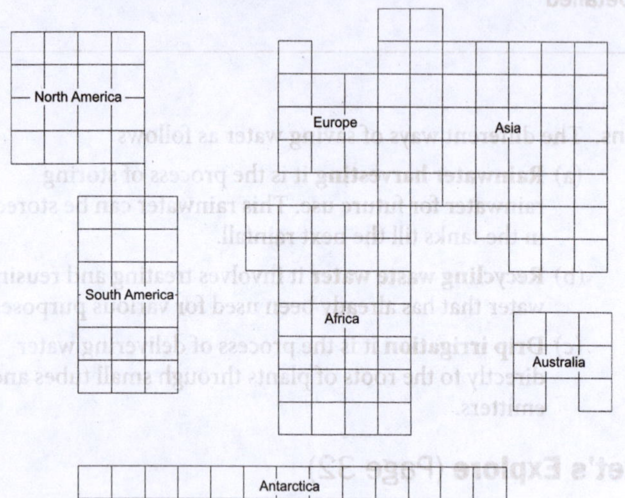

Ans. Asia is the largest continent as there are 44 blocs in Asia. Australia is the smallest with 8 blocs.

Q.2 Which one is larger–North America or South America, Africa or North America, Antarctica or Australia?

Ans. South America is larger than North America, Africa is larger than North America and Antarctica is larger than Australia.

Q.3 Re-colour the diagram by having a single colour for Europe and Asia and rename the result as 'Eurasia'. Compare its size with the continent of South America.

Ans. The blocs in Eurasia will be 47 and in South America are 18. There will be a difference of 29 blocks between the two continents. Hence, Eurasia will be more than double of South America's size.

Q.4 Write down the list of continents from the smallest to the largest.

Ans. The list of continents from smallest to the largest is as follows

1. Australia
2. Europe
3. Antarctica
4. North America
5. South America
6. Africa
7. Asia

Questions, Activities and Projects

Q.1 Explain the following terms

(a) Continent (b) Ocean (c) Island

Ans. (a) A continent is a large continuous expanse of land. On a map, continents are depicted as extensive landmasses that cover a significant portion of the Earth's surface. They are surrounded by water but are not considered islands due to their vast size. The seven widely accepted continents are Africa, Antarctica, Asia, Australia, Europe, North America and South America.

(b) An ocean is a large body of saltwater that covers a significant portion of the Earth's surface. Oceans are the largest water bodies on the globe, covering almost three-fourths of the Earth's surface. There are five main oceans, the Pacific Ocean, the Atlantic Ocean, the Indian Ocean: the Arctic Ocean and the Southern (or Antarctic) Ocean.

(c) An island is a smaller piece of land surrounded by water on all sides. Unlike continents, islands are not large enough to be considered landmasses. Islands can vary greatly in size, with some being large enough to host significant populations and infrastructure, while others may be small and uninhabited. An example of a large island is Greenland, the largest in the world.

Q.2 Let us draw–Without looking at the maps in this chapter, draw the continents free hand on a sheet of paper and colour them. Then compare your drawing with the map of oceans and continents in the chapter.

Ans. Do it yourself

Q.3 Let us do–On the outline map of the world given below, label all the continents and oceans.

Ans.

Arctic Ocean
North America
Eurasia
Atlantic Ocean
Pacific Ocean
Africa
Pacific Ocean
South America
Indian Ocean
Australia
Southern Ocean
Antarctica

Q.4 **Solve this Crossword**

Across

1. **Abundantly produced by the oceans**
3. **A large expanse of landmass**
6. **A large continent of which India is a part**
8. **A major source of pollution of the oceans**
10. **The coldest continent**

Down

2. **The largest island on Earth**
4. **A huge destructive wave from the ocean**
5. **The smallest continent**
7. **The largest body of water on the Earth**
9. **A landmass (but not a continent) surrounded by the sea or ocean**

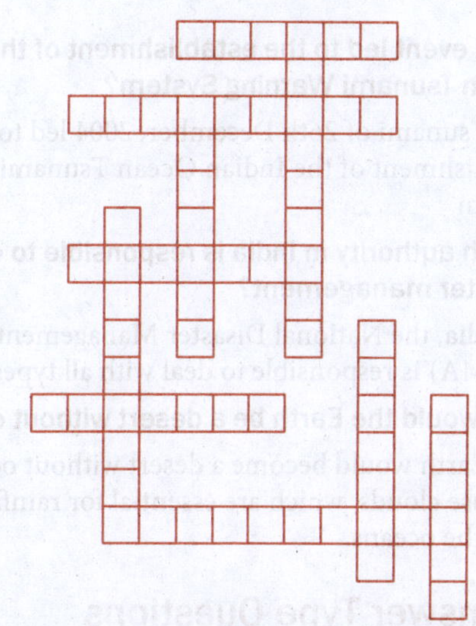

Ans. 1. Oxygen 2. Greenland 3. Continent 4. Tsunami 5. Australia 6. Eurasia 7. Pacific 8. Plastic 9. Island 10. Antarctica

REVIEW EXERCISE

Including Competency Based Questions

Part-I

Very Short Answer Type Questions

1. **What colour do early astronauts associate with Earth and why?**

Ans. The early astronauts associated Earth with blue colour due to the abundance of water bodies on the Earth.

2. **Which deity is invoked in the motto of the Indian Navy?**

Ans. The deity Varuna is invoked in the Motto of the Indian Navy. He is the god of water and Air.

3. **In which hemisphere is the majority of Earth's water located?**

Ans. The majority of Earth's water is located in the Southern Hemisphere.

4. **What kind of water is found in glaciers, rivers, lakes and underground, and why is it important?**

Ans. The freshwater is found in glaciers, rivers, lakes and underground water. It is important because it is fit for human use.

5. **What kind of life forms are sustained by the seawater that flows across different oceans?**

Ans. Various marine flora and fauna are sustained by the seawater that flows across different oceans. For example, algae, seaweeds, etc.

6. **What two parts of the Indian Ocean are found to the West and East of India?**

Ans. The two parts of the Indian Ocean around India are the Arabian Sea in the West and the Bay of Bengal in the East.

7. **What causes tsunamis and what are their potential impacts on coastal areas?**

Ans. Earthquake waves cause tsunamis and they have the potential to destroy the coastal areas.

8. **How many continents are generally listed and what are they named?**

Ans. Generally there are 7 continents. They are named as Asia, Africa, South America, North America and Antarctica, Europe and Australia.

9. **Which island is known as the largest in the world?**

Ans. Greenland is considered as the largest island in the world.

10. **What is the purpose of the Indian Antarctica Programme?**

Ans. The purpose of the Indian Antartica Programme is to conduct research on the evolution of climate over time.

11. What event led to the establishment of the Indian Ocean Tsunami Warning System?

Ans. The Tsunami of 26th December, 2004 led to the establishment of the Indian Ocean Tsunami Warning System.

12. Which authority in India is responsible to deal with disaster management?

Ans. In India, the National Disaster Management Authority (NDMA) is responsible to deal with all types of disaster.

13. Why would the Earth be a desert without oceans?

Ans. The Earth would become a desert without oceans because clouds, which are essential for rainfall, form over the oceans.

Short Answer Type Questions

1. Describe the geographical significance of the Arabian Sea and the Bay of Bengal to India.

Ans. The Arabian Sea lies to the West of India, while the Bay of Bengal is situated to the East. These two parts of the Indian Ocean play significant roles in India's climate, trade routes and maritime activities. The Arabian Sea is key to India's trade with the Middle East and Africa, while the Bay of Bengal connects India with South-East Asia. Both water bodies influence the monsoon patterns, which are vital for India's agriculture and overall economy.

2. What was the impact of the 26th December, 2004 tsunami on countries around the Indian Ocean, and what measures were taken afterwards?

Ans. The tsunami on 26th December, 2004, triggered by a massive undersea earthquake, caused widespread devastation in countries around the Indian Ocean, including India, Indonesia, Sri Lanka and Thailand. The natural disaster resulted in significant loss of life, property and infrastructure.

In response to this catastrophe, efforts were made to establish the Indian Ocean Tsunami Warning System to provide early warnings and reduce future impacts. This system aims to improve preparedness and response to potential tsunamis, enhancing safety for coastal communities.

Multiple Choice Questions (MCQs)

1. How many continents are there in the world?

(a) 8 (b) 10
(c) 7 (d) 6

2. Which of the following continents lies completely in the Northern Hemisphere?

(a) Australia (b) Europe
(c) South America (d) Africa

Long Answer Type Questions

1. Discuss the ecological importance of the various life forms found within the different zones of the ocean, from the Sun-lit surface to the dark depths.

Ans. The ocean is divided into different zones, each supporting distinct forms of life. The Sun-lit surface zone hosts photosynthetic organisms like phytoplankton, which form the basis of the marine food web. This zone also supports a diverse range of fish, marine mammals and birds.

As we move deeper into the ocean, light reduces. It supports life forms adapted to high pressure and cold temperatures, such as certain species of squid and anglerfish. The deepest parts of the ocean have unique creatures like tube worms and deep-sea jellyfish. Each zone's biodiversity is crucial for the overall health of marine ecosystems, contributing to nutrient cycling, carbon sequestration, and supporting fisheries that humans rely on.

2. Explain the role and significance of the Indian Ocean Tsunami Warning System established after the 2004 tsunami.

Ans. The Indian Ocean Tsunami Warning System (IOTWS) was established in response to the devastating tsunami of 26th December, 2004, which caused massive loss of life and property in multiple countries.

The system is designed to provide early warnings of potential tsunamis, enabling timely evacuations and other safety measures.

When a potential threat is identified, alerts are sent to national and regional authorities who then warn the public. The IOTWS has significantly improved the preparedness and response capabilities of countries around the Indian Ocean, reducing the risk of future tsunami-related casualties and damage.

By boosting international collaboration and enhancing local capacity for disaster management, the IOTWS plays a critical role in safeguarding coastal communities.

Part-II

3. Which of the following is the smallest continent?

(a) Australia (b) Europe
(c) Antarctica (d) Africa

4. Where is 97 % of water found on the Earth?

(a) In seas
(b) Underground
(c) In lakes
(d) In oceans

5. **Which of the following is the largest ocean?**

(a) Pacific Ocean (b) Atlantic Ocean
(c) Indian Ocean (d) Antarctica Ocean

6. **Arrange the following oceans according to their sizes from larger to smaller.**

I. Arctic Ocean II. Atlantic Ocean
III. Indian Ocean IV. Pacific Ocean

Codes

(a) I, II, III, IV (b) II, I, III, IV
(c) IV, II, I, III (d) IV, II, III, I

7. **Arrange the following continents according to their sizes from smaller to larger.**

I. Europe II. Asia
III. Africa IV. Antarctica

Codes

(a) I, IV, III, II (b) I, II, III, IV
(c) III, IV, I, II (d) II, IV, I, III

8. **Identify the continent that is being talked about in the following statements.**

(i) It is a huge continent that lies completely in the Southern Hemisphere.

(ii) There are no permanent human settlements.

(iii) Two Indian research stations: Maitri and Dakshin Gangotri are located there.

Codes

(a) Europe (b) Africa
(c) Antarctica (d) Asia

Answers

1. (c) **2.** (b) **3.** (a) **4.** (d) **5.** (a)
6. (d) **7.** (a) **8.** (c)

Fill in the Blanks

1. Almost three-fourths of the Earth's surface is covered with............... .

2. The continent Asia lies in the .... Hemisphere.

3. The shape of the Pacific Ocean is ....

4. Oceans have nourished the cultures of .... people all over the world.

5. Oceans play a crucial role in regulating the .... and sustaining life on Earth.

Ans. 1. water 2. Northern
3. circular 4. coastal 5. climate

True or False

1. The Earth appears mostly blue from outer space because most of its surface is covered with land.

2. The oceans hold most of the Earth's freshwater.

3. There are five oceans on Earth: the Pacific, Atlantic, Indian, Arctic and Southern (or Antarctic) Oceans.

4. A tsunami is a powerful wave generally caused by a strong earthquake or volcanic eruption at the bottom of the ocean.

5. The continents of Europe and Asia are often considered a single continent called Eurasia by geologists.

Ans. 1. False 2. False 3. True 4. True 5. True

Match the Following

1.

List I		List II
A. Oceans	1.	The plant life is found in the oceans.
B. Continents	2.	The large continuous expanse of land on Earth.
C. Water cycle	3.	The process by which water circulates between the Earth's oceans, atmosphere and land.
D. Marine flora	4.	Large bodies of saltwater cover most of the Earth's surface.
E. Marine fauna	5.	Animal life is found in the oceans.

Codes

	A	B	C	D	E		A	B	C	D	E
(a)	4	2	3	1	5	(b)	1	2	3	4	5
(c)	5	4	3	2	1	(d)	2	3	1	5	4

Ans. (a)

Assertion-Reason

1. **Assertion** (A) Oceans cover nearly three-fourths of the Earth's surface.

Reason (R) The Earth is called the 'blue planet' because of its extensive water coverage.

Codes

(a) Both A and R are true and R is the correct explanation of A

(b) Both A and R are true, but R is not the correct explanation of A

(c) A is true, but R is false

(d) A is false, but R is true

2. **Assertion** (A) Tsunamis can travel thousands of kilometers and cause widespread damage.

Reason (R) Tsunamis are caused by strong earthquakes or volcanic eruptions at the bottom of the ocean.

Codes

(a) Both A and R are true and R is the correct explanation of A

(b) Both A and R are true, but R is not the correct explanation of A

(c) A is true, but R is false

(d) A is false, but R is true

3. **Assertion** (A) Freshwater makes up a large proportion of the planet's water resources.

Reason (R) Most of the freshwater is found in glaciers, rivers, lakes, atmosphere and underground.

Codes

(a) Both A and R are true and R is the correct explanation of A

(b) Both A and R are true, but R is not the correct explanation of A

(c) A is true, but R is false

(d) A is false, but R is true

Ans. 1. (a) 2. (a) 3. (d)

Case Based Questions

1. **Read the paragraph given and answer the following questions.**

Oceans and continents are vital parts of the environment and affect most aspects of our lives, even if we do not notice it. We have mentioned that oceans send rain to the continents; this is part of the Earth's water cycle, which you will further study in science.

Without oceans, for instance, there would be no rainfall! The Earth would be a desert. Moreover, more than half of the world's oxygen is produced by the oceans' flora, which is why they are called 'the planet's lung's. The oceans, therefore, play a crucial role in regulating the climate and sustaining life on Earth. Oceans have deeply impacted humanity in many other ways. From early times, people have used oceans and seas to migrate to other regions, to trade in all kinds of goods, to conduct military campaigns, and as a source of food through fishing. Oceans have also nourished the cultures of coastal people all over the world. Almost all of them have tales and legends about the sea, sea gods and goddesses, sea monsters and treasures from the sea the oceans' dangers but also their blessings.

(i) How do oceans contribute to the Earth's water cycle, and what would happen to the Earth without oceans?

(ii) What is the significance of the flora in the oceans concerning the Earth's oxygen supply?

(iii) How have oceans historically impacted human activities and civilisations?

Ans. (i) Oceans send rain to the continents as part of the Earth's water cycle. Without oceans, there would be no rainfall, and the Earth would become a desert.

(ii) The ocean flora have a significant role to play in Earth's oxygen supply as more than half of the world's oxygen is supplied by the ocean flora. Hence, oceans are often called 'the Planet's lungs'.

(iii) Oceans have impacted humanity by enabling migration, trade, military campaigns and providing food through fishing. They have also nourished coastal cultures with tales, legends and resources.

2. **Read the passage given below and answer the following questions.**

They are large masses of clouds. Such clouds bring rain to the continents; for instance, the monsoon rains we in India expect every summer originate in the ocean–without such rains, our agriculture and all life will suffer. But oceans often also give rise to storms–violent events with extreme rainfall or very strong winds, such as cyclones, which can cause widespread damage to coastal regions of the world. A tsunami is another natural disaster that originates in the ocean. It is a huge and powerful wave generally caused by a strong earthquake or a volcanic eruption at the bottom of the ocean. Tsunamis can travel thousands of kilometres and submerge coastal areas, causing widespread damage.

(i) What natural phenomenon originating in the ocean is essential for agriculture in India during the summer?

(a) Cyclones (b) Tsunamis

(c) Monsoon rains (d) Volcanic eruptions

(ii) How do large masses of clouds formed over oceans contribute to agriculture in regions like India?

(a) By creating high-pressure systems

(b) By enhancing photosynthesis directly

(c) By providing essential rainfall during the monsoon season

(d) By reducing soil erosion

(iii) Why are monsoon rains important for India?

(a) They bring strong winds

(b) They originate from the ocean

(c) They are essential for agriculture and life

(d) They cause cyclones

(iv) Cyclones are characterised by which of the following features?

(a) Very strong winds and heavy rainfall

(b) Mila breezes and light rain

(c) Extremely low temperatures

(d) Gentle waves and calm weather

Ans. (i) (c), (ii) (c), (iii) (c), (iv) (a)

Competency Based Questions

1. **Depending on our choice, we may list any number of continents between four and seven. Why and how?**

Ans. The number of continents can vary between four and seven depending on how we choose to classify them. The variation in counting depends on whether we consider certain landmasses as combined or separate based on their historical and cultural evolution or geographical boundaries.

The different number of continents are given below:

Four continents	Africa-Eurasia, America, Antarctica, Australia
Five continents	Africa, America, Antarctica, Australia, Eurasia
Six continents	Africa, Antarctica, Australia, Eurasia, North America, South America
Seven continents	Africa, Antarctica, Asia, Australia, Europe, North America, South America

2. Continents do not include all landmass. Some smaller pieces of land are left out; surrounded by water on all sides. What are such landmasses called? Does India have any of them? Discuss.

Ans. The smaller pieces of land that are left out of the continents are surrounded by water from all sides are known as islands.

India has more than 1,300 small islands. Those islands are part of two major groups–Andaman and Nicobar Islands in the Bay of Bengal and Lakshadweep Islands in the Arabian Sea. The Andaman and Nicobar Islands are known for their unique biodiversity, including endemic species and diverse marine life. The Lakshadweep islands are renowned for their coral reefs and marine biodiversity.

3. Evaluate the significance of the Earth's water bodies, including both saltwater and freshwater bodies, in supporting life and regulating the planet's climate.

Ans. All the water bodies on the Earth play a major role in supporting life and regulating the planet's climate. The following statements support this fact

- Saltwater bodies, such as oceans and seas, cover about 71% of the Earth's surface and are home to diverse ecosystems that support marine life and global fisheries.
- Oceans act as a major heat reservoir, absorbing solar radiation and distributing heat through currents, which moderates global temperatures and influences weather patterns.
- Freshwater bodies, including rivers, lakes, glaciers and groundwater, provide essential drinking water, support agriculture, and are vital for numerous terrestrial ecosystems.
- Freshwater bodies participate in the water cycle too, involving evaporation, condensation and precipitation.

All the water bodies are interconnected systems that are fundamental to Earth's environmental stability and the well-being of all living organisms.

4. "Rahul Roy is a businessman from India and he has to travel from New Delhi (Asia) to Brazil (South America) for his business meetings. He chooses to take a flight and therefore, he has to cross different continents and oceans." Choose the option of continents/oceans that will come in his journey.

(a) Asia, Indian Ocean, Africa, Atlantic Ocean, South America.

(b) Asia, Indian Ocean, Europe, Atlantic Ocean, South America

(c) Indian Ocean, Africa, Atlantic Ocean, South America

(d) Asia, Africa, Atlantic Ocean, South America

Ans. (a) Asia, Indian Ocean, Africa, Atlantic Ocean, South America.

Skill Based Questions as per NEP 2020

1. Create a simple plan to conserve water at home. Outline three practical steps and explain how each step contributes to water conservation.

Ans. To conserve water at home, my plan includes three practical steps: installing water-efficient fixtures, practising mindful water usage and reusing water. These are discussed below

- First, I would install low-flow showerheads and faucets, as these fixtures reduce water flow without compromising functionality, saving significant amounts of water daily.
- Second, I would ensure that all family members practice mindful water usage, such as turning off the tap while brushing their teeth and taking shorter showers, which directly reduces water waste.
- Lastly, I would set up a system to collect and reuse greywater from sinks and showers for gardening purposes. This step not only reduces the demand for freshwater but also provides a sustainable way to maintain plants without additional water use. These measures collectively contribute to water conservation by minimising waste and optimising the use of available water resources.

2. Assess the impact of human activities on the oceans. What are two major threats to ocean health, and what measures can be taken to mitigate these threats?

Ans. Human activities have significantly impacted ocean health, with pollution and overfishing being two major threats. Pollution, including plastic waste and chemical runoff, harms marine life and disrupts ecosystems. Overfishing depletes fish populations and alters food webs.

To mitigate these threats, measures such as reducing plastic use, improving waste management, establishing marine protected areas, and enforcing sustainable fishing practices are essential. These actions can help preserve marine biodiversity and ensure the long-term health of ocean ecosystems.

3. Create a detailed diary entry from the perspective of an explorer navigating the oceans during the Age of Exploration. Describe the challenges and discoveries made during the journey.

Ans. "Today marks our third month at sea since departing from Lisbon. The vast expanse of the Atlantic Ocean stretches endlessly before us. The crew is growing weary, but our spirits remain high with the promise of new lands and riches.

Navigating these treacherous waters is no easy feat-unpredictable storms and strong currents test our resolve daily. Yesterday, we encountered a pod of dolphins, a sight that lifted the men's spirits. Supplies are running low, and freshwater is scarce, but we press on, driven by the dream of reaching India and establishing new trade routes. The stars guide us by night, and by day, we chart our course with the astrolabe. Each dawn brings new challenges and the hope of discovery. May the seas be kind to us as we continue our voyage."

4. Research and present a case study on the Andaman and Nicobar Islands, focusing on their geographical features, biodiversity, and the impact of the 2004 tsunami.

Ans. The Andaman and Nicobar Islands are a group of islands located in the Bay of Bengal. Geographically, they are characterised by hilly terrain and dense rainforests, which support a rich biodiversity, including unique species of flora and fauna. The islands are home to several indigenous tribes who have preserved their traditional ways of life.

The 2004 tsunami, triggered by an undersea earthquake near Indonesia, had a devastating impact on these islands, causing significant loss of life and property. The disaster highlighted the need for effective early warning systems and disaster preparedness strategies.

ASSESSMENT EXERCISE

Objective Type Questions

1. Which continent is permanently covered with ice?

(a) Australia
(b) North America
(c) Antarctica
(d) Europe

2. Name the continent which is surrounded by water bodies from three sides.

(a) Asia (b) Europe
(c) Antarctica (d) Australia

3. Which planet is known as a 'blue planet'?

(a) Venus (b) Mars
(c) Earth (d) Neptune

4. Assertion (A) The Earth's climate is regulated by the oceans.

Reason (R) Oceans play a role in maintaining the water cycle.

Codes

(a) Both A and R are true and R is the correct explanation of A
(b) Both A and R are true, but R is not the correct explanation of A
(c) A is true, but R is false
(d) A is false, but R is true

5. From early times, people have used oceans and seas to .... to other regions, to trade in all kinds of goods, and as a source of food through ....

6. The Earth's water cycle involves processes such as .... , ... and .... , which are driven by the oceans.

7. Oceans do not play a significant role in regulating the Earth's climate. (True or False)

8. Without oceans, there would still be adequate rainfall to sustain life on Earth. (True or False)

Subjective Questions (VSA, SA & LA)

1. Name the second largest continent after Asia.

2. What is the most widespread colour seen from space when looking at Earth?

3. Which research station was established by India in Antarctica?

4. Which disasters are associated with oceans?

5. Explain how in different ways we can calculate the continents.

6. Describe two ways in which oceans regulate the Earth's climate.

7. How does the distribution of oceans and continents differ between the Northern and Southern Hemispheres?

8. Suggest two measures that can be taken to protect and preserve ocean ecosystems.

9. Analyse the effects of tsunamis on coastal regions with examples.

CHAPTER 3

Landforms and Life

The land has many forms and features. The appearance of land changes a lot from one region to another. For example, if you are travelling by road from Chhota Nagpur region in Jharkhand to reach Almora in Uttarakhand via Prayagraj in Uttar Pradesh, you will see very different landscapes on the way.

3.1 Landforms

- A **landform** is a physical feature on the surface of our planet Earth.
- The landforms take shape over millions of years and have a significant connection with the environment and life.
- Landforms have different climates and are home to a variety of **flora** and **fauna**.
- Humans are similar to most of the **mammals** that live on land. They have adapted to all landforms, but the number of people living on different kinds of landforms varies throughout the world.
- Human **adaptation** and **resilience** to the landforms are represented by the various ways in which people have settled on different landforms.
- Landforms can broadly be divided into three categories i.e., **mountains**, **plateaus** and **plains**. However, there are few more landforms according to experts such as **deserts**.

Mountains

- The landforms that are much higher than the surrounding land are considered as mountains. Mountains can be recognised by a broad base, steep slopes and a narrow summit.
- The features of mountains vary according to their altitude (height). The high-altitude mountains are generally covered with snow while, at lower altitudes, the snow melts every summer and turns into water. This water flows down towards the plain as rivers. Therefore, many rivers originate from mountainous regions.
- The **Ganga** is the **largest river** in India. It originates from the Himalayas. The Ganga is nearly 2,500 km long. The Ganga has numerous tributaries. Some of them are the Yamuna and the Ghagara. These two tributaries also originated from the Himalayas. Other tributaries like the Son or Sone, originate from the Vindhya Range to the South of the Ganga plain.
- Highlands with lower heights, less steep slopes and rounded tops are called hills.
- Most of the world's mountains are grouped in mountain ranges, such as the **Himalayas** in Asia, the **Alps** in Europe and the **Andes** in South America. Some of these ranges stretch for thousands of kilometres.

What is Snow?

In most of India, **precipitation** is in the form of **rain** and **hail**. But at higher altitudes, precipitation is in the form of snow. It covers the landscape in a soft and beautiful white blanket. **Snow** and **hailstones** are precipitation of water in a solid state.

Some Major Mountains of the World

- **Mount Everest** between Tibet (China) and Nepal, and **Kanchenjunga** between Nepal and the Indian state of Sikkim are the two highest peaks of the Himalayan range.
- **Mount Aconcagua** in South America is the highest peak of the Andes.
- **Mount Kilimanjaro** in Eastern Africa is an isolated mountain that is not part of any range.
- **Mont Blanc** in Western Europe is the highest mountain of the Alps.

- **Anamudi** in Kerala, also known as Anai Peak, is the highest mountain in South India.

A sketch showing the relative heights of six mountains of the world

Young and Older Mountains

- Mountains with tall and sharp peaks, like the Himalayas, are relatively **young**. They were formed recently in Earth's history. They are called young because they are still in the developmental stage and their height is increasing continuously.
- Mountains that are short and have rounded tops, like the Aravallis are considered **'old mountains'**. Due to continuous erosion, their peaks are rounded.

Mountain Environment

- Mountain slopes are often covered with a type of forest called **montane forests**. In these forests, conifer trees such as pines, firs, spruce and deodar are common.
- Conifer trees are tall and cone-shaped, with thin, pointed leaves. At higher altitudes, only **grasses**, **mosses** and **lichens** are found.
- Deep forests, flowing rivers, lakes, grasslands and caves in the mountains are home to diverse fauna, for example, the golden eagle, the peregrine falcon, the Canadian lynx, the mountain hare, etc.

Life in the Mountains

Agriculture

- The mountain terrain is usually **rugged** or **rough** and has steep slopes. Hence, agriculture can be practised only in a few valley regions in the mountains.
- Cultivation is practised on the slopes by cutting steps into the slope. This is called **terrace farming**.
- In many mountainous regions of the world, herding is preferred as an occupation over agriculture.

Tourism

- **Tourism** is an important source of income for the people living in the mountains.
- The scenic beauty of the mountains attracts numerous tourists. Some tourists also go to the mountains for sports such as skiing, hiking, mountaineering and paragliding.

  However, when more tourists visit the mountains, it puts pressure on the environment of the mountains.

Culture

- For many centuries, people have also travelled to the mountains for pilgrimages to holy sites. **Mount Kailash** in **Tibet** is believed to be sacred by followers of **Hinduism**, **Buddhism**, **Jainism** and **Bon** (an ancient Tibetan religion).
- Most traditional communities worldwide consider the mountains as sacred places and worship them.
- **Mount Everest** is the highest mountain in the world at 8,849 m. It is known by many names like 'Chomolungma' in Tibet, which means **Mother Goddess of the World**. It is also known as **Sagarmatha** in Nepal which means **Goddess of the Sky**. Thus, it is worshipped by Tibetans and Nepalis.

Women Climbers of India

- **Bachendri Pal** was the **first Indian woman** to climb Mount Everest in 1984. She was awarded Padma Shri in 1984 and Padma Bhushan in 2019. She started climbing mountains from a young age and led many women's climbing expeditions.
- **Arunima Sinha** lost a leg in an accident when she was 31. With Bachendri Pal's encouragement and training, she managed to climb Mount Everest in 2013. She has climbed the highest peak of every continent, including **Mount Vinson** in Antarctica. She was awarded Padma Shri in 2015.

Try These

1. **Which landform is characterised by high elevation and flat surface?**
2. **Which type of forest are mainly found on the mountain slopes? Give an example of flora found there.**
3. **Which type of precipitation is common at higher altitudes?**

Plateaus

- A **plateau** is a landform that is higher from the surrounding land and has a flat surface. Some of its sides are often steep slopes.
- The height of plateaus can vary from a few hundred metres to several thousand metres.
- Like mountains, plateaus can be young or old in terms of the Earth's history.
- Two examples of plateaus are
  (i) **Tibetan Plateau** It is the **world's largest plateau.** The average altitude of the Tibetan plateau is 4,500 m, therefore it has been nicknamed the **Roof of the World.** From East to West, it is nearly 2,500 km long, which is equal to the distance from Chandigarh to Kanyakumari.
  (ii) **Deccan Plateau** The Deccan Plateau of Central and South India is one of the **oldest plateaus** in the world. It was formed through volcanic activity millions of years ago.

Minerals

- Just like mountains, plateaus are rich in mineral deposits. They are called **storehouses of minerals.** Therefore, mining is a major activity on plateaus.
- For example, the East African Plateau is famous for gold and diamond mining. In India, huge reserves of **iron, coal** and **manganese** are found in the Chhota Nagpur Plateau.
- The plateau environment is very diverse across the world. Many plateaus have rocky soil and they are less fertile than plains. Hence, plateaus are less favourable to farming. However, farming can be done in lava plateaus (that is, formed through volcanic activity), as they are often rich in black soil.

Waterfall

- Numerous waterfalls can be seen in the plateau regions. The Victoria Falls on the Zambezi River in Southern Africa, the **Hundru Falls** on the Subarnarekha River in the Chhota Nagpur Plateau and the Jog Falls on the Sharavati River in the Western Ghats are some examples of waterfalls.
- The **Nohkalikai Falls** in Cherrapunji Plateau (Meghalaya) has a height of 340 meters.

Plains

- Plains are areas of land that are mostly flat or have very gentle slopes. They do not have any large hills or deep valleys.
- The height of plains is generally not more than 300 metres above sea level. Plains also support a variety of flora and fauna.
- **Floodplains** are a type of plains which is formed by rivers originating in mountain ranges.
- Floodplains are formed where the rivers collect particles of rock, sand and silt called **sediments.** These sediments make the soil very fertile. Therefore, these plains are ideal for growing all kinds of crops.

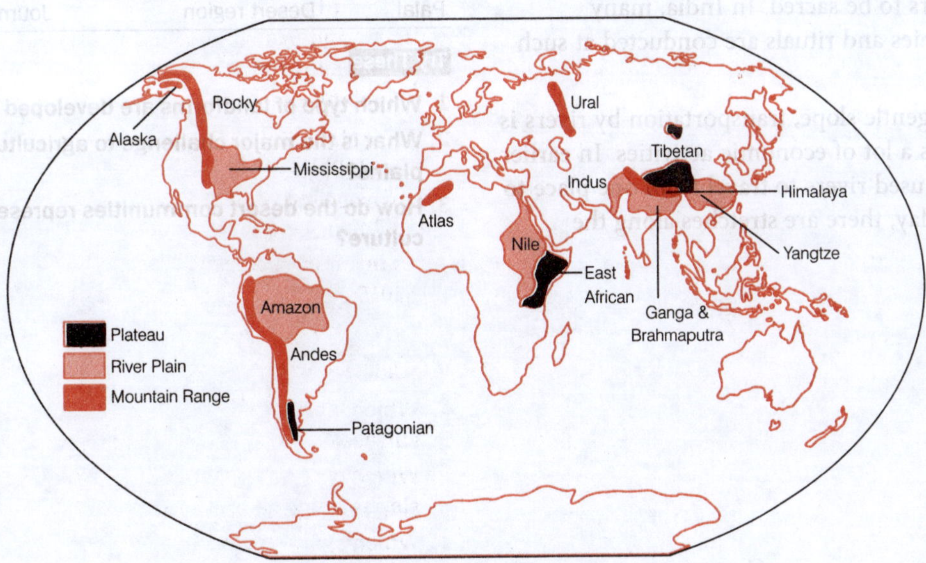

This world map shows a few major mountain ranges, plateaus and plains

Life in the Plains

- A large population of the world resides within the plain areas.
- About 40 crore people of the total population in India, live in **Ganga plain** (often called the **Gangetic plain**). Thus, it is affected by the problems of high population and pollution.

Agriculture

- Cultivation was developed in the fertile regions of plains thousands of years ago. In most of the plains of the world, the major occupations of people are river fishing and agriculture.
- In Gangetic plains, agriculture is the major occupation. Food crops such as rice, wheat, maize, barley and millet are grown in this region. Fibre crops such as cotton, jute and hemp are also grown in the Gangetic plain.
- Traditionally agriculture is mostly rainfed (land is irrigated by rainfall) but in recent decades, irrigation facilities like networks of canals or groundwater are used to water the fields.
- Irrigation has increased agricultural production, but it has also contributed to the depletion (or decrease) of groundwater. This is a challenge for the future of agriculture in the region.

Culture and Economy

- Rivers in mountain ranges or plains around the world have immense cultural value. Many communities have considered a river's source and its confluence with one or two other rivers to be sacred. In India, many festivals, ceremonies and rituals are conducted at such locations.
- As plains have a gentle slope, transportation by rivers is easy and supports a lot of economic activities. In earlier days, people also used rivers to travel from one place to another. Even today, there are stretches along the Ganga where people prefer to use boats to move from one place to another.

Deserts

- Deserts are considered to be large and dry landforms with very little precipitation. They also have a unique flora and fauna.
- There are two types of deserts- **hot and cold.** Examples of hot deserts are the **Sahara Desert** in Africa or the **Thar Desert** in the North-West of the Indian subcontinent. Examples of cold deserts include the **Gobi Desert** in Asia. Some experts also consider the Antarctica continent as a desert.
- Humans have adapted to most of the deserts irrespective of their harsh living conditions.
- In India, communities living in the Thar Desert, or migrating through it, have rich cultural traditions related to the desert such as folk songs and legends.

Five Tinais

In ancient Tamil Sangam poetry, there are five tinais. These tinais are five landforms that are related to specific gods, and lifestyles, moods or emotions. The following table shows the main occupation of the five landforms

Tinai	Landform	Main Occupation
Kurinji	Mountainous regions	Hunting and gathering
Mullai	Grassland and forests	Cattle rearing
Marudam	Fertile agricultural plains	Farming
Neydal	Coastal region	Fishing and seafaring
Palai	Desert region	Journeying and fighting

Try These

1. **Which type of landforms are developed by rivers?**
2. **What is the major challenge to agriculture in Gangetic plains?**
3. **How do the desert communities represent their vibrant culture?**

Glossary

Altitude The height of an object above sea level. Examples: the altitude of a mountain, the altitude of a bird or plane in flight, and the altitude of a satellite.

Montane forest A type of forest that grows in mountainous regions.

Moss A small green plant without flowers or true roots, often spreading in a cushion-like cover.

Lichen A plant-like organism that generally clings to rocks, walls or trees.

Terrain A piece or stretch of land, from the point of view of its physical features.

Adaptation Adaptation is a change or evolution in an animal or plant that helps it survive better in its environment.

Valley A valley is a low area of land between hills or mountains, often where a river or stream flows.

Flash floods A sudden local flood, often caused by a cloudburst.

Landslides The sudden collapse of a mass of Earth or rock from a mountainside.

Avalanche The sudden fall of snow, ice or rocks from a mountainside often occurs when the snow starts melting.

Cloudburst A sudden violent rainstorm.

Tributaries The rivers and streams that join the other larger rivers.

Erosion It is the process by which natural forces like wind, water, and ice break the rocks and soil, gradually moving them from one place to another.

Precipitation Precipitation is any form of water that falls from the sky. It includes rain, snow, sleet and hail.

Confluence It is the place where two or more rivers or streams meet and combine into one.

Expedition A journey that is meant for a specific reason, like adventure, research, etc.

Undulating surface Such a surface is identified as one that has a smooth, wavy shape with gentle rises and falls.

Sea level It is the average height of the ocean's surface, used as a standard to measure the elevation of land and the depth of the sea.

Sediments Sediments are small particles of rock, soil and other materials that are carried by wind, water, or ice.

Resilience It is the capacity to meet challenges and difficulties, adapt to them or overcome them.

LANDFORMS AND LIFE

Major Mountain Ranges

- Mount Everest and Kanchenjunga are the highest peaks of Himalayan range.
- Mount Aconcagua is the highest peak of the Andes.
- Mount Blanc is the highest peak of Alps.

Types of Mountains

- **Young Mountains** These mountains have steep slopes and high altitudes. For example, The Himalayas
- **Old Mountains** These mountains have lesser altitude and rounded top. For example, The Aravallis.

Mountain Environment

- Mountain slopes are covered with Montane forest.
- Conifers trees like pines, firs, spruce and deodar are common in these forests.
- At higher altitudes only grasses, mosses and lichen are found.
- Fauna of mountains include- Grey fox, yak, Ibex, leopard and black bear etc.

Mountains

- A landforms that are higher than surrounding lands are known as mountains.
- Highlands with lower height, less slopes and rounded tops are called hills.

Life in the Mountains

- Terrain is usually rugged or rough.
- Agriculture is possible in valley regions only.
- Terrace farming is common.
- Tourism is an important source of income.

Plains

- A landform with vast flat or gently undulating surface.
- Flood plains are formed by rivers originated in mountain ranges. The river soils makes them fertile.
- Agriculture is main occupation in plains.

Life in Plains

- About one-fourth of India's population lives in Gangetic plains.
- Crops like-cotton, jute, rice, wheat, maize are grown.

Culture

- The confluence of two or more rivers is considered as sacred.
- In India many festivals, ceremonies and rituals are conducted at such locations.

Plateaus

- A landform that is higher than surrounding landforms, with flat surface mostly.
- The height of plateaus can vary from a few hundred metres to several thousand metres.
- Tibet is the highest plateau of the world.
- Plateaus are often called 'storehouses of minerals'.

Plateau Environment

- Many plateaus have a rocky soil, which makes them less fertile.
- Lava plateaus that are formed through volcanic activity have rich black soil.
- Waterfalls are common feature of plateaus. For example,
  - The Victoria Falls - Zambezi river in Southern Africa
  - The Hundru Falls - Subarnarekha river in Chhota Nagpur plateau.
  - The Jog Falls - Sharavati river in Western Ghats.

NCERT FOLDER

Detailed Answers of All NCERT Questions

Lets's Explore (Page 42)

Q.1 As a class activity, form groups of four or five students and observe the school's surroundings. What kind of landscape do you see? Will the landscape change a few kilometres away? Or within some 50 kilometres? Compared with other groups.

Ans. The following landscape can be observed in the surroundings

(a) Plains (b) Plateaus

(c) Mountains

Landscape may or may not be changed within 50 kilometres.

Q.2 In the same groups, discuss a journey that any of you has made through a region of India. List the different landscapes seen on the way. Compare it with other groups.

Ans. The following landscapes can be observed during the journey in India

(a) Mountains (b) Plains

(c) Plateaus (d) Deserts

(e) Coastal region

Lets's Explore (Page 46)

Q.3 Here are two verses from a long poem by Kalidasa, who lived at least 1,500 years ago and is often considered to be the greatest poet of ancient India. The poem, Kumarasambhava, begins with an invocation to the Himalayas. (This is a simplified translation from Sanskrit.)

In the North rises Himalaya, the Lord of mountains, like a living god, who measures the Earth and stretches from the Western to the Eastern oceans. .... From it the wind comes down, carrying spray from descending Ganga, shaking the deodar trees, opening the peacocks' tail feathers and cooling the mountain people after they hunt deer. Discuss the verses and the following questions in class.

(a) What are the 'Western to the Eastern oceans'? Can you locate them as well as the 'Lord of mountains' on given figure?

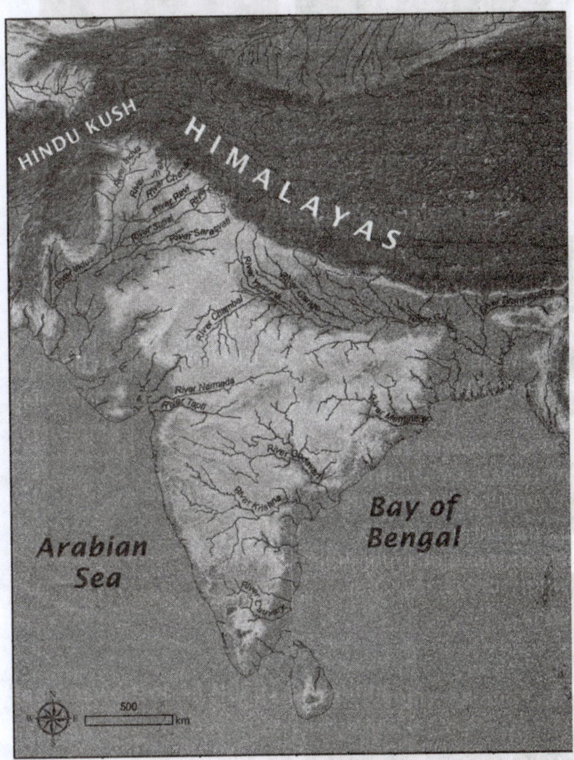

Ans. The Western ocean is Arabian sea and Eastern ocean is Bay of Bengal. 'Lord of mountains' is the Himalayas.

(b) Why is Ganga river mentioned?
(Hint: There could be several reasons.)

Ans. Ganga river is mentioned because

- Most of the population lives in the Ganga plains.
- It is most important in terms of agriculture.
- It is the sacred river in India.

Lets's Explore (Page 49)

Q.3 The images given below depict a few challenges that people living in the mountains may face. Discuss them in groups in the class and write one paragraph on each. Also discuss why, despite many such challenges, people still choose to live in the mountains.

Flash Flood, Landslide, Uncontrolled Tourism, Avalanche, Heavy Snowfall, Cloudburst, Cold Weather

Ans. The above given pictures depict the problems for people living in mountains. These are discussed below

(i) **Flash Flood** Flash flood is the sudden flood in a local region due to cloud burst. Sudden heavy rain can quickly turn mountain streams into dangerous floods. It can damage homes and roads.

(ii) **Uncontrolled Tourism** Too many visitors can put pressure on local resources and disturb mountain ecosystems, harming both the environment and local communities.

(iii) **Landslide** Soil and rocks sliding down slopes can destroy homes and block roads in mountain areas.

(iv) **Avalanches** It is a landslide due to heavy snowfall. Large snow slides can damage villages and disrupt travel in snowy mountain regions.

(v) **Heavy Snowfall** Excessive snow can block roads, limit access, and cause damage to houses in mountain areas.

(vi) **Cloudburst** Intense, short bursts of rain can lead to sudden floods and erosion in mountainous regions.

(vii) **Cold Weather** Extremely cold temperatures can make daily life and travel very difficult in the mountains.

People still prefer to live in mountainous regions because they are sacred to them. Mountains are a great source of tourism activity and many more natural resources.

Let's Explore (Page 53)

Q.4 Use the colour code in the map given below to add a landform to each name. For instance, 'Tibetan Plateau', 'Rocky range', 'Nile plain'. (You do not have to remember the names in this map.)

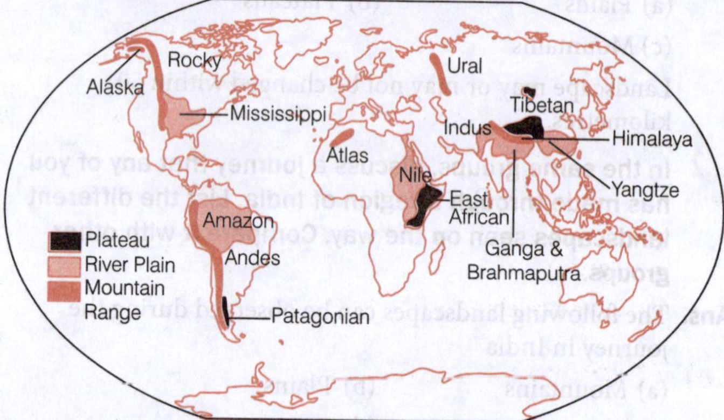

Ans. Do it yourself

Let's Explore (Page 54)

Q.5 The picture given below has been taken from a satellite. It captures a portion of North India from a high altitude. Observe and discuss the image as a class activity.

(a) Which colour is the Ganga plain?

(b) What does the white expanse represent?

(c) What does the brown expanse at the bottom left of the image represent?

Ans. (a) The Ganga plain is represented through green colour.

(b) The white expanse represents the Himalayan range.

(c) The brown expanse in the bottom left corner represents the Deccan plateau.

Let's Explore (Page 55)

Q.6 Can you give examples of river sources or confluences from your region that are regarded as sacred by any community?

Ans. Following are some examples of places that are sacred because they are source of river or confluence of river:

(a) **Gangotri** origin place of river Ganga

(b) **Yamunotri** origin place of river Yamuna

(c) **Allahabad** confluence of river Ganga, Yamuna and Saraswati

(d) **Devprayag** confluence of river Alaknanda and Bhagirathi

Q.7 Visit a nearby river and observe all activities there, whether economic or cultural. Note them down and discuss with your classmates.

Ans. The common economic and cultural activities near rivers are as follows

(a) Agriculture (b) Pilgrimages

(c) Sacred celebrations (d) Industries

Let's Explore (Page 56)

Q.8 Name some popular tourist destinations in India and identify the category of landform they are associated with.

Ans. Some popular tourist destinations in India and their landforms are as follows

(a) Leh-cold desert (b) Mussoorie-mountains

(c) Thar safari-hot desert (d) Kochi-sea coast

(e) Varanasi-plains

Questions, Activities and Projects

Q.1 In what type of landform is your town / village / city located? Which features mentioned in this chapter do you see around you?

Ans. Do it yourself

Q.2 Let us go back to our initial trip from Chhota Nagpur to Prayagraj and Almora. Describe the three landforms you came across on the way.

Ans. The three landforms from Chhota Nagpur to Prayagraj and Almora were plateaus, plains and mountains. These are described as follows

(a) **Plateaus** A plateau is a landform that rises from the surrounding land and has a more or less flat surface; some of its sides are often steep slopes. The height of plateaus can vary from a few hundred metres to several thousand metres.

(b) **Plains** Plains are landforms that have an extensive flat or gently undulating surface. They do not have any large hills or deep valleys. They are generally not more than 300 metres above sea level.

(c) **Mountains** Mountains are landforms that are much higher than the surrounding landscape. A broad base, steep slopes and a narrow summit can recognise them. Depending on their height, some mountains are covered with snow.

Q.3 List a few famous pilgrimage spots in India along with the landforms in which they are found.

Ans. Some of the famous pilgrimage site in India with their landforms type are as follows

(a) Vaishno Devi : mountains

(b) Amarnath Cave Temple : mountains

(c) Gangotri Temple: mountains

(d) Badrinath Temple : mountains

(e) Rameswaram : coastal region

(f) Tirupati: hills

(g) Shirdi : plains

(h) Haridwar: plains

Q.4 State whether true or false.

(a) The Himalayas are young mountains with rounded tops.

(b) Plateaus usually rise sharply at least on one side.

(c) Mountains and hills belong to the same type of landform.

(d) Mountains, plateaus and rivers in India have the same types of flora and fauna.

(e) Ganga is a tributary to the Yamuna.

(f) Deserts have unique flora and fauna.

(g) Melting snow feeds rivers.

(h) Sediments from rivers deposited in the plains make the land fertile.

(i) All deserts are hot.

Ans. (a) False (b) True

(c) True (d) False

(e) False (f) True

(g) True (h) True

(i) False

Q.5 Match words in pairs

Mount Everest	Africa
Rafting	Roof of the world
Camels	Rice fields
Plateau	Desert
Gangetic plains	River
Waterway	Ganga
Mount Kilimanjaro	Tributary
Yamuna	Climbing

Ans.

Mount Everest	climbing
Rafting	River
Camels	Desert
Plateau	Roof of the world
Gangetic plains	Rice fields
Waterway	Ganga
Mount Kilimanjaro	Africa
Yamuna	Tributary

REVIEW EXERCISE

Including Competency Based Questions

Very Short Answer Type Questions

1. Why is terrace farming practiced in mountainous regions?

Ans. Terrace farming is practiced in mountainous regions due to the steep slopes of hills and mountains.

2. Excessive tourism is a concern for mountain environments. How?

Ans. The excessive tourism might be a concern for mountain environments due to the fragile nature of the mountains and increased pollution due to tourism.

3. How do plateaus differ from plains in terms of their surface features?

Ans. The plateaus differ from plains in terms of their surface features as plateaus have at least one side with a steep slope, while plains are vast undulating land.

4. What makes floodplains ideal for agriculture?

Ans. Floodplains are ideal for agriculture because they are fertile due to the sediments deposited by the rivers.

5. How has the Ganga river influenced cultural practices in India?

Ans. The river Ganga is considered sacred and hence several festivals and cultural activities revolve around the river and places associated with it.

6. Early civilisations often located near rivers in plains. Why?

Ans. Early civilisation were often located near the river in plains because it is a fertile region and supports various crop cultivation.

7. Increased irrigation poses for agriculture in the Gangetic plains. How?

Ans. Increased irrigation facilities have boosted agriculture in Gangetic plains, but in the near future, it will lead to depletion in groundwater sources.

8. What evidence suggests mountains held spiritual significance in many cultures?

Ans. The following evidence suggests mountains hold a spiritual significance in many cultures

- Mount Everest is the highest mountain in the world at 8,849 m. It is known by many names. Tibetans name it 'Chomolungma', which means 'Mother Goddess of the World', Nepalis call it 'Sagarmatha', meaning 'Goddess of the Sky'. Thus, it is worshiped by Tibetans and Nepalis.
- Mount Kailash in Tibet is held sacred by followers of Hinduism, Buddhism, Jainism and Bon.

9. What distinguishes cold deserts from hot deserts?

Ans. The cold and hot deserts can be distinguished based on the temperature.

Short Answer Type Questions

1. What are the major types of landforms and their significance to life and culture?

Ans. The major types of landforms are mountains, plateaus, and plains. Their significance to life and culture is as follows

- Mountains offer natural beauty and resources.
- Plateaus are rich in minerals.
- Plains provide fertile soil for agriculture, each supporting diverse human cultures and activities.

2. What are mountain forests, and where are they commonly found? What are common animals found there?

Ans. Mountain forests are types of forests found in mountainous regions, characterised by coniferous trees like pines and firs. These forests are commonly found in the Himalayas and other high-altitude areas around the world. At higher altitudes only grasses, mosses and lichens are found.

Some typical animals found in mountain habitats are: the golden eagle, peregrine falcon, canadian lynx, snow leopard, ibex, Himalayan tahr, mountain hare, yak, grey fox and black bear.

3. What is terrace farming and why is it practised in mountainous regions?

Ans. Terrace farming is the form of agriculture seen in mountainous regions. In terrace farming, slopes of the mountains are made flat by cutting them. This type of farming is common in North-East India to grow tea leaves.

It is practiced in mountainous regions to prevent soil erosion and water runoff, which are major concerns in hilly areas. The mountain is made into steps that slows down the speed of rainwater preventing the damage to the crops.

4. What challenges do people face living in mountainous areas?

Ans. The following challenges are faced by the people living in mountainous areas

- **Flash Flood** Flash flood is the sudden flood in a local region due to cloud burst. Sudden heavy rain can quickly turn mountain streams into dangerous floods. It can damage homes and roads.
- **Landslide** Soil and rocks sliding down slopes can destroy homes and block roads in mountain areas.
- **Avalanches** It is a landslide due to heavy snowfall. Large snow slides can damage villages and disrupt travel in snowy mountain regions.
- **Heavy Snowfall** Excessive snow can block roads, limit access, and cause damage to houses in mountain areas.
- **Cloudburst** Intense, short bursts of rain can lead to sudden floods and erosion in mountainous regions.

Long Answer Type Questions

1. Describe the characteristics and significance of plateaus, with examples.

Ans. The following are the characteristics and significance of plateaus

- Plateaus are elevated flatlands with one or more sides having steep slopes.
- Plateaus vary in height from a few hundred to several thousand meters. The Tibetan Plateau is the largest and highest in the world. Its average altitude is 4,500 meters. It is also known as the 'Roof of the World'.
- The Deccan Plateau in India, one of the oldest, was formed through volcanic activity millions of years ago.
- Plateaus are rich in minerals, making mining a major activity. For example, the East African Plateau is famous for gold and diamond mining, while the Chhota Nagpur Plateau in India has vast reserves of iron, coal, and manganese.

2. Explain the importance of plains for human habitation and agriculture.

Ans. The plains are important for human habitation and agriculture because

- Plains are extensive flat or gently undulating areas, generally not more than 300 meters above sea level.
- Plains are formed by river deposits that create fertile soil ideal for agriculture.
- Floodplains, a type of plain, are created by sediments deposited by rivers originating in mountains.
- Plains are fertile areas that support intensive farming, which is a major economic activity.
- Plains also support diverse flora and fauna, and they have been home to many of the world's earliest civilisations.
- In India, the Ganga Plain supports over 40 crore people, showcasing its significance for human habitation and agricultural productivity.

3. What are the main types of landforms, and how do they differ from each other?

Ans. The main types of landforms are mountains, plateaus and plains. Mountains are elevated areas with steep slopes. They are generally part of ranges like the Himalayas or the Andes.

Plateaus are elevated flatlands with steep sides. They are rich in minerals. Most of the plateaus are formed by volcanic activity or tectonic movements.

Plains are flat or gently undulating landforms. The plains formed by river deposits are fertile and suitable for agriculture. All these landforms are different in their formation processes, elevation, and suitability for various human activities.

4. Give an overview of the cultural and economic significance of the Thar Desert.

Ans. The Thar Desert, located in North-West India, has a unique cultural and economic significance.

Culturally, it is home to rich traditions, including folk songs and legends.

They reflect the life and struggles of people living in deserts. Economically, the Thar Desert supports activities such as animal husbandry. Drought-resistant crops such as millet, sorghum and pulses are also grown. Irrigation methods, like rainwater harvesting and drip irrigation, are used to increase crop yields. The resilience of the people living in this harsh environment is evident in their ability to sustain and develop their livelihoods despite the challenging conditions. This adaptability highlights the interdependence between humans and their environment.

Part II

Multiple Choice Questions (MCQs)

1. The Andes Mountains are located in which continent?
(a) South America (b) North America
(c) Europe (d) Australia

2. .... is the tallest in the world, attracts climbers globally.
(a) Mount Kilimanjaro (b) Mount Everest
(c) Mount Elbrus (d) Mount McKinley

3. Which highland, referred to as the 'Roof of the World,' influences the climate of Asia?
(a) Deccan Plateau (b) Patagonian Plateau
(c) Tibetan Plateau (d) East African Plateau

4. About 40 crore people of the total population of India live in the plains of..............
(a) Nile (b) Amazon
(c) Ganga (d) Mississippi

5. Which desert is known for its vibrant cultural practices, including folk songs and legends in India?
(a) Sahara Desert (b) Thar Desert
(c) Gobi Desert (d) Arabian Desert

6. Which famous waterfall, located on the Zambezi river, is known for its scenic beauty?
(a) Hundru Falls (b) Victoria Falls
(c) Jog Falls (d) Nohkalikai Falls

7. Which plateau in India is known for its fertile black soil and volcanic origin?
(a) Chhota Nagpur Plateau (b) Deccan Plateau
(c) East African Plateau (d) Patagonian Plateau

8. Mountains are considered sacred in many traditions. Which mountain is considered holy by Hindus and Buddhists?
(a) Himalayas (b) Andes
(c) Rockies (d) Mount Kailash

9. There are two types of deserts namely, hot and cold. Which of the following is an example of the cold desert?
(a) Sahara Desert (b) Thar Desert
(c) Gobi Desert (d) Arabian Desert

10. In ancient Tamil Sangam poetry which landform is associated with cattle rearing?
(a) Kurinji (b) Mullai
(c) Marudam (d) Neydal

11. Which region in India is home to the famous Hundru Falls?
(a) Western Ghats (b) Cherrapunji Plateau
(c) Chhota Nagpur Plateau (d) Patagonian Plateau

12. .... are most suitable for large-scale agriculture due to its fertile soil.
(a) Mountains (b) Plateaus
(c) Plains (d) Deserts

13. This elevated landform is often rich in mineral resources and supports mining. Identify the land form.
(a) Mountains (b) Plateaus (c) Plains (d) Deserts

14. Arrange the following mountains according to their heights from smaller to larger.
I. Mount Everest II. Mount Aconcagua
III. Mount Kilimanjaro IV. Mont Blanc
Codes
(a) II, I, III, IV (b) II, III, I, IV
(c) IV, I, II, III (d) IV, III, II, I

15. Which of the following statements is/are incorrect?
I. South America has the Andes mountains.
II. Africa has Ural mountains.
III. Ural mountain divides Europe and Africa.
Codes
(a) Only I (b) Both I and II
(c) Only II and III (d) I, II and III

Answers

1. (a)	2. (b)	3. (c)	4. (c)	5. (b)
6. (b)	7. (b)	8. (d)	9. (c)	10. (b)
11. (b)	12. (c)	13. (b)	14. (d)	15. (c)

Fill in the Blanks

1. .... farming is practised on the slopes of mountains by cutting steps into the slope.
2. The river .... originates in the Himalayas and is considered the largest river in India.
3. The .... are a range of young fold mountains that stretch across the North-Eastern states of India.
4. .... is the largest delta in the world, formed by the confluence of the Ganges and Brahmaputra rivers.
5. The .... river basin is known for its extensive alluvial deposits and rich agricultural land.
6. .... are broad, flat valleys formed due to the down-cutting of rivers over millions of years.
7. The .... plateau is known for its rich deposits of minerals such as iron ore and coal.

Ans. 1. Terrace 2. Ganga 3. Purvanchal Hills 4. Sundarbans 5. Indo-Gangetic 6. Plains 7. Chhota Nagpur

True or False

1. The Aravalli Range is an example of a relatively young mountain range.
2. Mount Everest is the highest mountain in the world, located between Tibet and Nepal.

3. The Deccan Plateau is rich in mineral deposits, making mining a major activity in the region.
4. The highest mountain peak in the world is Mount K2.
5. The Western Ghats and the Eastern Ghats are mountain ranges that run parallel to the coasts of India.
6. Plains are characterised by high elevation and rugged terrain.
7. The Indo-Gangetic plains are some of the most fertile lands in the world.
8. The Deccan Plateau is bordered by the Western Ghats on the West and the Eastern Ghats on the East.

Ans. 1. False 2. True 3. True 4. False 5. True 6. False 7. True 8. True

Match the Following

1. Match the landfoms with its characteristics.

	List I		List II
A.	Mountains	1.	Landform with a flat surface that rises above the surrounding land
B.	Plateaus	2.	Low-lying landform, often fertile and suitable for agriculture
C.	Plains	3.	Elevated landform with steep slopes and a narrow summit

Codes

	A	B	C		A	B	C
(a)	3	1	2	(b)	1	2	3
(c)	2	1	3	(d)	3	2	1

2. Match the landform with its characteristic.

	List I		List II
A.	Himalayas	1.	Delta region known for its mangrove forests
B.	Western Ghats	2.	Ancient fold mountains in North-West India
C.	Indo-Gangetic Plains	3.	Mountain range running parallel to the western coast of India
D.	Sundarbans	4.	Fertile plain formed by major Indian rivers
E.	Aravalli Range	5.	Young fold mountains in northern India

Codes

	A	B	C	D	E		A	B	C	D	E
(a)	5	3	4	1	2	(b)	2	1	3	4	5
(c)	3	2	4	1	5	(d)	4	2	5	1	3

Ans. 1. (a) 2. (a)

Assertion-Reason

1. **Assertion** (A) Mountains with tall and sharp peaks are relatively 'young'.

   Reason (R) These mountains were formed recently in the Earth's history.

   Codes

   (a) Both A and R are true and R is the correct explanation of A
   (b) Both A and R are true, but R is not the correct explanation of A
   (c) A is true, but R is false
   (d) A is false, but R is true

2. **Assertion** (A) The Deccan Plateau is one of the oldest plateaus in the world.

   Reason (R) The Deccan Plateau was formed through volcanic activity millions of years ago.

   Codes

   (a) Both A and R are true and R is the correct explanation of A
   (b) Both A and R are true, but R is not the correct explanation of A
   (c) A is true, but R is false
   (d) A is false, but R is true

3. **Assertion** (A) Mount Kilimanjaro is part of a mountain range.

   Reason (R) Mount Kilimanjaro is located in Eastern Africa.

   Codes

   (a) Both A and R are true and R is the correct explanation of A
   (b) Both A and R are true, but R is not the correct explanation of A
   (c) A is true, but R is false (d) A is false, but R is true

Ans. 1. (a) 2. (a) 3. (d)

Case Based Questions

1. **Read the following paragraph and answer the questions that follow**

   Mountains with tall and sharp peaks, like the Himalayas, are relatively 'young', which means that they were formed recently in the Earth's history–but that is still millions of years ago! Shorter and more rounded mountains and hills, like the Aravalli Range, are much older and have been rounded by erosion. Sometimes, as with the Himalayas, upliftment as well as erosion continue to this day.

   (i) Himalayas are tall and have sharp peaks because they are ....
   (a) ancient mountains (b) young mountains
   (c) eroded hills (d) coastal ranges

   (ii) The Aravalli Range is an example of old mountain because of ....
   (a) tall and sharp (b) recently formed
   (c) erosion (d) continually uplifting

   (iii) The statement "some mountains of the world, like the Himalayas, are still growing in height" implies that these mountains are
   (a) Eroding rapidly (b) Forming new valleys
   (c) Experiencing upliftment
   (d) Located in coastal regions

(iv) **The erosion affects the appearance of older mountain ranges like the Aravalli Range by**
(a) making them taller
(b) sharpening their peaks
(c) making them shorter and more rounded
(d) adding volcanic features

Ans. (i) (b) (ii) (c) (iii) (c) (iv) (c)

2. Read the following paragraph and answer the questions that follow.

Thousands of years ago, the first civilisations developed around rivers in fertile plains. In our times too, a large part of the world's population lives in plains. About 40 crore people, more than one-fourth of the total Indian population, live in India's Ganga plain (often called the 'Gangetic plain'). As with many other plains of the world, the major occupations of people in this region include river fishing and agriculture.

Food crops such as rice, wheat, maize, barley and millet are grown. Fibre crops such as cotton, jute and hemp are also grown in the Gangetic plain.

Traditional agriculture has been mostly rainfed (that is, watered through rainfall). In recent decades, however, agriculture has turned to irrigation, with water brought to the fields through networks of canals or pumped from groundwater. While irrigation has increased agricultural production, it has also contributed to the depletion (or decrease) of groundwater. This presents a challenge for the future of agriculture in the region. Some of the other problems affecting the Ganga plains include high population and pollution. Whether in mountain ranges or plains, rivers around the world have carried immense cultural value. In particular, many communities have considered a river's source and its confluence with one or two other rivers to be sacred. In India, numerous festivals, ceremonies and rituals are conducted at such locations.

Because plains have a gentle slope, river navigation is easy and supports a lot of economic activities. In earlier days, people also used rivers extensively to travel from one place to another.

(i) **Why did the first civilisations develop around rivers in fertile plains?**

(ii) **How has agriculture changed in the Gangetic plain in recent decades?**

(iii) **Why do rivers hold immense cultural value for many communities?**

Ans. (i) The first civilisations developed around rivers in fertile plains because these areas were ideal for agriculture due to their fertile soil and availability of water.

(ii) Agriculture in the Gangetic plain has shifted from being mostly rainfed to relying on irrigation, with water brought to the fields through canals or pumped from groundwater.

(iii) Rivers hold immense cultural value because many communities consider a river's source and its confluence with other rivers to be sacred, and numerous festivals, ceremonies, and rituals are conducted at these locations.

Competency Based Questions

1. Tibetan Plateau is known as the 'Roof of the World'. Why?

Ans. The Tibetan Plateau, known as the 'Roof of the World', is the largest and highest plateau with an average altitude of 4,500 meters. It influences the climate of Asia and is home to unique biodiversity and cultural heritage.

2. Plateaus are sometimes referred to as "storehouses of minerals." Why?

Ans. Plateaus are sometimes referred to as 'storehouses of minerals' because

- They are rich in mineral deposits.
- The world's largest mines are found on the plateaus.

3. How do mountains contribute to river formation? How does it impact the fertility of floodplains?

Ans. Mountains contribute to river formation through the melting of snow and glaciers, which provides a continuous source of water that flows down the slopes, forming rivers. Formation of rivers make the floodplains highly fertile because rivers deposit nutrient-rich sediments during floods, creating ideal conditions for agriculture and supporting diverse ecosystems.

4. Human adaptation and resilience are represented by various ways in which people settle in different ways. How?

Ans. Human adapt and become resilient to challenges in various landforms in the following ways

(a) **Mountains** Mountains do not support agriculture at large scale. But humans have adapted the method of terrace farming. To reduce the risk of damage from snow, houses in mountains have slanting roofs.

(b) **Plains** Most of the plains are densely populated and face issues like pollution. Traditionally agriculture was rainfed but new irrigation facilities are developed to reduce dependence on rainfall.

(c) **Plateaus** Plateaus are not very fertile landforms. People living in plateau regions are engaged in mining activities as plateaus are a storehouse of minerals.

(d) **Deserts** People living in deserts are mostly migration tribes, they move from one place to another in search of water and other resources.

Skill Based Questions as per NEP 2020

1. Evaluate the challenges and opportunities presented by mountain regions for human settlement and development.

Ans. Mountain regions present challenges for human settlement and development due to their rugged terrain, limited arable land, and harsh climatic conditions. However, they also offer opportunities such as tourism, due to their scenic beauty and adventure sports potential. Additionally, mountain regions are often rich in natural resources like minerals and forests.

2. Imagine you are part of a community living near the Ganga Plain. Describe how the river influences your daily life and activities.

Ans. Living near the Ganga plain, the river is a central part of our daily life and activities. We rely on it for freshwater, which is essential for drinking, cooking, and washing. The fertile soil along the riverbanks allows us to grow a variety of crops, such as rice, wheat, and vegetables, which are our main sources of food and income. Fishing in the river provides an additional food source and livelihood for many families. The river also holds cultural and religious importance; we conduct rituals and celebrate festivals at the riverbanks, believing in its sacredness and purifying qualities. The Ganga is truly the lifeblood of our community, sustaining both our physical and spiritual needs.

3. Evaluate the impact of human activities on desert ecosystems and the measures needed to mitigate negative effects.

Ans. Human activities such as overgrasing, deforestation, and unsustainable water use can lead to desertification, loss of biodiversity, and soil degradation. Mitigating these effects requires sustainable land management practices, such as controlled grazing, reforestation, and efficient water use. Conservation efforts to protect native species and restore degraded land are also essential.

ASSESSMENT EXERCISE

Objective Type Questions

1. Which of the following rivers is a tributary of the Yamuna?
   (a) Ganga (b) Chambal
   (c) Godavari (d) Krishna
2. Which landform is referred to as the 'Roof of the World'?
   (a) Sahara Desert
   (b) Tibetan Plateau
   (c) Deccan Plateau
   (d) Gobi Desert
3. **Assertion** (A) Deserts have unique flora and fauna.
   Reason (R) Deserts receive very little precipitation, making the environment harsh for most life forms.
   Codes
   (a) Both A and R are true and R is the correct explanation of A
   (b) Both A and R are true, but R is not the correct explanation of A
   (c) A is true, but R is false
   (d) A is false, but R is true
4. **Assertion** (A) The Himalayas are young fold mountains.
   Reason (R) The Himalayas have been formed through the collision of tectonic plates millions of years ago.
   Codes
   (a) Both A and R are true and R is the correct explanation of A
   (b) Both A and R are true, but R is not the correct explanation of A
   (c) A is true, but R is false
   (d) A is false, but R is true
5. The meeting point of two or more rivers is called a ....
6. The highest mountain in the world is called .... by Tibetans.
7. Plateaus usually rise sharply at least on one side. (True/False)
8. Ganga is a tributary to the Yamuna. (True/False)

Subjective Questions (VSA, SA & LA)

1. Give an example of a hot and a cold desert.
2. What are the main occupations in the Neydal landscape according to Tamil Sangam poetry?
3. Differentiate between young and old mountains.
4. Tourism is an important source of income for people living in the mountains. How?
5. Describe the main characteristics of plateaus.
6. What are the five tinais in ancient Tamil Sangam poetry and their associated landscapes?
7. Analyse the environmental challenges faced by the Gangetic Plain due to modern agricultural practices.
8. Discuss the importance of river sources and confluences in Indian culture and economy.
9. Explain the impact of different landforms on human activities and culture in India.
10. Describe how the physical geography of the Gangetic Plain supports its large population and diverse economic activities.

CHAPTER 4

Timeline and Sources of History

We can learn about the past through various sources. There are some specialists who study these sources and analyse these sources to understand the history.

These sources are important as they throw light on the lives of the people who lived millions of years ago. Many of the activities and practices of today, trace their roots to the past.

4.1 Learning about the Past

Earth has a long history in which humans play a very small role. Many people study Earth's history to understand the past.

The specialists who study history are as follows

- **Geologists** They study Earth's physical features such as soil, stones, hills, mountains, rivers, seas and oceans.
- **Palaeontologists** They study plants, animals and human remains from millions of years ago. These are known as **fossils**.
  - **Anthropologists** They study human societies and cultures from ancient times to the present.
  - **Archaeologists** They study the past by digging remains left by people, plants and animals. These remains include tools, pots, beads, figurines, toys, bones, teeth, burnt grains, and parts of houses or bricks.

4.2 Measuring Time in History

- Every society and culture has its own methods of measuring time.
- Major events, such as the birth of an important person or the start of a ruler's reign, have often marked the beginning of a new era.

Calendar

- The calendars, such as Hindu, Muslim, Jewish and Chinese, are used to mark festivals and important events of their religion.
- The traditional calendars in India are based on the positions of the Sun and the Moon.
- A **panchanga** is a book that lists the days of each month and includes important astronomical data. This includes predictions for solar and lunar eclipses and times for sunrise and sunset.
- Panchangas are still commonly used in India and often provide weather forecasts for the year, as well as dates and timings for festivals.
- The **Gregorian calendar** is widely used around the world. In most of the Western countries, this calendar starts from the year when Jesus Christ was born.
- The years after Jesus Christ's birth are counted forward and used to be marked with **'AD'**. This stands for a Latin phrase **Anno Domini** which means 'in the year of our Lord.' This period is called the **Common Era** (CE) now. For example, India's independence in 1947 can be written as 1947 AD or 1947 CE.
- The years before the birth of Jesus are counted backwards. They were previously marked with **'BC'** (Before Christ) but now known as **Before Common Era** (BCE). For example, 560 BCE is an approximate year for the birth of Gautama Buddha.

Timeline

- It is a tool that displays a sequence of dates and events for a specific period. Timelines help in understanding the order in which historical events took place.
- Timeline shows dates and important events from the beginning of human history to the present.

Terms for Longer Duration of Time

Along with a year and a decade (a period of ten years), we often use other terms to understand longer durations of time. Following terms are quite commonly used when learning about history

- **Century** It refers to a period of 100 years. Centuries are counted starting from the year 1 CE. The 21st century CE spans from 2001 to 2100 CE. For BCE, the counting goes backward from 1 BCE. For example, the 3rd century BCE includes the years 300 BCE to 201 BCE.
- **Millennium** It represents a period of 1,000 years. Millenniums are counted starting from the year 1 CE. The current 3rd millennium CE, which started in 2001 CE will last until 3000 CE. Millenniums BCE are also counted backward from 1 BCE. For example, the 1st millennium BCE covers the years 1 BCE to 1000 BCE.

Try These

1. **Who would study the remains of plants and animals from millions of years ago?**
2. **How do historians use newspapers when studying history?**
3. **What marks the beginning of a new era in many societies?**
4. **What does "AD" stand for in the context of dating years?**

4.3 Sources of History

- There are various sources to study history. The historians gather information from many sources. For example, they consult various sources while studying about a king or queen from 1,500 years ago, an ancient monument, a war or trade items. They try to recreate the history of the period they are studying.
- Historians use newspapers when studying recent history (usually from the last two to three centuries). Electronic media like television and the internet have become valuable sources of information in the last few decades.

Sources of the history can be classified in four groups these are as follows

(i) **Oral Sources** These sources do not have any written evidence. These might be stories, folklore, rhymes that are transferred from one generation to another.

(ii) **Literary Sources** These sources are written evidence of history. They are helpful for understanding the chronological order of events in history. Some of the examples of literary sources are, Vedas, Ramayana, research papers of scientists, plays and poems, etc

Foreign accounts are aslo included in literary sources. These sources are provided by the foreign travelers or traders who visited the different countries.

(iii) **Artistic Sources** The painting and sculptures from the various periods are a great source of history. They help us to understand the technological advancements, use of raw materials and ideology of that period.

(iv) **Archeological Sources** These sources are based on the findings of pottery, tools, fossils of animals and plants, buildings, etc.

- Many experts contribute to these sources of history. These include historians, archaeologists, epigraphists, anthropologists and experts in literature and languages.
- From the last 50 years, scientific studies in history have gained importance. They provide a large amount of information to help understand the past. For example, studies of ancient climates, chemical analysis of excavated materials, and genetics of ancient people have provided new information. This supplements our existing sources of information.

4.4 The Beginnings of Human History

- Around 300,000 years ago, the modern humans (Homo sapiens) arrived on the Earth. This seemed to be a very long time but it is a very short part of Earth's history.
- Information about the lives of early humans can be acquired through rock paintings found in hundreds of caves worldwide. Some of these paintings depict figures or symbols of scenes with animals or humans.
- Early humans faced many challenges from nature. They used to live in groups to support each other.
- They were dependent on **hunting** and **gathering** for their survival.
- They had certain beliefs about the natural elements and the idea of the afterlife.
- They used to live in temporary camps, rock shelters or caves. They used to communicate to each other in languages which are not in use in today's time.
- They used fire and also learnt to make stone axes, blades, arrowheads and simple ornaments like shell beads, pendants made of animal teeth. These objects made their lives easier.

The First Crops

- The climate of Earth has gone through many changes. For a certain period of time, the Earth was covered with ice and this period was called 'ice age'. The last ice age lasted from over 100,000 years ago to 12,000 years ago.
- Gradually, when the climate warmed up, most of this ice melted and existing rivers and oceans originated.
- When living conditions of humans improved, they started to settle down and cultivate cereals and grains. They also domesticated animals such as cattle, goats, etc. They grow in size and number with the availability of more food.
- Most of these communities settled near rivers not only for availability of water but also because of fertile soil which made the process of growing crops easier.

Growth of Settlements

- Development of cultivation of crops resulted in many changes in the early societies. Social complexity of communities increased with their size. The small group of settlements grew up as villages. They started to exchange goods like food, clothing and tools.
- There were leaders or chieftains who were responsible for the well-being of the people. Everyone was collectively responsible for the community's welfare. For example, there was no individual owner of land. The community sowed and harvested the land collectively.
- Gradually small settlements or villages grew into large villages that exchanged goods like food, clothing and tools. Networks of communication and exchange were established among those villages, and some of them grew as small towns.
- New technologies like **pottery** for making pots and other clay objects were developed. The use of metals (copper first, iron later) was also increased to make durable tools, objects of daily use and ornaments.
- Thus, early humans faced many challenges in developing civilisation. Most of the species disappeared in this process of development.

Try These

1. **Through what sources archaeologists gather information about the past?**
2. **Early humans used to live in groups. Mention any two reasons.**
3. **What led to the development of small towns from villages in early civilisations?**

Glossary

History It is the study of the human past.

Fossils Fossils are impressions of footprints, or parts of plants or animals that are found preserved within layers of soil or rocks.

Era A distinct period of time.

Astronomical It is the term used for the celestial bodies in the solar system.

Solar Eclipse It occurs when the moon comes between the Sun and the Earth. It blocks the sunlight from reaching the Earth's surface.

Lunar Eclipse It occurs when the Earth comes between the Sun and the Moon. It blocks the sunlight from reaching the Moon's surface.

Gregorian Calendar The worldwide used calendar; it has 12 months in a year, with 365 days. It has a leap year every four years. For example, century years 1800, 1900, and 2000 century years are leap years only if they are multiples of 400.

Auspicious An event or person that is favourable or brings luck.

Source of History A place, person, text or an object from which we gather information about some past event or period.

Historian A person who studies and writes about the past.

Genetics It is the branch of biology that studies how certain features and characteristics of plants, animals or humans transfer from one generation to the next.

Afterlife A life that begins after death.

Welfare It is an act of maintaining health, growth and well-being.

Hamlet A small settlement or small village.

Hunting It is the act of chasing and killing wild animals for food.

Gathering It is an activity of collecting fruits and vegetables for food.

Epigraphists A person who studied the inscriptions or rock edicts, to understand the history.

TIMELINE AND SOURCES OF HISTORY

Study of Past

- **Geologists** Study physical feature of the Earth like, soil, stone, hills, mountains, rivers, seas, etc.
- **Palaeontologists** Study the remains of plants, animals and humans in form of fossils.
- **Anthropologists** Study human societies and cultures from oldest time to present.
- **Archaeologists** Study the past by digging up remains that people, plants and animals left-behind, such as tools, pots, beads, figurines, toys, bones, etc.

Measuring the Time

- Major events are marked as beginning of new era.
- Gregorian calendar is used worldwide.
- The years before Jesus birth are marked with BCE or Before Common Era.
- The years after Jesus birth are marked with CE or Common Era.

Timeline

It is a tool to mark events of a particular period in a sequence.

Beginning of Human History

- Modern human arrived on Earth about 3,00,000 years ago.
- Early humans used to live in groups under temporary rock shelters or caves.
- They used to make simple stone tools for hunting.
- Their lifestyle can be examined through rock paintings made by them.

Settlements and the First Crops

- Earth was once covered with the ice. It was called as the 'Ice Age'
- Last ice age lasted from over 1,00,000 years ago to around 12,000 years ago.
- With improved living conditions, human started settling down and cultivating cereals and grains.
- Most of them settled around river for water availability and fertile soil for agriculture.
- Chieftains were responsible for well-being of people.
- The small groups slowly became villages through communication and exchange.
- New technologies of pottery, using a metal were also developed.

Sources of History

- Historians studies multiple sources to examine the event.
  - → Oral sources
  - → Literary sources
  - → Artistic sources
  - → Archaeological sources

NCERT FOLDER

Detailed Answers of All NCERT Questions

Think About It (Page 60)

Q.1 What is the earliest memory you can recollect? Do you remember how old you were at that time? Those memories together are a part of your past, maybe going five or six years back.

Ans. Do it yourself

Q.2 How do you think understanding the past will help us understand the present world?

Ans. We can understand the present world by understanding the past in following ways

- We can understand why people choose to live in particular areas earlier and how those choices are still relevant in the present time.
- We can learn about the political system of the past and compare it with today's political system.

Let's Explore (Page 63)

Q.3 Such calculations are simple, but there is a catch. In the Gregorian calendar, there is no 'year zero'. The year 1 CE follows immediately the year 1 BCE. Draw a simple timeline marking every year from 2 BCE to 2 CE; you will see that because of the absence of a year zero, only 3 years have passed between those two dates.

Ans.

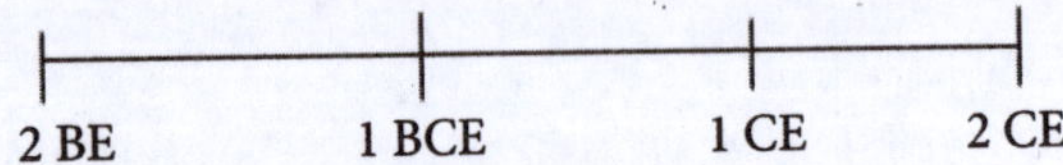

By observing the timeline between 2 BCE to 2 CE, it is visible that only three years have passed between two dates.

Q.4 So to calculate the number of years between a BCE date and a CE date, you should add them but subtract 1– in the above case, 2 + 2 – 1 = 3.

Ans. Do it yourself

Let's Explore (Page 65)

Q.5 Create a timeline stretching from 1900 CE to the current year and place the dates of birth of your grandparents, parents, siblings and yourself. Also, mark the years that the 20th century CE begins with and ends with.

Ans. The 20th century began from the year 1901 and ended in the year 2000.

Think About It (Page 67)

Q.6 Have you ever seen old coins, books, clothes, jewellery or utensils in and around your house? What type of information can we gain from such objects? Or from old houses or buildings?

Ans. Objects like old coins, books, clothes, jewellery or utensils, old houses or buildings, give information about the past, the clothes people used to wear, and what kind of utensils they used. They all are archeological sources of history.

Let's Explore (Page 68)

Q.7 There are a few images of different sources of history. What do you think the objects represent? Write down in the boxes next to the images any information that you get from these objects.

Ans.

1. **Coins** They are archaeological sources of history. The engravings on the coins offer information about the identity of the authority which issued them.
2. **Sculpture** They are an artistic source of history. This image looks like a sculpture from a temple wall. They give information about the faiths and beliefs by the people in the past.

3. **Emblem** It is also an archaeological source of history. It is part of Sarnath's pillar engraved by the king Ashoka in the past. It is the source of information about the rules and regulations passed by the king.

Let's Explore (Page 70)

Q.8 In the picture below, look at some activities of early humans in a rock shelter. Which ones can you recognise? Give a brief description for each.

Ans. The following activities can be observed in the picture given

- **Painting** People used to paint the stories of their daily life on the rocks. They used to make them using simple figures or symbols. They used to show scenes with animals and humans.
- **Tool Making** Early humans used to make tools like axes and arrowheads using stones. These tools were used in hunting animals.
- **Fire** Early humans discovered the fire. They learnt to control fire to make food, keep their shelters warm and keep wild animals away from their shelters.

Let's Explore (Page 71)

Q.9 Observe the following scene. It depicts an agricultural community from a few millenniums ago. List the main activities you can identify.

Ans. The following activities can be observed from the given image

- **Harvesting** The people are working in fields for harvesting the crops.
- **Sheep Rearing** The people used to domesticate the sheeps and goats for wool and meat.
- **Gathering** People used to gather fruits and vegetables for food.
- **Small Settlement** Early humans used to live in small groups. Initially they started to live in small settlements.

Think About It (Page 72)

Q.10 Both in this earlier picture of a rock shelter and in this one men and women are given certain roles. While they may appear to be 'natural', they are not necessarily correct and do not cover all situations. For instance, in a rock shelter, women may have helped prepare colours for painting the rock or may have done some of the painting. In both scenes, men may have done some of the cooking or may have helped take care of children. Keeping in mind that we have only limited information, think about such roles and situations, and discuss in class.

Ans. The various roles of men and women that can be observed from the above given images are as follows

Men	Women
Men used to do hunting	Women used to do gathering
Men used to do control the fire	Women used to cook the food
Men used to rear the sheep	Women used to harvest the crops

There can be many more combinations of activities that were performed by the men and women. There is no clear division of activities between the men and women.

Questions, Activities and Projects

Q.1. As a project, write the history of your family (or village if you live in one), using sources of history at your disposal. Ask your teacher to guide you.

Ans. Do it yourself (Hint: Write about the birth place of your grandparents, their job, then your parents birth place, their education and their jobs)

Q.2. Can we compare historians to detectives? Give reasons for your answers.

Ans. Yes, historians can be compared to detectives for several reasons. Some of them are as follows

(a) **Investigation of Evidence** Just like detectives gather evidence to solve a case, historians collect and examine various sources of information such as documents, utensils and coins to understand the past.

(b) **Analysis and Interpretation** Detectives analyse the evidence to piece together a narrative of what happened. Similarly, historians analyse historical data to interpret events, understand causes and effects, and construct coherent narratives about past events.

(c) **Use of Multiple Sources** Detectives use multiple sources of information, such as witness statements, forensic evidence and surveillance footage, to build a case. Historians also use a variety of sources, including written records, archaeological findings, oral histories and more, to piece together historical narratives.

Q.3. A few exercises with dates

(a) **Place these dates chronologically on the timeline: 323 CE, 323 BCE, 100 CE, 100 BCE, 1900 BCE, 1090 CE and 2024 CE.**

Ans.

323 BCE, 100 CE, 1090 CE (above the timeline)

1900 BCE, 100 BCE, 323 CE, 2024 CE (below the timeline)

(b) **If king Chandragupta was born in 320 CE, which century did he belong to? And how many years was that after the Buddha's birth?**

Ans. If king Chandragupta was born in 320 CE he would belong to the 4th century. This event will be after 879 (560+320-1) years of the Buddha's birth.

(c) **Rani of Jhansi was born in 1828. Which century did she belong to? How many years was that before India's Independence?**

Ans. Rani of Jhansi belonged to the 19th century as she was born in 1828. This event was 119 years before the independence of India.

(d) **Turn '12,000 years ago' into a date.**

Ans. '12,000 years ago' into date is approximately 10,000 BCE.

Q.4. Plan a visit to a nearby museum: the visit should be prepared with some prior research on the kind of exhibits the museum holds. Keep notes during the visit. Write a brief report afterwards, highlighting what was unexpected / interesting / fun about the visit and the exhibits.

Ans. Do it yourself

Q.5. Invite to your school an archaeologist or a historian and ask them to speak on the history of your region and why it is important to know it.

Ans. Do it yourself

REVIEW EXERCISE

Including Competency Based Questions

Part I

Very Short Answer Type Questions

1. What role do newspapers and electronic media play in studying recent history?

Ans. Newspapers and electronic media provide information for studying recent history, especially the last few decades.

2. There are some people who are trained to uncover the secrets left beneath the Earth's surface and help us learn about the past. Name any three of them.

Ans. The people who are trained to uncover the secrets left beneath the Earth's surface and help us learn about the past are as follows

- **Geologists** They study physical features of the Earth, like rocks, mountains, rivers, etc.

- **Paleontologists** They study the fossils of plants and animals.
- **Archaeologists** They study the remains of tools, pots, beads, figurines, toys, bones, etc.

3. How is the beginning of a new era marked?

Ans. The beginning of a new era is marked with the birth of an important person or the start of the ruler's reign.

4. Differentiate between common era and before common era.

Ans. The years after the birth of Jesus are marked as Common Era (CE) on the other hand (BCE) the years before the birth of Jesus are marked as 'Before Common Era'.

5. How scientific research is contributing to studying the past?

Ans. Scientific research is contributing in studying the past in following ways

- It supports the studies of ancient climate.
- It helps in chemical studies of excavated materials
- It studies the genetics of ancient people.

6. When was the last 'ice age' observed?

Ans. The last ice age was observed between 100,000 years ago to 12,000 years ago.

7. Which type of technologies were developed with the development of large villages and towns?

Ans. The following type of technologies were developed with the development of large villages and towns

- **Pottery** The techniques of making pots and other clay objects.
- **Use of Metals** They used copper and iron for making tools and other objects of daily use. It increased the durability of these objects.

Short Answer Type Questions

1. Mention two changes in the life of early man after the discovery of agriculture.

Ans. The changes in the life of early man after the discovery of agriculture were

- As people began to grow plants, they had to stay in the same place for a long time. It was not possible for them to migrate frequently as before. Crops took a long time to grow and produce grains.
- In some parts of the sub-continent, people started making large clay pots, baskets, or dug pits into the ground in order to store grains for both food and seed.

2. What could be the reasons behind the continued use of traditional calendars for religious and cultural events even though the common era calendar is widely adopted?

Ans. Traditional calendars are often deeply intertwined with the religious and cultural practices of a community. They carry significant meaning for calculating the dates of festivals, rituals and other auspicious events. Despite the global adoption of the common era calendar for most practical purposes, these traditional calendars preserve cultural heritage and ensure that important events are celebrated in a manner consistent with longstanding traditions.

3. What can be inferred about the significance of the first crop cultivation in human history?

Ans. The cultivation of the first crops marked a significant shift from nomadic lifestyles to settled agricultural communities. This development allowed humans to produce surplus food, leading to population growth and the establishment of permanent settlements.

It also paved the way for advancements in technology, social structures and trade. The first crops thus played a crucial role in the development of complex societies and civilisations.

4. What role did geographical factors play in the domestication of the first crops?

Ans. Geographical factors played a crucial role in the domestication of the first crops, as certain regions offered favourable conditions for agriculture, such as fertile soil, a stable climate and access to water sources. The availability of wild plant species suitable for domestication also influenced where early farming began. These geographical advantages allowed early humans to experiment with and eventually master agricultural practices, leading to the spread of farming techniques to other areas.

Long Answer Type Questions

1. What are the methods used to measure historical time, and why is it important?

Ans. Historical time is measured using different calendars and timelines. Different calendars are based on marking significant events like the birth of important figures or the beginning of eras. The Gregorian calendar, widely used today, counts years from the birth of Jesus Christ. Other calendars, like the Hindu, Muslim, and Jewish ones, are also used.

Importance of Timeline Timelines help us understand the sequence of events, such as the birth of Buddha before Jesus. This chronological understanding is crucial for understanding the chronology and context of historical events, helping us learn from the past to understand the present better.

2. What is the difference between a millennium and a century in terms of their duration and how do these time periods help us understand historical events?

Ans. A millennium refers to a period of 1,000 years, while a century is a period of 100 years. This distinction is significant in historical studies as it allows us to categorise and analyse events over different time scales.

For example, the 21st century spans from the year 2001 to 2100, while the 3rd millennium covers the years from 2001 to 3000. Understanding these time frames helps historians contextualise major developments, such as the rise and fall of civilisations, technological advancements, and significant cultural shifts. By examining events within a millennium, historians can identify broader trends and patterns that may not be apparent when looking at shorter periods like a century. This long-term perspective is crucial for understanding the complexities of human history and how different eras influence one another over time.

3. What types of sources do historians use to gather information about the past, and how do these sources contribute to our understanding of history?

Ans. Historians are dependent on several types of sources to gather information about past events, including archaeological sources, oral sources, artistic sources and literary sources. These sources can be described as follows

- Archaeological sources include artifacts such as tools, pottery, and remains of ancient structures, which provide tangible evidence of how people lived, worked, and interacted in their environments.
- Oral sources consist of stories, traditions, and memories passed down through generations, offering insights into cultural practices and societal values that may not be documented in written form.
- Artistic sources, such as paintings and sculptures, reflect the beliefs, emotions and daily lives of people in different historical periods, helping us understand their perspectives and experiences.
- Literary sources encompass written texts, including historical accounts, poems and religious scriptures, which provide context and details about events, thoughts and philosophies of the time.

By analysing these diverse sources, historians can piece together a more comprehensive and nuanced understanding of history, revealing the complexities of human experiences across different cultures and eras.

Part II

Multiple Choice Questions (MCQs)

1. Which discipline is primarily concerned with the study of human societies and cultures?

(a) Geology
(b) Anthropology
(c) Archaeology
(d) Paleontology

2. Why is it important to use multiple sources when studying history?

(a) To confuse the reader
(b) To gather a comprehensive understanding and verify facts
(c) To limit the information available
(d) To focus on a single perspective

3. The significance of the Gregorian calendar in historical time measurement is that it

(a) is based solely on lunar cycles.
(b) is used worldwide for organising dates.
(c) only counts years in the common era.
(d) was established in ancient Rome.

4. Artifacts such as tools and pottery contribute to our understanding of history by

(a) providing entertainment for historians.
(b) offering insights into the daily lives and cultures of past societies.
(c) serving as decorative items in museums.
(d) confusing the timeline of events.

5. When considering the evolution of human societies, one can conclude that

(a) all early humans were nomadic throughout history.
(b) the development of agriculture led to permanent settlements.
(c) technology had no impact on social structures.
(d) humans have always lived in large cities.

6. In the context of historical studies, the term "BCE" is used to indicate

(a) years after the birth of Jesus Christ.
(b) years before the common era.
(c) the beginning of the ice age.
(d) a specific calendar used in Europe.

7. The role of historians in studying the past can best be described as

(a) collecting artifacts without analysis.
(b) engaging in a dialogue between the present and the past.
(c) focusing solely on written documents.
(d) ignoring oral histories and traditions.

8. The transition from hunting and gathering to agriculture primarily resulted in

(a) a decrease in population.
(b) increased social complexity and community organisation.
(c) a return to nomadic lifestyles.
(d) the extinction of various animal species.

9. **In the study of history, timelines are particularly useful for**
   (a) memorising historical dates without context.
   (b) visualising the sequence and relationships between events.
   (c) focusing only on significant figures.
   (d) ignoring less important events.

10. **The emergence of chieftains in early societies indicates that**
   (a) leadership was unnecessary in small communities.
   (b) social structures became more complex as populations grew.
   (c) all individuals had equal roles and responsibilities.
   (d) communities relied solely on trade for survival.

11. **Palaeontologists primarily focus on**
   (a) the study of ancient human cultures.
   (b) the analysis of fossils to understand past life forms.
   (c) the exploration of historical texts.
   (d) the examination of geological features.

12. **The concept of "millennium" refers to a period of**
   (a) 100 years (b) 500 years
   (c) 1,000 years (d) 10 years

13. **Consider the following statements.**
   I. **The last ice age lasted from over 100,000 years ago to around 12,000 years ago.**
   II. **Early civilisations settled around rivers only because of water availability.**
   III. **Leaders or 'chieftains' were responsible for the well-being of people in the community.**

   Which of these statements is/are true?
   (a) I only (b) I and II
   (c) I and III (d) II and III

Answers

1. (b) **2.** (b) **3.** (b) **4.** (b)
5. (b) **6.** (b) **7.** (b) **8.** (b)
9. (b) **10.** (b) **11.** (b) **12.** (c)
13. (c)

Fill in the Blanks

1. In history, a period of 100 years is called a ....
2. The first examples of rock art in the world date back to around .... BCE.
3. Paleontologists study the remains of plants, animals and humans in the form of ....
4. The conventional year for Jesus Christ's birth is taken as the starting point for the .... calendar.
5. Leaders or .... were responsible for the well-being of the People.

Ans. 1. century 2. 40,000 3. fossils
4. Gregorian 5. Chieftains

True or False

1. The Gregorian calendar is the only calendar that has ever been used to measure time.
2. Historians can use sources other than written documents, such as oral traditions and artifacts, to study history.
3. Geologists study human artifacts to understand past human behaviour.
4. The Common Era (CE) follows immediately after 1 BCE in the Gregorian calendar.
5. The examples of oral sources of history are paintings and sculptures.

Ans. 1. False 2. True 3. False 4. True 5. False

Assertion-Reason

1. **Assertion** (A) Archaeologists play a crucial role in reconstructing the history of human societies.
   Reason (R) Archaeologists study fossils to understand the physical characteristics of ancient humans.
   Codes
   (a) Both A and R are true and R is the correct explanation of A
   (b) Both A and R are true, but R is not the correct explanation of A
   (c) A is true, but R is false
   (d) A is false, but R is true

2. **Assertion** (A) Palaeontologists help us understand the evolution of life on Earth.
   Reason (R) Palaeontologists excavate and study artifacts from ancient civilisations.
   Codes
   (a) Both A and R are true and R is the correct explanation of A
   (b) Both A and R are true, but R is not the correct explanation of A.
   (c) A is true, but R is false
   (d) A is false, but R is true

3. **Assertion** (A) The Gregorian calendar does not have a year zero.
   Reason (R) Years in the Gregorian calendar are counted from 1 BCE directly to 1 CE.
   Codes
   (a) Both A and R are true and R is the correct explanation of A
   (b) Both A and R are true, but R is not the correct explanation of A
   (c) A is true, but R is false
   (d) A is false, but R is true

Ans. 1. (c) 2. (c) 3. (a)

Case Based Questions

1. Read the following paragraph and answer the questions that follow

The calendar is commonly used worldwide; side by side, Hindu, Muslim, Jewish, Chinese and other calendars are also used for calculating the dates of festivals and other auspicious events.

In the West, the conventional year for Jesus Christ's birth has generally been taken to be the starting point for this calendar. Years are counted forward from this point and used to be marked with 'AD' (an abbreviation for a Latin phrase that refers to the years after Jesus' birth).

However, this is now called the Common Era or CE across the world. For example, 1947, the year India gained independence, can be written as 1947 AD (sometimes AD 1947) or 1947 CE. Similarly, the years before the conventional date for the birth of Jesus are counted backward and used to be marked with BC (or Before Christ). They are now called Before Common Era or BCE. For example, 560 BCE is an approximate year of birth of Gautama Buddha.

(i) In what ways might the use of different calendars create challenges for historians trying to align dates of events across cultures?

(ii) Why might the terminology for years have shifted from "AD" and "BC" to "CE" and "BCE"?

(iii) Let us assume that a turtle was born in year 450 CE. How many years ago this event took place if this is the year 2024?

Ans. (i) The use of different calendars can complicate the work of historians who attempt to align dates of events across various cultures. Converting dates between calendars requires a deep understanding of how each system operates, including knowledge of leap years, lunar cycles, and other calendar-specific details. This can lead to confusion when trying to establish a common timeline for global history.

(ii) The shift from "AD" and "BC" to "CE" and "BCE" likely reflects a growing recognition of the need for a more inclusive, secular way of marking time that can be universally accepted regardless of religious beliefs. This change allows for a more neutral terminology that still acknowledges the same historical reference points but does so in a way that is respectful of diverse cultures and religions.

(iii) If the turtle was born in 450 CE then this event took place (450+ 2024-1) 2,473 years ago.

2. Read the following paragraph and answer the questions that follows

Early humans faced many challenges from nature and lived in bands or groups to help each other. They were constantly seeking shelter and food, and were mainly hunters and gatherers; this means that they relied on hunting and collecting edible plants and fruits for their survival.

Our early ancestors also had certain beliefs about the natural elements and possibly also some notion of afterlife. These groups lived in temporary camps, rock shelters or caves, and communicated with each other using languages that are now lost. They used fire and started making objects that made their lives easier, like improved stone axes and blades, arrowheads and other tools. Aspects of their life are visible in rock paintings found in hundreds of caves all over the world. Some of those paintings depict simple figures or a few symbols; others are more detailed and represent scenes with animals or humans. In time, these early humans learned to make simple ornaments such as stone or shell beads, pendants made of animal teeth, and sometimes exchanged them with other groups.

(i) What might be the reason early humans lived in groups or bands rather than alone?

(a) To establish permanent settlements
(b) To ensure better protection and cooperation in finding food and shelter
(c) To develop complex languages
(d) To practice agriculture

(ii) What might have been the purpose of the rock paintings created by early humans?

(a) To decorate their living spaces
(b) To record their daily activities, beliefs or significant events
(c) To serve as blueprints for construction
(d) To document agricultural techniques

(iii) Why is it likely that early humans began to improve tools such as stone axes and blades?

(a) They had access to better materials over time
(b) Improved tools made hunting and gathering more efficient
(c) They were influenced by other cultures
(d) They needed to build permanent homes

(iv) The early humans used to do painting on their rock caves. What could be the possible reasons for this activity?

(a) They wanted to beautify their walls
(b) They draw to mark the sign of authority
(c) They draw to make sure animals stay away from their shelters
(d) They used to draw to mark the ceremonies, gathering or their achievements

Ans. (i) (b) (ii) (b) (iii) (b) (iv) (d)

Competency Based Questions

1. How early humans supported each other by living together?

Ans. Early humans supported each other by living together in the following ways

- They used to communicate with each other using languages.
- They used fire to make tools that made their lives easier.
- They learnt to make simple ornaments and sometimes exchanged them with the other groups.

2. The early communities often settle down near the rivers. Why?

Ans. The early communities often settle down near the rivers due to following reasons

- They settled near rivers for the availability of water for various purposes.
- The other reason for settling down near the rivers was the fertile soil near rivers which supported agriculture.

3. Oral histories and inscriptions on monuments enhance our understanding of ancient civilisations. Justify the statement?

Ans. Oral histories and inscriptions on monuments both play a crucial role in enhancing our understanding of ancient civilisations by preserving cultural narratives and official records. Oral histories capture traditions, stories and experiences passed down through generations, offering personal and communal perspectives on historical events.

Inscriptions on monuments provide formal and often official records, such as decrees, commemorations and dedications, that offer direct evidence of significant events and figures.

Combining these sources allows historians to validate oral traditions with physical evidence and understand the broader socio-political context of ancient societies.

4. It is important for historians to use multiple sources when studying the past. Why?

Ans. Using multiple sources is essential for historians to ensure accuracy and comprehensiveness in their work. Different sources provide various perspectives and types of information. For example, archaeological findings offer physical evidence, while written records provide narrative accounts.

Studying multiple sources helps historians verify facts, identify biases, and construct more reliable historical narratives. It also allows for a more holistic understanding of past events, as each source type contributes unique insights and details.

5. Analyse the challenges faced by early humans in adapting to changing environmental conditions and the strategies they employed to ensure their survival. How did these adaptations contribute to the development of more complex societies over time?

Ans. Early humans lived in a constantly changing environment, facing challenges such as fluctuating climates, limited resources and threats from predators. To cope with these challenges, they developed strategies such as forming small, mobile groups for mutual support and protection, and relying on a diverse range of food sources through hunting and gathering.

As the climate warmed after the last ice age, many communities began to settle in fertile areas and adopt agriculture, leading to more stable food supplies and population growth. This transition allowed for the development of more complex social structures, as communities grew in size and individuals began to specialise in different tasks. Leaders emerged to manage resources and communal activities, while the establishment of trade networks facilitated the exchange of goods and ideas between different societies. As these communities became more prosperous and technologically advanced, they laid the foundations for the rise of early civilisations, with the development of writing, cities, and more sophisticated social and political institutions.

6. Given that every object or structure tells a story and is like a piece in a jigsaw puzzle, how do historians ensure they accurately reconstruct historical events from these diverse sources?

Ans. Historians ensure they accurately reconstruct historical events from diverse sources by employing a careful and methodical approach. They gather information from various types of evidence, including artifacts, written documents, oral histories and archaeological findings. Each source offers unique insights, much like pieces of a jigsaw puzzle that, when combined, create a fuller picture of the past. Historians critically evaluate these sources for reliability and context, looking for corroboration among them.

Sometimes, sources may present conflicting information, requiring historians to assess which sources are more credible based on factors such as the author's perspective, the time of creation, and the intended audience. They also consider the contributions of specialists, such as archaeologists and anthropologists, who provide additional context and expertise. By synthesising information from multiple sources, historians can construct a more nuanced understanding of historical events, ensuring that their interpretations are as accurate and comprehensive as possible. This process highlights the importance of diverse sources in piecing together the complex narratives of human history.

Skill Based Questions as per NEP 2020

1. Analyse the impact of the discovery of fire on early human societies. Write a brief essay discussing how fire influenced the diet, safety and social structure of early humans.

Ans. Analysing the impact of fire on early human societies involves understanding how this discovery transformed daily life. Fire provided warmth and protection from predators, allowing humans to inhabit colder regions. It also enabled the cooking of food, which made it easier to digest and unlocked more nutrients, contributing to physical and cognitive development.

Furthermore, the control of fire likely fostered social bonds as groups gathered around campfires, leading to more complex social structures.

2. Examine the role of technology in the development of early human societies. How did advancements shape their interactions?

Ans. Technology played a crucial role in the development of early human societies by facilitating more efficient food production and enhancing daily life. The invention of tools, such as stone axes and later metal implements, allowed for better hunting, gathering and farming practices.

As communities became more adept at producing food, they could support larger populations and engage in trade. This technological advancement led to increased interactions between different groups, as surplus goods were exchanged.

Furthermore, innovations like pottery and weaving contributed to cultural exchanges and the establishment of social hierarchies, shaping the dynamics of early societies. Ultimately, technology was a driving force in the evolution of human interactions and societal structures.

3. Evaluate the statement: "History is an unending dialogue between the present and the past." What does this mean in the context of how we study history?

Ans. The above statement suggests that our understanding of history is continuously influenced by contemporary perspectives and societal changes. This means that historians do not simply study the past in isolation; they interpret historical events through the lens of current values, beliefs and knowledge.

As society evolves, the interpretation of historical events also evolves, which can lead to new insights or reevaluations of previously accepted narratives. This dynamic relationship emphasizes the importance of context in historical study, as what we consider significant or relevant can change over time.

Thus, history is not static; it is a living conversation that shapes and is shaped by the present.

4. Reflect on the importance of timelines in historical study. How do they aid in understanding the sequence and significance of events?

Ans. Timelines are essential tools in historical study, providing a visual representation of the sequence and duration of events over time. They help historians and students organise information chronologically, making it easier to understand how events relate to one another. By placing significant occurrences in order, timelines reveal patterns and connections that might otherwise be overlooked. For example, a timeline can illustrate how the birth of influential figures or the occurrence of major events influenced subsequent developments in society.

Additionally, timelines can highlight the relative scale of events, showing which were pivotal in shaping human history. Overall, they serve as a framework for contextualising historical narratives, allowing for a clearer understanding of the complexities of the past and its impact on the present.

ASSESSMENT EXERCISE

Objective Type Questions

1. What is the primary purpose of a panchanga?
   (a) To list historical events
   (b) To predict weather patterns
   (c) To provide astronomical data and predictions
   (d) To record literary works
2. Which calendar is commonly used worldwide today?
   (a) Hindu calendar
   (b) Gregorian calendar
   (c) Jewish calendar
   (d) Chinese calendar
3. How many years ago was Gautama Buddha born, if we are in the year 2024 CE?
   (a) 2560 years ago (b) 1583 years ago
   (c) 2583 years ago (d) 1524 years ago
4. **Assertion** (A) Archaeologists study human societies and cultures.

   Reason (R) They uncover secrets left beneath the Earths' surface.

   Codes
   (a) Both A and R are true and R is the correct explanation of A.
   (b) Both A and R are true, but R is not the correct explanation of A
   (c) A is true, but R is false
   (d) A is false, but R is true
5. The study of the human past is known as ....
6. .... are trained to study the physical features of the Earth.
7. The timeline shows events from the beginning of humanity to the present. (True/False)
8. Epigraphists study ancient inscriptions as part of historical research. (True/False)

Subjective Questions (VSA, SA & LA)

1. With the growth of hamlets, which type of technologies were developed?
2. What could be the possible reason for which early humans started living around rivers?
3. Early humans have faced many challenges from nature and lived in bands or groups to help each other. What could be the possible threats to early humans?
4. How have scientific studies contributed to the reconstruction of history?
5. Every object or structure tells a story and is like a piece in a jigsaw puzzle. Justify the statement.
6. Differentiate between century and millennium.
7. Discuss the significance of timelines in understanding historical events. Give examples.
8. How do archaeologists and anthropologists contribute to our understanding of history? Use examples to illustrate their roles.

CHAPTER 5

India, That is Bharat

Modern India is very different from the India that existed hundreds and even thousands of years ago. Today India has well defined borders, defined states and a known population. It has a well recognised name which was not the case earlier. The name of India was subjected to different interpretations and pronounciations by different people.

5.1 Naming of India by Indians

- In past, the Indian sub-continent has had many different names and shifting boundaries. India has been known by many names throughout history. These names are mentioned in ancient texts, accounts of travellers and pilgrims and inscriptions.
- Both inhabitants of India and visitors from outside (foreigners), have called India by various names.
- Rigveda is several thousand years old and it is the most ancient text of India. The North-West region of the sub-continent is named as 'Sapta Sindhava' in the Rigveda.
- 'Sapta Sindhava' means the 'land of the seven rivers'. The word 'Sindhava' originates from 'Sindhu', meaning the Indus river or a river in general.
- Later, the names for the other parts of India appeared in the literature. Mahabharata, one of the India's most famous texts mentions the name of many regions such as follows

Name of Region in Mahabharata	Modern name for the Region
Kashmira	More or less today's Kashmir
Kurukshetra	Parts of Haryana
Vanga	Parts of Bengal
Pragjyotisha	Roughly today's Assam
Kaccha	Kutch
Kerala	More or less today's Kerala

- The earliest known name for the entire Indian sub-continent appears in the Mahabharata, a poem written around a few centuries BCE. It uses the terms 'Bharatavarsha' and 'Jambudvipa'.
- The term **Bharatavarsha** refers to the entire Indian sub-continent. It means 'the country of the Bharatas'.
- The name 'Bharata' originates from the Rig Veda where it refers to one of the main Vedic groups of people. In the literature of the later period, it mentions several kings named as 'Bharata' are mentioned.
- '**Jambudvipa**' means 'the island of the fruit of the Jamun tree'. It is a native Indian tree which is also called as 'Jambul tree', 'Malabar plum tree' etc. Over time, it came to represent the Indian sub-continent.
- **Ashoka**, an Indian emperor who ruled around 250 BCE, used the term 'Jambudvipa' for whole of India in one of his inscriptions. At that time, India included the areas of present day Bangladesh, Pakistan and Afghanistan.
- A few centuries later, 'Bharata' became the widely accepted name for the Indian sub-continent.
- The ancient text, **Vishnu Purana**, defines Bharata as 'The country that lies North of the ocean and South of the snowy mountains is called Bharata'.
- The name Bharata is still used today. In North India, the term 'Bharat' is used while in South India the term 'Bharatam' is used.

- Different parts of the country had similar definitions for India. For example, a 2,000-year-old Tamil poem praises a king, whose name is known from Cape Kumari in the South, the great mountain (Himalayas) in the North and the oceans in the East and West. This shows that the ancient Indians had a clear understanding of their country's geography.

Must Know !

The Indian Constitution uses the phrase 'India, that is Bharat' at the beginning. The Hindi version of the Constitution also mentions the same as 'Bharat, arthath India'. This clearly indicates that 'India' and Bharat' are two names for the same country.

5.2 Naming of India By Foreigners

- Persians were the first foreigners to mention India. They were ancient inhabitants of Iran.
- In 6th century BCE, a Persian emperor conquered the Indus river region (earlier known as 'Sindhu'). Hence, this India was named as 'Hind', 'Hidu', or 'Hindu' in their earliest records and inscriptions. These names are adaptations of the term 'Sindhu'. It is notable that 'Hindu' was a geographical term, not related to the Hindu religion.
- Another term, **Hindustan** which is quite recent was first used by Persians 1,800 years ago. It was later adopted by invaders to refer to the Indian sub-continent.
- The ancient Greeks adopted the name from the Persians and called **India-Indoi** or **Indike**. This word originally comes from the term 'Sindhu' in the following way
  Sindhu → Hindhu → Indoi/Indike
- Greeks dropped the letter 'H' of 'Hindu' because this letter did not exist in the Greek language.
- The ancient Chinese called India **Yintu** or **Yindu**. This name is also derived from the term 'Sindhu' in the following way
  Sindhu → Hindhu → Indu → Yindu
- The Chinese also called India **Tianzhu**, meaning 'heavenly master'. This shows the respect the ancient Chinese had for India as the land of Buddha. This word is also derived from the term 'Sindhu'.

Xuanzang

- Xuanzang, a Chinese scholar, travelled to India in the 7th century.
- He explored India for 17 years, meeting scholars and collecting Buddhist texts.
- He then returned to China and translated the texts from Sanskrit to Chinese.
- Many Chinese scholars visited India after him.

Try These

1. The term 'Sindhu' is used for which river?
2. What was the ancient name of Assam as mentioned in the Mahabharata?
3. Shivani once went to a forest trip along with her teachers. They told her that jamun tree holds significance in the naming of India. What was the name of ancient India based on jamun tree?
4. Rakesh was listening carefully to a presentation on Chinese travellers in India, one of them was Xuanzang. He collected which texts in India?

Glossary

Inhabitants People living in a particular region or country (in this context, the people of India).

Jambudvipa The Indian sub-continent, meaning 'island of the Jamun tree'.

Bharata Region bounded by the ocean and Himalayas.

Constitution The foundational legal document of India, which establishes the country's framework, laws and principles and officially recognises 'India' and 'Bharat' as interchangeable names for the nation.

INDIA, THAT IS BHARAT

Naming by

Rig Veda (oldest text)

- The name 'Bharata' first appears in the Rig Veda.

Mahabharata

It mentions the following names

- Bharatavarsha (entire Indian sub-continent)
- Jambudvipa (island of jamun tree, represented Indian sub-continent)

It mentions many regions such as

- Kashmira (Kashmir)
- Kurukshetra (Haryana)
- Pragjyotisha (Assam)
- Kerala (Kerala)
- Vanga (Bengal)
- Kaccha (Kutch)

Vishnu Purana

- It mentions the name Bharata as the region bounded by ocean and Himalayas.

Naming by Foreigners

Persians (6th century BCE)

- Hind, Hidu, Hindu (derived from Sindhu)

Greeks

- Indoi, Indike (adopted from Persians)

Chinese

- Yintu, Yindu (derived from Sindhu)
- Tianzhu (meaning 'heavenly master')

Xuanzang

- A Chinese scholar who travelled to India in 7th century
- Explored India for 17 years
- Collected Buddhist texts
- Translated texts from Sanskrit to Chinese

Key Points

- India's name has evolved over time.
- Different regions had similar definitions.
- 'India' and 'Bharat' are used interchangeably.
- Constitution recognises 'India' and 'Bharat' as same country.
- Ashoka used 'Jambudvipa' for entire India (250 BCE).
- Bharata became widely accepted name for Indian sub-continent.
- Tamil poem (2000-years-old) describes India's geography.

NCERT FOLDER

Detailed Answers of All NCERT Questions

Think About It (Page 77)

Q.1 Consider the physical map of the Indian sub-continent at the start of the chapter. What are its natural boundaries that you can make out?

Ans. I can make out the following natural boundaries from the physical map of the Indian sub-continent at the start of the chapter

- **Northern and North-Eastern Boundary** This boundary is made by the Himalayas.
- **North Western Boundary** The Hindukush mountains form the North-Western boundary of the Indian sub-continent.
- **Bay of Bengal** It forms the Eastern boundary of the sub-continent.
- **Arabian Sea** It forms the Western boundary of the Indian sub-continent.

Let's Explore (Page 78)

Q.2 Do you recognise the names of any regions given in the map (Fig. 5.4) on page 79 in NCERT? List the ones that you have heard of.

Ans. I have heard the names of the following regions given in the map

- Gandhara
- Panchala
- Mahishmati

Most of these regions are related to the legendary folk tale of Mahabharata and some are connected with the lives of Buddha.

Think About It (Page 80)

Q.3 Have you identified the 'snowy mountains'? Do you think this brief description of Bharata is correct?

Ans. Yes, I have identified the 'snowy mountains'. It is used for the Himalayan mountain which is snow laden in most part of the year.

Yes, I think this brief description of Bharata is correct to a huge extent as the natural Southern boundary of India is made by the Indian ocean and the Northern boundary is made by the snow laden Himalayas.

Let's Explore (Page 81)

Q.4 In the given reproduction of the first page of the original Constitution of India, can you make out the phrase 'India, that is Bharat'?

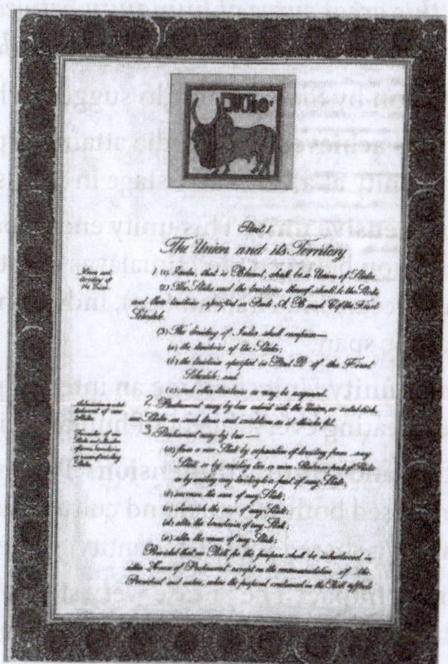

Ans. Yes, I can make out the following phrase from the first page of the original Constitution of India.

India, that is bharat, shall be a union of states. The states and the territories there of shall be the states and their territories specified in parts A, B and C of the first schedule ....

Let's Explore (Page 83)

Q.4 Can you complete this table of the many names of India?

Persian	
Greek	
Latin	India
Chinese	
Arabic & Persian	
English	India
French	Inde

Ans. The completed table is as follows

Persian	Hindhu
Greek	Indoi / Indike
Latin	India
Chinese	Yindu / Yintu
Arabic & Persian	Hindustan
English	India
French	Inde

Questions, Activities and Projects

Q.1 Discuss what could be the meaning of the quotation at the start of the chapter.

Ans. The quotation at the start of the chapter is as follows

In India at a very early time the spiritual and cultural unity was made complete and became the very stuff of the life of all this great surge of humanity between the Himalayas and the two seas. ~Sri Aurobindo

The quotation by Sri Aurobindo suggests that

- **Unity was achieved early** India attained spiritual and cultural unity at a very early stage in its history.
- **Comprehensive unity** This unity encompassed the entire region between the Himalayas and the two seas (Indian Ocean and Arabian Sea), indicating a vast geographic span.
- **Depth of unity** Unity became an integral part of daily life, permeating every aspect of human existence.
- **Spiritual and cultural dimensions** The unity encompassed both spiritual and cultural aspects, indicating a shared sense of identity, values and beliefs.
- **Enduring impact** The phrase 'very stuff of life' implies that this unity has had a lasting impact, shaping the essence of Indian society.

In essence, Sri Aurobindo's quotation highlights India's unique achievement of profound spiritual and cultural unity, transcending regional and geographical boundaries and becoming an integral part of its collective identity.

Q.2 True or False

(i) The Rigveda describes the entire geography of India.

Ans False

(ii) The Vishnu Purana describes the entire sub-continent.

Ans True

(iii) In Ashoka's time, 'Jambudvipa' included today's India, parts of Afghanistan, Bangladesh and Pakistan.

Ans True

(iv) The Mahabharata lists many regions, including Kashmir, Kutch and Kerala.

Ans True

(v) The term 'Hindustan' first appeared in a Greek inscription more than 2,000 years ago.

Ans False

(vi) In ancient Persian, the word 'Hindu' refers to the Hindu religion.

Ans False

(vii) 'Bharata' is a name given to India by foreign travellers.

Ans False

Q.3 If you were born some 2,000 years ago and had the chance to name our country, what name or names might you have chosen, and why? Use your imagination!

Ans If I were born 2,000 years ago, I would have chosen names that reflect the country's natural beauty, cultural richness and mythological significance.

Some of the names which I have would have chosen are as follows

- **Aryavarta** It is derived from the Sanskrit word 'Arya', meaning noble, to honor the ancient Indo-Aryan civilisation.
- **Bharatamrita** This word combines 'Bharata' and 'amrita', which together mean immortal, to signify the land's eternal essence.
- **Dharmakshetra** It refers to 'Land of Dharma', reflecting the country's spiritual and philosophical heritage.
- **Mahabhumi** It signifies 'Great Land' or 'Subcontinent,' acknowledging its vastness and majesty.
- **Swarnaloka** It translates to 'Land of Gold,' symbolising prosperity, richness, and cultural wealth.
- **Vidyodaya** It means 'Rise of Knowledge,' honoring the ancient wisdom, sciences and philosophies.

I would have also considered names that evoke the country's natural beauty, such as

- **Himalayagrama** It refers to'Village of the Himalayas,' acknowledging the majestic mountain range.
- **Gangaikonda** It is named after the sacred Ganges River, symbolising spiritual growth.
- **Marutvana** It means 'Forest of the Winds', reflecting the land's diverse ecosystems.

These names blend geography, culture, mythology and natural beauty, capturing the essence of ancient India.

Q.4 Why did people travel to India from various parts of the world in ancient times? What could be their motivations in undertaking such long journeys? (Hint: There could be at least four or five motivations)

Ans. People traveled to ancient India from various parts of the world for various reasons such as follows

- **Trade** To exchange goods like spices, textiles and precious stones.
- **Spirituality** To explore India's rich spiritual heritage and visit sacred sites.
- **Knowledge** To study subjects like mathematics, astronomy and medicine at esteemed universities.
- **Conquest** To expand empires and gain riches.
- **Cultural Exchange** To foster diplomatic relations and learn from India's culture.

Additionally, some traveled for adventure, economic opportunities, refuge, or health and wellness. India's diversity and richness attracted people from around the world.

REVIEW EXERCISE
Including Competency Based Questions

Part I

Very Short Answer Type Questions

1. What does 'Sapta Sindhava' mean?

Ans. 'Sapta Sindhava' means the land of the seven rivers. In the Rigveda, it refers to the North-West region of the Indian sub-continent. The term signifies the importance of rivers in ancient Indian geography and culture.

2. What is the meaning of 'Bharatavarsha'?

Ans. 'Bharatavarsha' refers to the entire Indian sub-continent, named after the ancient Vedic tribe 'Bharatas'. It means the country of the Bharatas, encompassing present-day India, Bangladesh, Pakistan and Afghanistan.

3. What does the Indian Constitution state about 'India' and 'Bharat'?

Ans. The Indian Constitution states that 'India' and 'Bharat' are interchangeable names for the same country. The Constitution's preamble affirms, 'India, that is Bharat', recognising the country's diverse cultural and historical heritage. This equivalence reinforces national unity, acknowledging the coexistence of multiple names for a single nation.

4. What is the origin of the name 'Bharata'?

Ans. The name 'Bharata' originates from the Rigveda, where it refers to an ancient Vedic tribe. The term gained significance through mentions of kings named Bharata in later literature. Over time, 'Bharata' became synonymous with the Indian sub-continent, representing the country's geographical and cultural identity.

5. Who were the first foreigners to mention India and what name did they use?

Ans. The Persians, ancient inhabitants of Iran, were the first foreigners to mention India. In the 6th century BCE, a Persian emperor conquered the Indus river region, known as 'Sindhu'. As a result, they named India 'Hind', 'Hidu', or 'Hindu' in their earliest records and inscriptions, adapting the term 'Sindhu'.

6. How did the ancient Greeks refer to India?

Ans. The ancient Greeks adopted the Persian name and called India 'Indoi' or 'Indike'. They dropped the letter 'H' as it didn't exist in their language, evolving the term from Sindhu to Hindhu to Indoi/Indike.

7. What names did the ancient Chinese use to refer to India?

Ans. The ancient Chinese used multiple names to refer to India, including 'Yintu' or 'Yindu', derived from 'Sindhu'. Additionally, they employed 'Tianzhu', meaning 'heavenly master', demonstrating respect for India as the land of Buddha.

Short Answer Type Questions

1. Describe the evolution of the name 'Bharatavarsha'.

Ans. Originating in the Mahabharata, the name 'Bharatavarsha' underwent significant evolution. Initially, it referred to the kingdom of the Bharatas, an ancient Vedic tribe. Over time, the term expanded to encompass the entire Indian sub-continent, including present-day India, Bangladesh, Pakistan and Afghanistan. This evolution reflects the dynamic nature of India's naming conventions, influenced by literary, cultural and geographical developments. The Mahabharata's usage of 'Bharatavarsha' solidified its significance, making it a widely accepted name for the region. The term's evolution demonstrates the complex and multifaceted nature of India's identity, shaped by various historical and cultural factors.

The name 'Bharatavarsha' has been used in various contexts, including ancient texts, inscriptions and literary works. Its evolution highlights the country's rich cultural heritage and the diverse perspectives of its inhabitants. The term's widespread acceptance underscores its significance in shaping India's national identity.

2. How did the concept of 'Jambudvipa' emerge? How it has been interpreted?

Ans. The concept of 'Jambudvipa' emerged gradually, initially referring to a specific region. Later, it came to represent the Indian subcontinent, symbolising the country's geographical and cultural identity. Ashoka's inscriptions mention 'Jambudvipa', highlighting its significance in ancient Indian thought. The term's evolution reflects India's diverse cultural and historical heritage, influenced by various literary and philosophical works. 'Jambudvipa' became synonymous with India, representing its unique blend of geography, culture and history.

The concept of 'Jambudvipa' has been interpreted in various ways, including geographical, cultural and spiritual perspectives. Its evolution demonstrates the dynamic nature of Indian thought, shaped by diverse influences and historical developments.

3. What is the significance of the Mahabharata in Indian history? What is the impact of this significance?

Ans. The Mahabharata holds immense significance in Indian history, providing profound insights into ancient Indian geography, culture and society. This epic text mentions various regions, shaping India's cultural and religious heritage. Its influence extends beyond literature, impacting art, philosophy and ethics. The Mahabharata's exploration of human nature, morality, and duty continues to resonate with Indians, making it a cornerstone of Indian identity.

The Mahabharata's significance extends to its impact on Indian art, architecture and performing arts. Its stories and characters have inspired countless works of art, literature and popular culture. The epic's themes and values continue to shape Indian thought and society.

4. What is the definition of Bharata according to Vishnu Purana? Mention the importance of this definition.

Ans. Vishnu Purana defines Bharata as the region bounded by the ocean and the Himalayas. This definition highlights the importance of natural features in shaping India's identity. Bharata refers to the entire Indian sub-continent, encompassing present-day India.

The Purana's definition emphasises the significance of Bharata's geographical boundaries, demonstrating the ancient Indian understanding of their country's physical and cultural landscape.

The definition of Bharata in Vishnu Purana underscores the importance of geography in shaping Indian identity. The text's emphasis on natural features highlights the country's diverse physical landscape and its impact on cultural development.

5. What was the significance of the Persian conquest of the Indus River region in the 6th century BCE and how did it impact the naming of India?

Ans. The Persian conquest of the Indus river region in the 6th century BCE marked a pivotal moment in India's history, with far-reaching consequences for its naming and global recognition. By adapting the term 'Sindhu' to create 'Hind', 'Hidu', or 'Hindu', the Persians established the first foreign reference to the sub-continent. Initially, these terms denoted the geographical region, not the religion. This naming convention influenced subsequent foreign references, shaping India's perception and identification by other civilisations.

The Persian conquest facilitated cultural exchange, trade and the spread of ideas, integrating India into the ancient world. The conquest's impact extended beyond naming, as it introduced Indian culture, philosophy and trade to the Persian Empire, fostering a rich cultural exchange.

Long Answer Type Question

1. Discuss the impact of foreign invaders and scholars on the naming and perception of India in ancient times. How did the Persians, Greeks and Chinese contribute to India's global recognition?

Ans. Foreign invaders and scholars played a pivotal role in shaping India's global recognition in ancient times, with the Persians, Greeks and Chinese significantly contributing to its perception as a spiritual and cultural hub in the following ways

- The Persians, who conquered the Indus river region, named India 'Hind', 'Hidu', or 'Hindu', adapting the term 'Sindhu', reflecting cultural exchange and trade.
- The Greeks adopted this name, calling India 'Indoi' or 'Indike', demonstrating the spread of ideas and cultural exchange.
- The Chinese referred to India as 'Yintu' or 'Yindu', derived from 'Sindhu' and 'Tianzhu', meaning 'heavenly master', showcasing their reverence for Indian spiritual heritage. Scholars like Xuanzang further facilitated cultural exchange, translating Buddhist texts and introducing Indian knowledge to China.

These interactions

- contributed to India's global recognition, shaping its perception as a spiritual and cultural hub
- demonstrated the enduring legacy of Indo-Persian, Indo-Greek and Indo-Chinese cultural exchange
- highlighted India's significance in ancient global networks of trade, ideas, and cultural exchange.

The names given by these civilisations reflect the profound impact of foreign invaders and scholars on India's global recognition, underscoring the country's enduring cultural and spiritual significance in ancient times.

Part II

Multiple Choice Type Questions (MCQs)

1. What does the term 'Sapta Sindhava' mean?
(a) Land of the seven rivers
(b) Land of the seven mountains
(c) Land of the seven oceans
(d) Land of the seven forests

2. Which ancient Indian text defines Bharata as 'The country that lies North of the ocean and South of the snowy mountains'?
(a) Rigveda (b) Mahabharata
(c) Vishnu Purana (c) Bhagavad Gita

3. What does the term 'Jambudvipa' mean?
(a) Land of the rose apple tree
(b) Island of the fruit of the jamun tree
(c) Land of the mango tree
(d) Island of the coconut tree

4. According to the Indian Constitution, what are the two names used to refer to the same country?
(a) India and Hindustan
(b) India and Bharat
(c) Bharat and Hindustan
(d) Hindustan and Jambudvipa

5. How did the ancient Greeks modify the name 'Hindu'?
(a) Added the letter 'H' (b) Dropped the letter 'H'
(c) Changed it to 'Indoi' (d) Kept it unchanged

6. What was the Chinese term for India, meaning 'Heavenly Master'?
(a) Yintu (b) Yindu (c) Tianzhu (d) Sindhu

7. Who was the Chinese scholar who traveled to India in the 7th century?
(a) Xuanzang (b) Buddha
(c) Confucius (d) Lao Tzu

8. Which of the following statements are correct?
I. The first foreigners to mention India were the Persians.
II. Xuanzang traveled to India and translated Buddhist texts from Sanskrit to Chinese.
III. The ancient Greeks named India 'Indoi' or 'Indike' without modifying the original name.
Options
(a) I and II only (b) II and III only
(c) I and III only (d) All of these

9. Consider the following statements.
Statement I The Rigveda is the most ancient text of India.
Statement II Bharatavarsha refers to the entire Indian Subcontinent.
Which of the above statements is/are correct?
Options
(a) Both statements are true
(b) Both statements are false
(c) Statement I is true, statement II is false
(d) Statement I is false, statement II is true

Ans. 1. (a) 2. (c) 3. (b) 4. (b) 5. (b) 6. (c) 7. (a) 8. (a) 9. (a)

Fill in the Blanks

1. In the course of history, India has been called by many names, both by its .... and by visitors from outside.
2. Historical names of India are found in the accounts of .... and ....
3. The Indian Constitution begins by stating ".............., that is Bharat".
4. Kurukshetra, listed in the Mahabharata, corresponds to parts of present-day ....
5. Xuanzang, a Chinese scholar, spent .... years exploring India, meeting scholars and collecting Buddhist texts.
6. The term "Hindustan" was first used by the Persians .... years ago to refer to the Indian sub-continent.

Ans. 1. inhabitants 2. travellers, pilgrims 3. India 4. Haryana 5. 17 6. 1,800

True or False

1. Ashoka used the term "Bharatavarsha" to refer to India.
2. The Persians were the first foreigners to mention India and they named it "India" in their earliest records.
3. This name, 'Bharata' remains in use even today.
4. The Indian Constitution, was first written in English

Ans. 1. False 2. False 3. True 4. True

Match the Following

1. Match the region mentioned in Mahabharata with its modern-day equivalent.

	List I		List II
A.	Kashmira	1.	Parts of Bengal
B.	Kurukshetra	2.	Parts of Haryana
C.	Vanga	3.	Roughly today's Assam
D	Pragjyotisha	4.	More or less today's Kashmir

Codes

	A	B	C	D		A	B	C	D
(a)	2	4	1	3	(b)	4	2	1	3
(c)	4	2	3	1	(d)	1	2	3	4

Ans. (b)

Assertion-Reason

1. **Assertion** (A) The term 'Jambudvipa' was used by Ashoka to refer to the entire Indian Subcontinent.

   Reason (R) This is a common tree native to India.

   Codes

   (a) Both A and R are true and R is the correct explanation of A

   (b) Both A and R are true, but R is not the correct explanation of A

   (c) A is true, but R is false

   (d) A is false, but R is true

2. **Assertion** (A) The Indian Constitution recognises only "India" as the official name of the country.

   Reason (R) The Constitution begins by stating "India, that is Bharat".

   Codes

   (a) Both A and R are true and R is the correct explanation of A

   (b) Both A and R are true, but R is not the correct explanation of A

   (c) A is true, but R is false

   (d) A is false, but R is true

3. **Assertion** (A) The name "Bharata" originates from the Rig Veda.

   Reason (R) The Rig Veda mentions the names of several rivers and peoples.

   Codes

   (a) Both A and R are true and R is the correct explanation of A

   (b) Both A and R are true, but R is not the correct explanation of A

   (c) A is true, but R is false

   (d) A is false, but R is true

4. **Assertion** (A) The ancient Indians had a clear understanding of their country's geography.

   Reason (R) A 2,000-year-old Tamil poem praises a king, saying his name is known from Cape Kumari in the South, the great mountain (Himalayas) in the North, and the oceans in the East and West.

   Codes

   (a) Both A and R are true and R is the correct explanation of A

   (b) Both A and R are true, but R is not the correct explanation of A

   (c) A is true, but R is false

   (d) A is false, but R is true

5. **Assertion** (A) The Rigveda gives the North-West region of the subcontinent the name 'Sapta' Sindhava.

   Reason (R) The Persian emperor conquered the Indus River region and adapted the term "Sindhu" to create these names.

   Codes

   (a) Both A and R are true and R is the correct explanation of A

   (b) Both A and R are true, but R is not the correct explanation of A

   (c) A is true, but R is false

   (d) A is false, but R is true

Ans. 1. (b) 2. (d) 3. (a) 4. (a) 5. (b)

Case Based Questions

1. **Read the source given below and answer the questions that follow.**

   It is interesting to note that different parts of the country adopted a similar definition for India. For instance, a poem of ancient Tamil literature, from about 2,000 years ago, praises a king whose name is known "from [Cape] Kumari in the South, from the great mountain in the North, from the oceans on the East and on the West..."

   You can now recognise 'the great mountain in the North', and it should not be difficult to identify 'Cape Kumari'. It looks like ancient Indians knew their geography well!

   (i) What value is reflected in the ancient Tamil poem's description of the king's realm?

   (a) Military conquest

   (b) Geographical unity

   (c) Cultural diversity

   (d) Economic prosperity

   (ii) What does the poem reveal about ancient Indian culture's attitude towards geography?

   (a) Indifference to geographical boundaries

   (b) Importance of trade routes

   (c) Value of geographical knowledge

   (d) Focus on religious sites

   (iii) What cultural value is showcased in the poem's praise of the king's widespread recognition?

   (a) Regionalism

   (b) National pride

   (c) Religious tolerance

   (d) Social hierarchy

   (iv) What does the ancient Tamil literature indicate about the knowledge of geography in ancient India?

   (a) Ancient Indians had limited geographical knowledge.

   (b) Ancient Indians had a detailed and accurate understanding of their geography.

   (c) Ancient Indians were unaware of their geographical boundaries.

   (d) Ancient Indians confused the locations of various geographical features.

Ans. (i) (b) (ii) (c) (iii) (b) (iv) (b)

2. Read the source given below and answer the questions that follows.

But when do we come across a name for the entire Indian sub-continent? Because ancient Indian texts are difficult to date, this is not an easy question to answer. The Mahabharata uses the terms 'Bharatavarsha' and 'Jambudvipa', and scholars generally agree that this long poem was written from a few centuries BCE onward.

The first term, 'Bharatavarsha', clearly extends to the entire Subcontinent, and the text includes the names of numerous rivers and peoples. 'Bharatavarsha' means 'the country of the Bharatas'. 'Bharata' is a name that first appears in the Rigveda, where it refers to one of the main Vedic groups of people. In later literature, several kings named 'Bharata' are mentioned.

(i) What are the challenges faced by the scholars in determining when the Indian sub-continent was first referred to by a single name?

(ii) How does the term 'Bharatavarsha' contribute to our understanding of ancient Indian geography and identity?

(iii) What significance does the name 'Bharata' hold in ancient Indian literature and how does its evolution reflect the development of Indian identity?

Ans. (i) Scholars face significant challenges while determining the exact time when the Indian sub-continent was first referred to by a single name, primarily due to the difficulty in dating ancient Indian texts with precision. The ambiguity surrounding the chronology of these texts makes it hard to determine the earliest occurrence of a unified name for the sub-continent.

(ii) The term 'Bharatavarsha' significantly enhances our understanding of ancient Indian geography and identity by denoting the entire sub-continent, encompassing diverse regions, rivers and peoples. This comprehensive designation implies a unified identity, showcasing ancient Indians' thorough understanding of their vast territory and its various components. Moreover, 'Bharatavarsha' highlights the existence of a collective consciousness, transcending regional boundaries and fostering a sense of shared heritage.

(iii) The name 'Bharata' is deeply meaningful in ancient Indian literature, reflecting the growth of Indian identity. Initially, it referred to a specific tribe, then became linked to legendary kings, symbolising leadership. Eventually, 'Bharata' represented the entire sub-continent, embodying a unified national identity. This evolution shows how Indian identity expanded from tribal to national, highlighting the lasting impact of 'Bharata' on India's collective identity.

Competency Based Questions

1. 'Hindustan' is a common term used for India today. What is the origin of the term 'Hindustan'?

Ans. The term 'Hindustan' originated with the Persians around 1,800 years ago. Initially, it referred to the Indian sub-continent, encompassing present-day India, Pakistan and Bangladesh. Later, invaders adopted the term to describe the region. 'Hindustan' is a relatively recent name compared to other foreign designations for India, such as 'Hind' or 'Indoi'.

2. Comment on the significance of the Rigveda. How its significance impacted the Indian philosophy, spirituality and culture?

Ans. The Rigveda's significance lies in its status as India's most ancient text, providing invaluable insights into ancient Indian geography, culture and society. Mentioning 'Sapta Sindhava', it highlights the region's early naming conventions.

As a foundational text, the Rigveda shapes India's cultural and religious heritage, influencing subsequent literary and philosophical works. Its ancient wisdom continues to inspire and inform Indian thought and identity, demonstrating the enduring relevance of this sacred text.

The Rigveda's significance extends to its impact on Indian philosophy, spirituality and culture. Its hymns and verses have inspired countless generations of Indians, shaping their worldview and values. The text's exploration of human existence, nature, and the divine continues to resonate with Indians, making it a cornerstone of Indian civilisation.

3. How did the ancient Chinese demonstrate their respect for Indian culture and spirituality through their naming conventions?

Ans. The ancient Chinese exhibited profound reverence for Indian culture and spirituality through their naming conventions, reflecting a deep admiration for India's spiritual and philosophical heritage. By calling India 'Tianzhu', meaning 'heavenly master', they acknowledged India as the land of Buddha and a spiritual hub. The use of 'Yintu' or 'Yindu', derived from 'Sindhu', further demonstrated their respect.

Chinese scholar Xuanzang's 17-year exploration of India, collection of Buddhist texts, and translations from Sanskrit to Chinese solidified cultural ties. This reverence reflects the significant impact of Indian spirituality and culture on ancient Chinese thought and society, underscoring the enduring legacy of Indo-Chinese cultural exchange.

4. Comment on the geographical understanding of ancient Indians.

Ans. Ancient Indians possessed a clear understanding of their country's geography, as evident from texts like the Rigveda, Mahabharata and Vishnu Purana. These texts describe the region's boundaries, rivers, and mountains, showcasing a comprehensive knowledge of the sub-continent's geography.

The Rigveda mentions 'Sapta Sindhava', highlighting the significance of rivers in shaping India's identity. The ancient Indians' geographical understanding was not limited to physical features; they also recognised the cultural and regional diversity within the sub-continent. The Mahabharata mentions various regions, such as Kashmira, Kurukshetra and Vanga, demonstrating an awareness of India's complex geography. This understanding reflects a sophisticated appreciation of the sub-continent's ecological, cultural and political landscape. Additionally, ancient Indians recognised the strategic importance of geographical features, such as the Himalayas and the Indian Ocean, in shaping the sub-continent's climate, trade and cultural exchange.

Skill Based Questions as per NEP 2020

1. Imagine you are a traveller in ancient India. Write a story about your journey across the Indian sub-continent, mentioning the different regions you visit.

Ans. The following is the story of my journey as a traveller across the ancient Indian sub-continent

My travels took me to the majestic Kashmira, nestled in the Himalayas, where I wandered through lush meadows, discovering ancient temples and mysterious ruins that whispered tales of a bygone era.

From Kashmira, I ventured to Kurukshetra, the legendary battlefield of the Mahabharata. As I walked, I felt the weight of history beneath my feet. I visited the sacred lake of Brahmsar, where the Pandavas are said to have camped, and the Jyotisar, where Krishna delivered the divine sermon of the Bhagavad Gita.

Next, I journeyed to Vanga, where I sailed along the rivers, watching artisans weave magic on their looms. I listened to the sweet melodies of the veena and savored the flavors of local delicacies, like the sweet rice cakes and spicy fish curries.

In Pragjyotisha, I discovered a hub of ancient wisdom, where sages shared secrets of the universe and scholars debated the mysteries of life. I attended discourses on the Vedas and learned about the intricacies of Ayurveda, the traditional Indian system of medicine.

As I traveled South, I braved the scorching deserts of Kaccha, where resilient nomads shared their stories of survival and courage.

Finally, I arrived in Kerala, a tropical paradise of swaying palms and serene backwaters. I cruised along the tranquil waters marveling at the intricate carvings on the ancient temples.

Throughout my journey, I encountered diverse cultures, languages and traditions, yet a common thread of warmth and hospitality bound them together. Ancient India's rich tapestry left an indelible mark on my heart, and I carried its memories with me forever.

2. You are a historian tasked with explaining the evolution of India's names to a curious reader. Write a clear and concise explanation.

Ans. India's names have evolved over time, reflecting its diverse cultural, geographical and historical contexts as follows

- 'Sapta Sindhava' (Land of Seven Rivers) in the Rigveda (1500 BCE) referred to the North-Western region, emphasising the importance of rivers in ancient Indian civilisation.
- 'Bharatavarsha' (Country of the Bharatas) and 'Jambudvipa' (Island of the Jamun Tree) in the Mahabharata (400 BCE) denoted the entire sub-continent, highlighting its geographical boundaries and cultural identity.
- Foreigners adapted these names, reflecting their perspectives and interactions with ancient India
  - **Persians** (6th century BCE): 'Hind', 'Hidu', or 'Hindu' (from Sindhu/Indus river), emphasising the region's connection to the Indus Valley.
  - **Greeks** (3rd century BCE): 'Indoi' or 'Indike' (dropping the 'H' sound), showcasing their phonetic adaptations.
  - **Chinese** (2nd century BCE): 'Yintu' or 'Yindu' (from Sindhu), demonstrating their cultural exchange and trade.
  - **Tianzhu** (Heavenly Master) term of respect, highlighting India's reputation as a land of spiritual wisdom.

This evolution of names reflects the dynamic interplay between ancient India's internal developments and external interactions, shaping its identity and legacy.

ASSESSMENT EXERCISE

Objective Type Questions

1. Who among the following used the term 'Jambudvipa' to refer to India?
   (a) Ashoka (b) Rigveda
   (c) Mahabharata (d) Vishnu Purana
2. What is the name of the ancient Indian text that mentions the North-West region of the subcontinent as 'Sapta Sindhava'?
   (a) Mahabharata (b) Rigveda
   (c) Vishnu Purana (d) Bhagavad Gita
3. Who were the first foreigners to mention India?
   (a) Greeks (b) Persians
   (c) Chinese (d) Romans
4. What was the origin of the name 'Hind' or 'Hindu'?
   (a) Derived from the Indus River
   (b) Adapted from the term 'Sindhu'
   (c) Named by the ancient Greeks
   (d) Named by the ancient Chinese
5. **Assertion** (A) Today, the India we know is a modern nation.
   Reason (R) It has defined borders, defined states and a known population.
   Codes
   (a) Both A and R are true and R is the correct explanation of A
   (b) Both A and R are true, but R is not the correct explanation of A
   (c) A is true, but R is false
   (d) A is false, but R is true
6. The Rigveda is .... years old.
7. The Chinese called India '...............', meaning 'heavenly master', showing respect for India as the land of Buddha.
8. In South India, the term 'Bharatam' is often used. (True/False)
9. The Indian Constitution recognises only 'india' as the name of our country. (True/False)

Subjective Questions (VSA, SA & LA)

1. Which ancient Indian text mentions the names of several regions, including Kashmir and Kerala?
2. Who defined Bharata as "the country that lies North of the ocean and South of the snowy mountains"?
3. In the 6th century BCE, who launched a military campaign and gained control of the region of the Indus river?
4. What was the name used by the ancient Chinese to refer to India, showing respect for it as the land of Buddha?
5. What is the significance of the name 'Bharatavarsha' mentioned in the Mahabharata and who is it named after?
6. What are the two terms used in the Mahabharata to refer to the entire Indian sub-continent and what do they mean?
7. How did the ancient Chinese refer to India and what was the meaning of the term 'Tianzhu'?
8. What is the significance of the term 'Bharat' in modern times and how is it used in the Indian Constitution?
9. "The name 'Bharat' is an integral part of India's cultural and national identity." Justify.
10. A Chinese scholar is interested in exploring the cultural significance of India in ancient Chinese literature. How would Xuanzang's travels to India contribute to this scholar's understanding?

The Beginnings of Indian Civilisation

Over long ages, the Earth's climate has gone through many changes. As living conditions improved, the early humans or first human groups started to settle down. They also practised agriculture, and developed some technologies like construction, metallurgy and transport. These humans were moving towards making a civilisation.

6.1 Civilisation

- Civilisation is a term used for an advanced stage of human society. In different parts of the world civilisations started at different times.
- In the region known as **Mesopotamia** (modern Iraq and Syria), the civilisation developed about 6000 years ago. The Egyptian civilisation was settled centuries after it.
- The development of ancient civilisations leads to modern humanity and civilisation.

Characteristics of a Civilisation

- **Government and Administration** There is some form of government and administration in every civilisation. This system is established to manage the complex system of society and its activities.
- **Urbanisation** The practice of town planning is seen in civilisations. It generally includes the growth of cities and their management.
- **Crafts** Numerous crafts are developed within a civilisation. This may include management of raw materials (such as stone or metal) and the production of finished goods like ornaments and tools.
- **Trade** It is the exchange of goods. In a civilisation, both internal and external trade are done.
- **Writing** Writing was used to communicate and keep records.
- **Cultural ideas** The cultural ideas in the civilisations are expressed through art, architecture, literature, oral traditions or its social customs.
- **Agriculture** In a civilisation, the agricultural produce is enough for both villages and cities.

6.2 From Village to City

- In regions of Punjab and Sindh plains, villages and towns were developed near the 3500 BCE. The plains of Punjab and Sindh were fertile and supported agriculture.
- These plains used to get its water from river **Indus** and its tributaries. On its East, there was another river named **Saraswati** that used to flow from the foothills of Himalayas through Haryana, Punjab and parts of Rajasthan and Gujarat.
- By 2600 BCE, the villages in these plains grew into towns. Further these towns developed as cities by extending their trade and other exchanges. This development is also called the **first urbanisation of India.**
- This civilisation is known by different names by archaeologists like, Indus, Harappan, Indus-Sarasvati or Sindhu-Sarasvati civilisation. It is one of the oldest civilisations that developed in the world. The people who used to live in this civilisation are known as **Harappans**. They are called Harappans because, in 1920-21, Harappa was the first excavated site from this civilisation.

The Sarasvati River

- The Sarasvati river was first mentioned in the Rigveda. As per the text, it is worshipped both as a goddess and as a river flowing 'from the mountains to sea'. Later texts give information about the drying up of the river and its eventual disappearance.
- Today this river is known by the name of **Ghaggar** in India and **Hakra** in Pakistan. It is a seasonal river that flows only during the rainy season.

6.3 Town Planning

Harappa and Mohenjo-daro, now in Pakistan, were the first two cities of this civilisation which were discovered in 1924. Later, more sites were discovered in the Indus plains. That is why the civilisation was called the **Indus Valley Civilisation**. Some of the sites are

- Major cities such as Dholavira in Gujarat, Rakhigarhi in Haryana, Ganeriwala in the Cholistan desert of Pakistan.
- Many smaller sites such as Lothal in Gujarat, Farmana in Haryana, Kalibangan in Rajasthan, Bhirrana and Banawali in Haryana, etc.

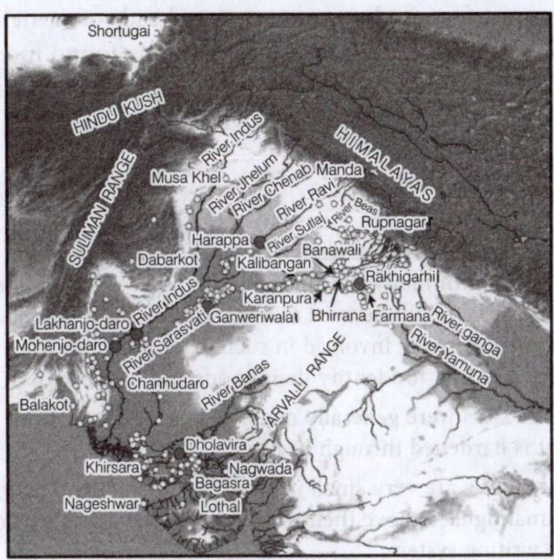

Some of the main settlements of the Indus Valley civilisation

- The large cities like Harappa were built according to precise plans. Some of the common features of cities of Indus Valley Civilisation are as follows
  - The streets were wide and often aligned with the cardinal directions (North, South, East and West).
  - Most of the cities were fortified. Cities were often divided in two parts, i.e, **upper town** and **lower town**. It is possible that the upper town was for the elites like administrators, trades and priests and the lower town was for the common people.
  - There were large community buildings like warehouses where goods were stored.
  - Various sized houses of individuals were built in streets and smaller lanes.
  - The quality of small and large houses were maintained. All of them were generally built of bricks.

Great Bath of Mohenjo-daro

- It was a small tank in Mohenjo-daro that measured around 12* 7 metres. It was made of waterproofing materials like natural bitumen.
- The tank was surrounded by small rooms. One of them had a well. There was a drain in one corner of the tank to empty it from time to time and refill it with freshwater.
- Archaeologists have proposed various purposes of such a structure. Some of them are
  - It might be a public bath for people.
  - It might be a bath of the royal family only.
  - It might be used for religious rituals.

Mohenjo-daro's Great Bath

Try These

1. **Which development is also known as the first urbanisation of India?**
2. **What could have been the purpose of the Great Bath in Mohenjo-daro?**
3. **What could have led to the transition from villages to cities in the Punjab and Sindh plains?**

6.4 Water Management

- The Harappans used to give importance to water management and cleanliness.
- They used to have separate areas for bathing in their home that were connected to a network of drains. These drains were generally laid below the streets and removed the wastewater.
- In Mohenjo-daro, people drew water from hundreds of wells made of bricks.
- In Dholavira, there were reservoirs (73 metres in length) to draw water. Six of these reservoirs were built with stones or even cut into rocks. Most of them were connected through underground drains for efficient water **harvesting** and distribution.

A large reservoir cut in the rock at Dholavira, measuring 33 meteres in length.

6.5 Harappan Food

- The diet of Harappan people was quite diverse. The remains of dairy products, turmeric, ginger and banana were found in Harappan sites.
- Most of the Harappan settlements were developed along the banks of large or small rivers. These sites were chosen due to availability of water as well as due to fertile soil around rivers.
- According to archaeological findings, Harappans grew cereals like barley, wheat, some millets, rice along with pulses and a variety of vegetables. They were also the first in Eurasia to grow cotton. This cotton was used to weave clothes.
- Harappans made farming tools like plough which is continued to be used by modern day farmers.
- The intense agricultural activities were managed by a number of small villages. The cities were dependent on the agricultural produce from rural areas for daily basis.
- Large number of animal and fish bones were found during excavation in Harappa. This refers to the fact that a number of animals were also domesticated by the Harappans for meat consumption. **Fishing** was also practised by Harappans in both rivers and in the sea.

6.6 A Lively Trade

- The Harappans were engaged in trade actively. They were not only trading within their civilisation but also with other civilisations and cultures within and outside India. To conduct this trade, they used both land and maritime routes.
- The settlements like Lothal in Gujarat were used as **dockyards**. There is a huge basin of 217 metres length and 36 metres width to receive and send boats for transportation of goods.
- Harappans used to export ornaments, timber, some objects of daily use and probably gold, cotton and some food items too. They most probably imported the copper.
- Harappans had mastered the art of using copper. They used to add tin to copper for making the harder metal called bronze. They used bronze to make tools, pots and pans, etc.
- The most favoured ornaments were beads of carnelian which was a reddish semi precious stone found mostly in Gujarat. They also made conch shells into beautiful shell bangles.

Seals

- There have been thousands of small seals found during excavation of many sites in the Indus Valley Civilisation. These seals might be used as a mark of identity. As the Harappans were involved in such extensive trade, they were required to identify their goods and other traders.
- These seals were generally made of steatite, a soft stone that is hardened through heating.
- These seals are very small in size. They generally depict animal figures above them with few signs that are part of the writing system.
- The symbolic meaning of the figures and signs on seals is yet to be understood, but it is clear that these seals were somehow related to the trade activities.

Harappan Seals

Objects Made and Used by Harappans

The following objects of daily use and cultural and symbolic importance were found from different sites of Harappan Civilisation.

- A bronze mirror, a terracotta pot, a few stone weights, a bronze chisel and a game board engraved on a stone, about 25 cm in length were found from Dholavira .
- A terracotta whistle, about 4 cm in length was found from Karanpura in Rajasthan.

- A statuette of a figure often called **Priest King**, a seal showing a swastika and a seal depicting a three-faced deity seated on a raised platform, surrounded by powerful animals were found.
- The **Dancing Girl**, a bronze figurine was found from Mohenjo-daro.
- A terracotta figurine seated in a 'namaste' and a design on a pot which seems to tell the story of the thirsty crow, who finds a clever way to drink water at the bottom of the pot were found from Lothal.

6.7 Decline of the Indus Valley Civilisation

- Around 1900 BCE, the Indus Valley Civilisation or Sindhu-Sarasvati civilisation or IVC began to decline.
- The cities were emptied one by one. The system of government or administration was lost and people were adopting the rural lifestyle due to change in climate.
- Slowly the Harappans were divided into hundreds of small rural settlements.
- There are several factors proposed by the archaeologists for the fall of civilisation. Some of them are as follows
  - Earlier invasions or warfare were thought to be the cause of the decline of Indus Valley Civilisation. But no traces of the army were seen in the civilisation. It might be a peaceful civilisation.
  - The other factor may be the climatic change that affected much of the world from 2200 BCE onwards. During this period, rainfall was reduced and places were dried up. This reduced the agricultural supply to the cities.
  - In the central basin of civilisation, the Sarasvati river dried up. Due to this cities like Kalibangan or Banawali were abandoned.
- There might be some other causes for the decline of the Indus Valley Civilisation but these causes represent how much we are dependent on climate and the environment for our well-being.
- Though the cities disappeared, much of the Harappan culture and technology survived and passed on to the next phase of Indian Civilisation.

Try These

1. **What metal did the Harappans import?**
2. **What type of shells were crafted into beautiful bangles?**
3. **The 'Dancing Girl' is a bronze figurine found at which site?**

Glossary

Metallurgy It includes the techniques of extracting metals from nature, purifying or combining them, as well as the scientific study of metals and their properties.

Tributary A river that flows into a larger river (or lake). For instance, the Yamuna is a tributary of the Ganga.

Fortification A massive wall surrounding a settlement or city, generally for the protection of the city.

Elite It refers to the higher layers of the society, such as rulers, officials, administrators and often priests.

Reservoir it is a large natural or artificial place where water is stored.

Pulses It includes crops like beans, peas and lentils (dal).

Harvesting It refers to collection and storage of rainwater or surface runoff for later use.

THE BEGINNINGS OF INDIAN CIVILISATION

Civilisation

- It is a general term used for an advanced stage of human societies.
- Mesopotamian civilisation developed about 6000 years ago and ancient Egypt civilisation followed it few centuries later.

Characteristics of a Civilisation

- Government and Administration
- Urbanisation
- Variety of crafts
- Trade
- Some form of writing
- Cultural ideas
- Agriculture

From Village to City

- In plains of Indus and Saraswati from about 3500 BCE, villages grew into towns.
- With increased trade and other exchanges, those towns grew into cities. This transformation happened around 2600 BCE.
- This civilisation is known by different names like
  - Indus Harappan
  - Indus-Saraswati or Sindhu-Saraswati
- It is one of the oldest civilisation of the world.
- It is also known as 'first urbanisation' in India.
- The people of this civilisation were known as 'Harappan'.

Water Management

- The Harappans used to have separate bathing areas in their houses.
- In Mohenjo-daro, people had well made of brick to fetch water.
- In regions like Dholavira there were large reservoirs, ponds, etc to fetch

Town Planning

Characteristics

- Wide streets
- Streets were aligned to cardinal directions
- Fortified boundaries
- Divided into upper town and lower town
- Huge community buildings like warehouse and Great Bath.

Major Towns

- Harappa (Pakistan)
- Mohenjo-daro (Pakistan)
- Dholavira (Gujarat)
- Rakhigarhi (Haryana)
- Lothal (Gujarat)
- Kalibangan (Rajasthan)

Food of Harappans

- Harappan created settlements near small or large rivers.
- They used to grow cereals like barley, wheat, rice and some millets along with pulses, vegetables and cotton.

A Brick Trade

- Harappans exported ornaments, timber, some of objects of daily use, gold, cotton and some food items.
- They used both land and maritime route.
- A dockyard like structure at Lothal is the evidence of Maritime trade.
- Seals were used as identity of goods and traders. They were generally made of steatite.

Decline of Civilisation

- Around 1900 BCE the civilisation began to fall.
- Cause of decline are not clear, there might be various factors, such as. There might be invasions or the warfare. The Saraswati river dried and land became barren.

NCERT FOLDER

Detailed Answers of All NCERT Questions

Think About It (Page 86)

Q.1 Which of the characteristics of civilisation do you think is the most fundamental, that is, a characteristic essential to the development of all others?

Ans. The system of government and administration and urbanism are fundamental characteristics for development of all other characteristics.

Let's Explore (Page 87)

Q.2 For each characteristic of a civilisation, can you make a list of professions or occupations that might exist in such a society?

Ans. A list of professions or occupations that might exist in such a society are as follows

A. **Government and Administration** King, chieftians and police man

B. **Urbanism** Sweeper, house-help, cook and gardner

C. **Craft** Goldensmith, blacksmith, artist and sculptor

D. **Trade** Vendors, exporter and importer

E. **Writing** Authors and sculptors

F. **Agriculture** Farmers

G. **Culture** Priest

Don't Miss Out (Page 88)

Q.3 Why are the inhabitants of this civilisation called 'Harappans' today?

Ans. The inhabitants of this civilisation are called 'Harappans' today because the city of Harappa (today in Pakistan's Punjab) was the first of this civilisation to be excavated, way back in 1920–21, over a century ago.

Let's Explore (Page 89)

Q.4 Some of the important cities of this civilisation are marked in the map. As a class activity, can you try to match these cities with the modern states or regions in the table?

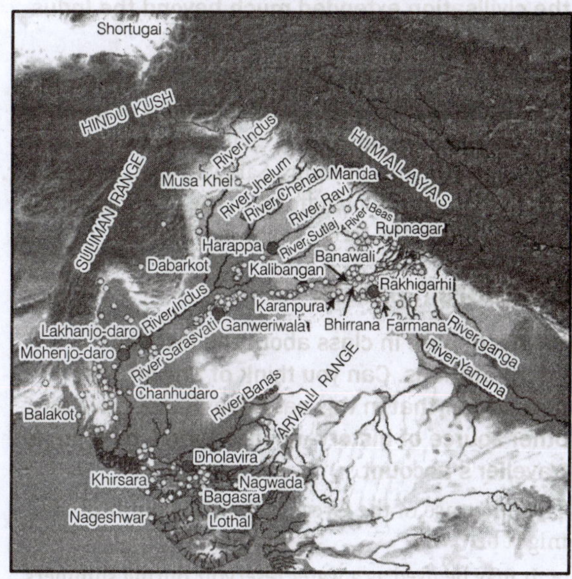

Harappan City	Modern State/Region
Dholavira	Punjab
Harappa	Gujarat
Kalibangan	Sindh
Mohenjo-daro	Haryana
Rakhigarhi	Rajasthan

Ans.

Harappan City	Modern State/Region
Dholavira	Gujarat
Harappa	Punjab
Kalibangan	Rajasthan
Mohenjo-daro	Sindh
Rakhigarhi	Haryana

Think About It (Page 91)

Q.5 You may have come across the term 'Indus Valley Civilisation' and noticed that we have not used it. A look at the map (Fig. 6.3 on page 89) explains why the term 'Valley' is obsolete, as we now know that the civilisation extended much beyond the Indus region.

Ans. The term valley is not suitable for civilisation as the civilisation was spread beyond the plains of the Indus river and its tributaries. The civilisation was spread between the plains of Indus, Sarswati and Ganga river. While the valley is a landform in the mountainous region. Hence, the term 'Valley' is obsolete.

Let's Explore (Page 93)

Q.6 Have a debate in class about the last two interpretations. Can you think of any others? Remember that in this case, we do not have any other source of history–no inscription, no text, no traveller's account.

Ans. The other use of the Great Bath of Mohenjo-daro might be

- It may be used as a water reservoir during summers.
- It may also be used as a source of irrigation.

Let's Explore (Page 95)

Q.7 As a class activity, measure the length of your classroom, a school corridor or a playground with the help of any measuring tape. Compare these lengths with the length of the largest reservoir in Dholavira.

Ans. Do it yourself

Think About It (Page 96)

Q.8 Imagine the large number of workers required to build such a network of reservoirs. Who do you think organised their work and gave them precise instructions? How do you think they were paid for their labour? (Hint: there was no money at that time in the way we have today.) Since the reservoirs needed to be cleaned from time to time, was there some local authority to manage their maintenance? What clues do we get from all this about this city's ruler and municipal administration?

Use your imagination and discuss with your teacher. Archaeologists also discuss these questions and the answers are not always final!

Ans. The construction of reservoirs might be organised by the government and administration. As there was no money, they might have been paid through cereals or some other goods. There might be a system of municipal administration that took care of cleanliness of reservoirs from time to time. As there is a system of government and administration, there will be authorities assigned to different sections in administration.

Let's Explore (Page 97)

Q.9 Imagine you cook a meal in a Harappan house. What dish or dishes would you prepare?

Ans. Based on the information, following dishes could be prepared in a Harappa house

- Dal and rice
- Fish
- Meat
- Chapati and vegetables
- Curd
- Pudding

Let's Explore (Page 99)

Q 10. Looking at these three Harappan seals with some writing signs, what goes through your mind? Would you like to suggest any interpretations? Let your imagination run!

Ans. On observing the above given seals followings thought comes to the mind

- The animals that are shown on these seals were known to the people in Harappa.
- These animals might be sacred to the people of Harappa.
- The name of the rulers might have been written.

Think About It (Page 102)

Q 11. Looking at the objects given in the chapter. Can you make out what activities or aspects of life were important for the Harappans?

Ans. Based on the objects given in the chapters, following activities might be important for the Harappans

- Jewellery making
- Pottery
- Sculpting
- Dancing
- Seal making

Let's Explore (Page 102)

Q 12. Complete the story found on the Lothal pot. How was such a story remembered for more than 4,000 years, in your opinion?

Ans. Such stories might be remembered through oral transfer from one generation to the other.

Q13. Consider the 'Dancing Girl' figurine. What do you make of the attitude the figurine expresses? Observe her bangles covering an entire arm, a practice still visible in parts of Gujarat and Rajasthan. Where else in this chapter can you spot bangles worn in this manner. What conclusion should we draw from this?

Ans. The figurine expresses the posture of waiting or dancing. In the Kalibangan site of Harappan civilisation such bangles could be spotted.

The conclusions from these facts are as follows

- The Dancing Girl figure might have been brought to Mohenjo-daro from Kalibangan.
- The bangles were traded between Mohenjo-daro and Kalibangan.

Questions, Activities and Projects

Q1. Why does the civilisation studied in this chapter have several names? Discuss their significance.

Ans. The civilisation in this chapter has several names based on the areas where it was discovered and settled.

Each name has its own significance. Some of them are as follows

- **Indus** The civilisation was settled mostly near the fertile plains of the river Indus and its tributaries.
- **Harappan** The civilisation was named Harappan because the very first site of this civilisation was discovered in Harappa city.
- **Indus-Sarswati or Sindhu- Saraswati** The name was given based on the widespread expanse of the civilisation over the vast fertile plains of Indus and Saraswati rivers.

Q2. Write a brief report (150 to 200 words) summing up some of the achievements of the Indus-Sarasvati Civilisation.

Ans. Some achievements of the Indus-Sarasvati Civilisation are as follows

- The large cities were built according to precise plans.
- Their streets were wide and aligned to the cardinal directions.
- They gave importance to water management and cleanliness.
- Most of the cities were fortified and divided into two parts, upper town and lower town. Upper town was for elite people and lower town was for common people.
- There were some large buildings like warehouses to store goods.
- They used to have separate areas for bathing in their homes that were connected to a larger network of drains.
- In Mohenjo-daro people have wells in their houses and others used to fetch water from ponds, nearby streams or human-made reservoirs.
- They were engaged in active trade between the civilisations and other civilisations in the world.

Q3. Imagine you have to travel from the city of Harappa to Kalibangan. What are your different options? Can you make a rough estimation of the amount of time each option might take?

Ans. If one has to go to the Kalibangan from Harappa, they can travel through river Ravi and reach the confluence of Ravi and Sutlej, from there take a land route to reach Kalibangan. The trip from Harappa to Kalibangan might take 10-15 days.

Q4. Let us imagine a Harappan man or woman being transported to an average kitchen in today's India. What are the four or five biggest surprises awaiting them?

Ans. The biggest surprises for a man or woman being transported to an average kitchen in today's India will be

- A refrigerator
- A microwave and oven
- Steel utensils
- Packed milk packets

Q5. Looking at all the pictures in this chapter, make a list of the ornaments/gestures/ objects that still feel familiar in our 21st century.

Ans. Following ornaments/ gestures/ objects can still found in 21st century

- Mirror
- Comb
- Pots
- Drainage system
- Plough
- Whistle
- Chess board

Q6. What mindset does the system of reservoirs at Dholavira reflect?

Ans. The system of reservoirs at Dholavira reflects the idea that

- People in Harappan civilisation were aware about water conservation.
- They used to store rainwater.
- Harappans gave much importance to water management and cleanliness.

Q7. In Mohenjo-daro, about 700 wells built with bricks have been counted. They seem to have been regularly maintained and used for several centuries. Discuss the implications.

Ans. The use of about 700 wells built with brick have several implications. Some of them are as follows

- The regular use of wells for several centuries will lead to decline in groundwater.
- It will reduce the water for irrigation.
- There may be wastage of water due to easy accessibility.

Q8. It is often said that the Harappans had a high civic sense. Discuss the significance of this statement. Do you agree with it? Compared with citizens in a large city of India today.

Ans. Yes, Harappans had a high civic sense. Some of the facts that support the statement are as follows

- They had a separate bathing area that was well connected with the network of drains.
- The waste used to flow through the drains.
- The houses were made of bricks only.
- People in Harappan cities were engaged in trading activities.

In today's large cities of India, the drainage system is not working very well due to over population and pollution. There are slum areas around the large cities these days which were not the feature of Harappan cities. Hence, in these ways Harappan cities were more civic than modern cities in India.

REVIEW EXERCISE

Including Competency Based Questions

Part I

Very Short Answer Type Questions

1. What term is used for an advanced stage of human society with urban planning and governance?

Ans. Civilisation is the term used for an advanced stage of human society with urban planning and governance.

2. Name the earliest city discovered in India.

Ans. Harappa was the first city to be discovered in India.

3. Which grains were produced by the Harappans?

Ans. Wheat, barley, pulses, peas, rice, sesame, linseed and mustard were the grains produced by the Harappans.

4. Where was the evidence of a dockyard found in Harappan cities?

Ans. Evidence of a dockyard has been found in Lothal, Gujarat, where a huge basin measuring 217 metres in length and 36 metres in width has been present. It is the place where the boats and ships came from the sea.

5. Name four excavation sites of Harappan civilisation.

Ans. Dholavira, Lothal, Mohenjodaro and Harrapan are the excavation sites of the Harappan civilisation.

6. What do you mean by the term urbanisation?

Ans. The practice of town planning which is seen in civilisations is known as urbanisation. It is the growth of cities, and their management. It also includes water management and a drainage system.

7. Name a few objects of daily use found from Dholavira.

Ans. Few objects of daily use found from Dholavira are a bronze mirror, a terracotta pot, a few stone weights, a bronze chisel and a game board engraved on a stone, about 25 cm in length were found from Dholavira.

Short Answer Type Questions

1. Explain the architectural features and the rituals which were offered in the Great Bath.

Ans. The architectural features of Great Bath are

- It is a special tank, which was lined with bricks, coated with water proofing material called bitumen.
- There were steps leading down to it from two sides, while there were rooms on all sides.
- The ritual offered in Great Bath was that people took a dip in the tank on special occasions.

2. What were the factors that contributed to the development of the Harappan civilisation?

Ans. The following factors contributed in the development of the Harappan civilisation

- The Harappan civilisation developed in the fertile plains of the Indus and Sarasvati rivers, which provided ample water for agriculture and supported a growing population.

- The availability of raw materials, the development of trade networks and advancements in metallurgy and craftsmanship contributed to its growth.
- The society had a form of governance to manage urban planning, trade and public utilities, which further facilitated the civilisation's development.

3. Describe the craft works of the Harappans.

Ans. The craft works of the Harappans were as follows

- Crafts in Harappa were made of stone, shell and metal, including copper, bronze, gold and silver.
- Copper, bronze, silver and gold were used to make tools, weapons, ornaments and vessels. Apart from these artefacts, beads, weights and blades were also made.

4. What are the probable factors that marked the decline of the Harappan civilisation?

Ans. The following factors marked the decline of the Harappan civilisation

- The cities were abandoned one by one.
- The inhabitants of cities started to live the rural lifestyle.
- A climatic change in the world from 2200 BCE onwards.

5. What are the defining characteristics of the Harappan civilisation's urban planning?

Ans. The characteristics that defines Harappan civilisation are

- Its advanced urban planning, which included grid-like street patterns.
- A well-planned drainage system.
- Use of standardised brick sizes for construction.
- Cities were divided into different sectors, with distinct areas for residential, administrative and religious activities.
- The presence of large public structures like the Great Bath in Mohenjo-daro and granaries indicates a high level of social organisation and state control over resources.

6. How did the Harappan civilisation contribute to the development of metallurgy?

Ans. The Harappan civilisation made significant advances in metallurgy, particularly in the crafting of tools and ornaments from copper, bronze and other metals. They developed techniques for casting and alloying metals, which were used to produce a variety of objects including tools, weapons and jewellery.

This expertise in metallurgy not only facilitated their daily life but also played a role in trade, as metal goods were likely exchanged with neighbouring regions.

7. What evidence suggests that the Harappan civilisation engaged in trade and with whom did they likely trade?

Ans. Evidence of trade in the Harappan civilisation comes from the discovery of standardised weights and measures, seals and artefacts made from materials not native to the region, such as lapis lazuli and marine shells.

These items suggest a wide trade network, possibly extending to Mesopotamia, Central Asia and the Persian Gulf. The presence of Harappan seals in Mesopotamian cities further supports the idea that the Harappans engaged in long-distance trade, exchanging goods like textiles, beads and crafts.

8. What role did agriculture play in the economy of the Harappan civilisation?

Ans. Agriculture was the backbone of the Harappan economy, with the cultivation of crops like wheat, barley, pulses and cotton providing the main sustenance for the population. The fertile plains of the Indus and Sarasvati rivers allowed for productive farming, supported by advanced irrigation techniques.

Surpluses generated from agriculture likely fueled urbanisation and trade, as excess goods could be stored in granaries and traded with other regions.

Long Answer Type Questions

1. Discuss the significance of urban planning in the Harappan civilisation. How did it reflect the administrative capabilities of the society?

Ans. Urban planning in the Harappan civilisation was highly advanced and reflects the administrative capabilities of the society in the following ways

- Cities like Harappa and Mohenjo-daro were planned, with wide streets laid out in a grid pattern and aligned with the cardinal directions.
- The cities were divided into different zones, including residential areas, public baths, granaries and administrative buildings, indicating a clear understanding of urban management.
- The uniformity in the size and construction of bricks across different cities suggests the existence of standardised regulations, possibly enforced by a central authority.
- The extensive drainage system, which included covered drains beneath the streets, points to the emphasis on hygiene and public health.
- The presence of large warehouses and granaries indicates organised storage and distribution of food, reflecting an efficient administrative system capable of managing large populations.
- This level of urban planning not only ensured the smooth functioning of the cities but also demonstrates the sophisticated governance that characterised the Harappan civilisation.

2. The diet of Harappans was quite diverse. Validate the statemtent.

Ans. The diet of Harappans was quite diverse. The statement can be validated through following facts

- Scientific examinations of clay pots found the remains of turmeric, ginger and banana.
- Some pots also validate the consumption of dairy products.

- They used to do fishing in both rivers and sea.
- They used to domesticate the animals to consume meat.
- Harappans used to cultivate cereals like barley, wheat, some millets, rice, pulses and a variety of vegetables.
- The Harappans engaged in trade with other regions, which likely introduced new food items into their diet.
- The presence of large granaries and storage facilities indicates the systematic collection and storage of various, food items.

3. The Harappans managed their trade networks and they had extensive trading relationships both within and outside their civilisation. What evidence supports this statement?

Ans. The Harappans managed their trade networks with a high level of organisation. Some of the evidences which support this statement are

- They engaged in both internal and external trade, exchanging commodities like pottery, beads, cotton, and metal goods.
- The presence of materials such as copper and tin, which were not locally available hence, they imported these resources.
- Harappan cities like Lothal in Gujarat served as major trading hubs, with a well-constructed dockyard that facilitated maritime trade. This indicates that the Harappans not only traded overland but also had established sea routes.
- The discovery of seals with inscriptions and animal motifs further points to their use in trade, possibly as a form of identification or ownership for goods.
- Trade goods from the Harappan civilisation have been found in distant lands that indicates extensive trading relationships of Harappans with other contemporary civilisations.
- The standardised system of weights and measures across the civilisation also highlights the organised nature of their trade.

Overall, the evidence of sophisticated trade networks and the presence of foreign goods in Harappan sites underline the significance of trade in the economic and cultural development of the civilisation.

Part II

Multiple Choice Questions (MCQs)

1. How old is the Harappa civilisation?
(a) About 4000 years old (b) About 3000 years old
(c) About 4700 years old (d) About 5500 years old

2. When was the first city of Harappa discovered by the archaeologists?
(a) About 80 years ago (b) About 150 years ago
(c) About 50 years ago (d) About 100 years ago

3. The Great Bath is a part of
(a) Mohenjo-daro (b) Lothal
(c) Dholavira (d) Kalibangan

4. Name the place where elites generally lived.
(a) Lower town (b) Upper town
(c) Middle town (d) None of these

5. Tin was mixed with ...... to produce bronze.
(a) aluminium (b) gold (c) copper (d) silver

6. The city of Lothal was located on the bank of a tributary of which river?
(a) Ganga (b) Yamuna (c) Saraswati (d) Sabarmati

7. Which material was most commonly used for constructing houses in Harappan cities?
(a) Stone (b) Wood (c) Brick (d) Clay

8. The discovery of weights and measures at Harappan sites indicates
(a) a lack of trade
(b) standardisation in trade practices
(c) the use of barter system
(d) no evidence of trade activities

9. What was one of the primary reasons for the growth of villages and towns in the Indus-Sarasvati region?
(a) Advancement in metallurgy
(b) Increased trade and exchanges
(c) Discovery of gold mines
(d) Development of art and architecture

10. Arrange the following places from North-South direction.

I. Lothal **II. Mohenjo-daro**
III. Harappa **IV. Kalibangan**

Codes
(a) I, II, III, IV (b) II, I, III, IV
(c) III, II, II, IV (d) III, IV, II, I

Answers

1. (c)	2. (d)	3. (a)	4. (b)	5. (c)
6. (d)	7. (c)	8. (b)	9. (b)	10. (d)

Fill in the Blanks

1. The ...... is the earliest city discovered in India.
2. The signs on the top of the seal are part of a ...
3. ...... and ...... were available around settlements.
4. The Harappan civilisation is also known as the .... civilisation.
5. The city of .... was the first Harappan site to be excavated in 1920-21.
6. The river .... was important to the Harappan civilisation and is known today as Ghaggar in India.

7. Harappan cities were known for their advanced .... system, which included covered drains.

8. .... was the first city to show evidence of cotton cultivation in the Harappan civilisation.

Ans. 1. Harappa 2. writing 3. Water, fertile soil 4. Indus- Sarasvati 5. Harappa 6. Sarasvati 7. drainage 8. Mohenjo-daro

True or False

1. Till date, no concrete reasons have been found for the decline of Harappan cities.
2. Most of the houses in Harappa had separate bathing areas.
3. The Harappan towns in the state of Gujarat have been found in Dholavira and Lothal.
4. The term "Indus Valley Civilisation" is no longer widely used because the civilisation extended beyond the Indus region.
5. The Harappan civilisation was characterised by its lack of urban planning.
6. The Great Bath at Mohenjo-daro was a large reservoir for storing drinking water.
7. The Harappan cities had a uniform construction style, regardless of the size of the house.
8. The Sarasvati river is mentioned in the Rigveda as both a goddess and a river.

Ans. 1. True 2. True 3. True 4. True 5. False 6. False 7. True 8. True

Assertion-Reason

1. **Assertion** (A) The Harappan civilisation had a highly organised urban planning system.

   Reason (R) The streets in Harappan cities were wide and aligned with the cardinal directions.

   Codes

   (a) Both A and R are true and R is the correct explanation of A

   (b) Both A and R are true, but R is not the correct explanation of A

   (c) A is true, but R is false

   (d) A is false, but R is true

2. **Assertion** (A) The Harappans were pioneers in the field of metallurgy.

   Reason (R) They imported tin to mix with copper to produce bronze, which was used to make tools and other artefacts.

   Codes

   (a) Both A and R are true and R is the correct explanation of A

   (b) Both A and R are true, but R is not the correct explanation of A

   (c) A is true, but R is false

   (d) A is false, but R is true

3. **Assertion** (A) The Harappan civilisation did not engage in long-distance trade.

   Reason (R) Lothal, one of the Harappan sites, had a well-constructed dockyard, indicating maritime trade activities.

   Codes

   (a) Both A and R are true and R is the correct explanation of A

   (b) Both A and R are true, but R is not the correct explanation of A

   (c) A is true, but R is false

   (d) A is false, but R is true

4. **Assertion** (A) The decline of the Harappan civilisation was caused solely by foreign invasions.

   Reason (R) Environmental changes, such as the drying up of the Sarasvati river, significantly impacted agriculture and led to the abandonment of cities.

   Codes

   (a) Both A and R are true and R is the correct explanation of A

   (b) Both A and R are true, but R is not the correct explanation of A

   (c) A is true, but R is false

   (d) A is false, but R is true

5. **Assertion** (A) Harappan seals were primarily used for religious rituals.

   Reason (R) The seals often depicted animals and symbols and were used in trade activities as a mark of identity.

   Codes

   (a) Both A and R are true and R is the correct explanation of A

   (b) Both A and R are true, but R is not the correct explanation of A

   (c) A is true, but R is false

   (d) A is false, but R is true

Ans. 1. (a) 2. (a) 3. (d) 4.(d) 5. (d)

Case Based Questions

1. **Read the following source and answer the questions that follow.**

The Harappans were engaged in active trade, not only within their own civilisation (other cities nearby or far away), but with other civilisations and cultures within and outside India. They exported ornaments, timber, some objects of daily use, probably also gold and cotton and possibly some food items. The most favoured ornaments were beads of carnelian, a reddish semi precious stone found mostly in Gujarat. What the Harappans imported in exchange of the exported goods is not so clear. It probably included copper, since this metal was not so common back home.

To conduct such a trade, they used land routes and rivers, and the sea for more distant destinations — this is the first intensive maritime activity in India. Indeed, quite a few Harappan settlements are located in the coastal regions of Gujarat and Sindh. Lothal, a small settlement in Gujarat. Harappan beads of carnelian beads excavated at Susa (present-day Iran).

(i) What does the evidence of Harappan carnelian beads found at Susa suggest about their trade activities?

(a) The Harappans used carnelian beads only for local decoration.
(b) The Harappans had trade connections extending beyond the Indian sub-continent.
(c) Susa was a Harappan city known for bead-making.
(d) Carnelian was imported by the Harappans from Susa.

(ii) Why is the large basin found in Lothal significant in understanding Harappan trade practices?

(a) It was used as a water reservoir for agricultural purposes.
(b) It indicates that Lothal was primarily a fishing village.
(c) It was likely a dockyard used for receiving and sending goods via boats.
(d) It was a ceremonial site for religious rituals.

(iii) What can be inferred about the Harappans' expertise in working with materials like shell and carnelian?

(a) They were only able to work with soft, easily shaped materials.
(b) They developed advanced techniques to handle hard and precious materials.
(c) Their crafts were limited to basic tools and implements.
(d) They imported all of their ornaments from other civilisations.

(iv) Which aspect of the Harappan civilisation indicates the beginning of maritime activities in India?

(a) The construction of large temples.
(b) The crafting of ivory combs found in Oman.
(c) The presence of coastal settlements and a dockyard at Lothal.
(d) The development of inland water reservoirs.

Ans. (i) (b) (ii) (c) (iii) (b) (iv) (c)

2. Read the following source and answer the questions that follow.

Harappa and Mohenjo-daro, now in Pakistan, were the first two cities of this civilisation to be discovered; their identification goes back to 1924, a century ago. Several sites followed in the Indus plains, which is why the civilisation was initially called 'Indus Valley civilisation'. The larger Harappan cities were built according to precise plans. They had wide streets, which were often oriented to the cardinal directions. Most cities seem to have been surrounded by fortifications and had two distinct parts – the 'upper town', where the local elite probably lived, and the 'lower town', where common people lived.

Some large buildings seem to have been used for collective purposes – for instance, warehouses where goods to be transported were stored. Individual houses of various sizes lined the streets and smaller lanes. Interestingly, the quality of construction was the same for small and big houses. All those buildings were generally made of bricks.

(i) Why might the discovery of Harappa and Mohenjo-daro have been significant?

(ii) How do the city layouts of Harappan cities reflect their planning and organisation?

(iii) Why might it be important that Harappan cities had similar construction quality for all buildings?

Ans. (i) The discovery of Harappa and Mohenjo-daro was significant because they were the first two cities found from the Indus Valley Civilisation. They provide us a glimpse into one of the earliest urban cultures in history.

(ii) The city layouts of Harappan cities, with wide streets oriented to cardinal directions and separate areas for elites and common people, reflect a well-planned and organised urban structure.

(iii) It is important because it suggests a uniform standard of living and construction practices. It indicates that there was no division in the quality of housing between different social classes.

Competency Based Questions

1. In what ways did the Harappan civilisation demonstrate advanced knowledge in water management?

Ans. The Harappan civilisation exhibited advanced knowledge in water management through their intricate systems of wells, reservoirs and drainage. Cities like Mohenjo-daro had a well-planned drainage system where wastewater was channelled away from homes into large brick-lined sewers.

2. The Harappans gave much importance to water management and cleanliness. How did it contribute to the civilisation's sustainability?

Ans. Water management was crucial for the Harappan civilisation. Their practice of water management and cleanliness contributed to the civilisation's sustainability in the following ways

- The Harappans developed sophisticated systems for harvesting and storing water, including wells, reservoirs, and a complex drainage system that maintained cleanliness and prevented flooding.

- This not only supported agriculture but also ensured a steady water supply for daily use.
- The efficient management of water resources was vital for the sustainability and growth of civilisation.

3. The geography of the Indus-Sarasvati region influenced the development of the Harappan civilisation. How?

Ans. The geography of the Indus-Sarasvati region influenced the development of the Harappan civilisation in the following ways

- The fertile plains of rivers provided an ideal environment for the growth of the Harappan civilisation.
- The rivers supported agriculture through irrigation, which supported urbanisation.
- The region's location also facilitated trade, connecting the Harappan civilisation with other contemporary cultures like Mesopotamia.
- However, changes in the course of these rivers may have contributed to the eventual decline of civilisation.

4. Around 1900 BCE, the Indus Valley Civilisation, began to fall apart. Examine the statement.

Ans. Around 1900 BCE, despite all its achievements, the Indus Valley Civilisation began to fall apart. The cities were abandoned one by one.

The remaining inhabitants adopted a rural lifestyle in the changed environment.

The factors of the decline of Indus Valley Civilisation are as follows

- Earlier, it was thought that warfare or invasions may have destroyed the cities, but there is no evidence of warfare or invasion have been found. Indeed, the Harappans do not seem to have kept any army or weapons of war.

  Harappa seems to have been a relatively peaceful civilisation. Thus, this reason is not taken much into consideration.
- A climatic change which affected much of the world from 2200 BCE onward, causing reduced rainfall and a drier phase affected the civilisation. This would have made agriculture more difficult and could have reduced food supply to the cities.
- The sudden drying up of Sarasvati river in its central basin severely impacted availability of food for the people. Also, cities such as Kalibangan or Banawali were abandoned.

Skill Based Questions as per NEP 2020

1. Compare the town-planning features of different Harappan cities like Harappa, Mohenjo-daro and Dholavira. What does this tell us about the civilisation's administrative structure?

Ans. Harappa and Mohenjo-daro featured wide streets, uniform brick houses, and advanced drainage systems, indicating centralised planning. Dholavira, on the other hand, had a unique layout with three distinct zones and stone foundations for buildings, showing variation in town planning within the civilisation. The consistent quality of construction and the presence of large public structures across these cities suggest a well-organised administrative structure capable of overseeing large-scale urban development.

2. Imagine you are an architect in the Harappan civilisation. Design a new city layout that improves upon existing features like drainage, water supply and housing. Explain your design and the rationale behind your improvements.

Ans. As an architect in the Harappan civilisation, I would design a new city layout that enhances the features we already have, like drainage, water supply and housing. Some of the development can be like this

- **Central Water Reservoirs** At the centre of the city, I would place large water reservoirs. These would collect rainwater and store it for the dry season.
- **Advanced Drainage** I would improve the drainage system by making it more efficient. Every house would have its own drain connected to the main street drain, which would be covered and lead to a central sewage system. This would keep the streets clean and prevent waterlogging during the monsoon season.
- **Housing** The houses would be made of uniform bricks, but I would introduce more variety in sizes to accommodate different family needs. Each house would have a courtyard for ventilation and a small garden for growing herbs or vegetables.

These development will support in the following manner

- **Water Management** By placing reservoirs in the centre, water would be easily accessible to everyone, and rainwater would be efficiently collected.
- **Cleanliness** The advanced drainage system ensures that waste is quickly removed from residential areas, keeping the city clean and healthy. This new layout would not only improve the living conditions in the city but also make it more sustainable and pleasant for future generations.

ASSESSMENT EXERCISE

Objective Type Questions

1. Which river was central to the Indus Valley Civilisation?
(a) Ganges (b) Yamuna (c) Indus (d) Brahmaputra

2. What was the primary material used for constructing houses in the Indus Valley Civilisation?
(a) Stone (b) Wood (c) Bricks (d) Mud

3. Which of the following was a major city of the Indus Valley Civilisation?
(a) Harappa (b) Pataliputra (c) Varanasi (d) Delhi

4. What script did the people of the Indus Valley Civilisation use?
(a) Devanagari (b) Hieroglyphics
(c) Brahmi (d) Undeciphered script

5. Which among the following is not a feature of the Indus Valley Civilisation?
(a) Advanced drainage system (b) Monumental architecture
(c) Trade with Mesopotamia (d) Iron tools

6. **Assertion** (A) The Indus Valley Civilisation had well-planned cities.

Reason (R) The cities were laid out in a grid pattern with advanced drainage systems.

Codes
(a) Both A and R are true and R is the correct explanation of A
(b) Both A and R are true, but R is not the correct explanation of A
(c) A is true, but R is false
(d) A is false, but R is true

7. **Assertion** (A) The Indus Valley people were skilled in metallurgy.

Reason (R) They used iron extensively in their tools and weapons.

Codes
(a) Both A and R are true and R is the correct explanation of A
(b) Both A and R are true, but R is not the correct explanation of A
(c) A is true, but R is false
(d) A is false, but R is true

8. The main crops grown by the Indus Valley people were .... and ....

9. The Great Bath was found in the city of ....

10. The Indus Valley Civilisation was contemporary with the ancient civilisations of Egypt and Mesopotamia. (True/False)

11. The script used by the Indus Valley people has been fully deciphered. (True/False)

Subjective Questions (VSA, SA & LA)

1. Name two major cities of the Indus Valley Civilisation.

2. Which material was commonly used for constructing the houses in the Indus Valley Civilisation?

3. What kind of script did the Indus Valley people use?

4. What was the primary occupation of the Indus Valley people?

5. Mention one feature of the drainage system in the Indus Valley cities.

6. Explain the significance of the Great Bath in Mohenjo-daro.

7. What were the main features of the economy of the Indus Valley Civilisation?

8. Describe the town planning of the Indus Valley Civilisation.

9. Discuss the decline of the Indus Valley Civilisation and the theories surrounding it.

10. Evaluate the social and cultural life of the Indus Valley Civilisation.

CHAPTER 7

India's Cultural Roots

Indian culture is thousands of years old. Some of its branches include art, literature, science, medicine, religion, governance and martial arts. There are also different 'schools of thought' which means groups of thinkers and **spiritual seekers** with similar ideas about human life and the world.

According to archaeologists and scholars, some of India's cultural roots trace back to Indus or Harappan or Sindhu-Sarasvati civilisation.

7.1 The Vedas and Vedic Culture

- The word 'Veda' comes from the Sanskrit term *vid* which means 'knowledge'.
- There are **four Vedas**, namely, the Rig Veda, the Yajur Veda, the Sama Veda and the Atharva Veda. They are the most ancient texts of India, and indeed among the most ancient in the world.
- The Vedas consist of thousands of hymns ,which are prayers in the form of poems and songs, that were recited orally. Hymns were composed in the Sapta Sindhava region.
- It is difficult to determine when the Rig Veda, the **oldest** of the four Vedas, was written. Experts suggest it was composed between the 5th and 2nd millennium BCE.
- Vedas have been memorised through strict training and passed on orally with almost no changes.
- The Vedic hymns were composed by ***rishis*** (male seers or sages) and ***rishikas*** (female ones) in an early form of the Sanskrit language.
- They were written in poetic form for many deities (gods or goddesses), such as Indra, Agni, Varuna, Mitra, Sarasvati, Ushas and many more. Together with the seers, these deities maintained *ritam*, which means truth and order in human life and in the 'cosmos'. The early *rishis* and *rishikas* saw those gods and goddesses as one, not separate beings.
- In this worldview, values like 'Truth' were especially important as it was often another name for God.
- The last *mantras* (verses) of the Rig Veda also emphasised the importance of unity among people.

Must Know !

In 2008, UNESCO recognised Vedic chanting as 'a masterpiece of the oral and intangible heritage of humanity'.

Vedic Society

- Early Vedic society was organised in different *janas* or 'clans' that is, larger groups of people. The Rig Veda alone lists over 30 such *janas*. For instance, the Bharatas, the Purus, the Kurus, the Yadus and the Turvashas, etc. Each clan was associated with a particular region of the North-West part of the sub-continent.
- There is not much information about how *janas* governed their society. The Vedas only mentioned words like *raja* (a king or ruler), *sabha* and *samiti*, both of which refer to a collective gathering or assembly. It is assumed through this information that, *raja* or *samiti* were involved in governing the vedic society.
- Many professions are mentioned in the Vedic texts, such as agriculturist, weaver, potter, builder, carpenter, healer, dancer, barber, priest, etc.

Vedic Schools of Thought

- Vedic culture developed many rituals (yajna, often read as *yagya*) which aimed towards various deities (gods or goddesses) for individual or collective benefit and well-being.
- Daily rituals were generally in the form of prayers and offerings to Agni, the deity associated with fire. The rituals became more and more complex with time.

- A group of texts known as **Upanishads** expanded the Vedic concepts. It introduced new concepts, such as rebirth (taking birth again and again) and karma (our actions or their results).
- According to one school of thought, generally known as **Vedanta**, everything ranging from human life, nature and the universe is one divine essence called **brahman** or ***tat*** ('that').
- The Upanishads also introduced the concept of atman or self. It is the divine essence that is found in every being, but is ultimately one with brahman. It follows that everything in this world is connected and interdependent. This explains a common prayer that begins with sarve *bhavantu sukhinah*, or "May all creatures be happy", and wish them all to be free from disease and sorrow.
- Early in the 1st millennium BCE, several more schools of thought grew out of the Vedas. One of them was **Yoga**.
- Yoga developed methods intended to achieve the realisation of brahman in one's **consciousness.** Together, these schools of thought became the foundations for what we call 'Hinduism' today.

Try These

1. **What are the two terms mentioned in the Vedas referring to a collective assembly?**
2. **What is a common prayer that wishes for the happiness of all creatures?**
3. **The Vedic hymns were composed by rishis (male seers) and rishikas (female seers) in an early form of the .... language.**

7.2 Buddhism

- Buddhism emerged as a distinct school of thought rejecting Vedic authority.
- About two-and-a-half millenniums ago, a young prince named **Siddhartha Gautama** was born in Lumbini (today in Nepal).There are different conclusions by scholars regarding the precise year of his birth.
- Siddhartha Gautama grew up living a protected life in the palace. One day, at the age of 29, he moved out to take a round of the city in a chariot. For the first time in his life, he came across an old man, a sick man and a dead body. He also saw an ascetic, who appeared to be happy and at peace. After this experience, Siddhartha decided to give up his palace life, leaving behind his wife and son.
- He travelled on foot as an ascetic, and met other ascetics and scholars. He searched for the root cause of suffering in human life. After meditating for many days under a pipal tree at Bodh Gaya (today in Bihar), he attained enlightenment.
- He realised that **avidya** (ignorance) and **attachment** are the source of human suffering and gave a method to remove these two causes. Siddhartha then came to be known as the 'Buddha', which means the 'enlightened' or 'awakened' one.
- The Buddha started teaching what he had realised. This included the idea of ahimsa, which is generally translated as 'non-violence', but originally means 'non-hurting'or 'non-injuring'.

The Buddha founded the Sangha, a community of *bhikshus* or **monks** (and, later *bhikhunis* or nuns).
They dedicated themselves to practising and spreading his teachings. His influence greatly impacted India and Asia.

This stone panel, some 800 years old, shows the Buddha teaching

7.3 Jainism

- Jainism is another important school of thought that became widespread at the same time as Buddhism. However, its roots are believed to be much older than Buddhism.
- Just like Siddhartha Gautama, Prince Vardhamana was born into a royal family in the early 6th century BCE. His birthplace was near the city of Vaishali, in modern-day Bihar.
- At the age of 30, he decided to leave his home and go in search of spiritual knowledge. He practised an ascetic discipline and, after 12 years, achieved 'infinite knowledge' or supreme wisdom. He became known as **Mahavira**, or 'great hero', and started preaching what he had realised.

- Jain teachings include ahimsa, **anekantavada** and **aparigraha**. These ideas, which are also important in Buddhism and Vedantic thought, are central to Indian culture.
- Jainism also insists on the interconnectedness and interdependence of all creatures, from humans to invisible organisms. They support each other and cannot live without one another.

A traditional painting of Mahavira

Must Know!

The word 'Jain' or jaina comes from Sanskrit word 'jina' which means 'conqueror'. This does not refer to the territory or enemies, but to conquer ignorance and attachments, so as to reach enlightenment.

Similarities Between Buddhism and Jainism

- In both Buddhism and Jainism, ahimsa means much more than refraining from physical violence against a person or an animal. It also means refraining from violence in thought, such as having ill feelings towards anyone.
- In both Buddhism and Jainism, monks and sometimes nuns too, began travelling across the land to spread their respective teachings far and wide. Some of them created new monasteries in faraway places, while others led ascetic lives in **rock cut caves**. Archaeological findings have revealed many traces of those monasteries.
- Buddhism and Jainism also shared some common concepts, such as dharma, karma, rebirth, the search for an end to suffering and ignorance, and many important values.

Caves cut into the rock at Ellora (Maharashtra) between the 6th and the 10th centuries CE. Some of the caves are Hindu, others are Buddhist and Jain.

Charvaka School of Thought

- Charvaka school (sometimes also 'Lokayata'), believed that this material world is the only thing that exists. Therefore, there can be no life after death.
- This school does not seem to have gained much popularity and it disappeared with time.

Try These

1. .... means 'ignorance' in Buddhism.
2. Jainism insists on the interconnectedness and .... of all creatures, from humans to invisible organisms.
3. What does the term 'Buddha' signify?
4. What are the key principles of Jainism?

7.4 Folk and Tribal Roots

India has rich 'oral traditions', that is, teachings or practices transmitted through everyday practice, without written texts. These include many folk traditions passed down by common people and tribal traditions passed down by tribes.

Meaning of Tribe

- A tribe is a group of families or clans sharing a tradition of common descent, a culture and a language. They live as a close-knit community under a chief and hold no private property.
- Tribes were simply different janas (groups of people) who lived in particular places, like forests or mountains.
- The Constitution of India uses the terms 'tribes' and 'tribal communities' in English, and 'janjati' in Hindi.
- According to official figures, in 2011 India had 705 tribes. They are spread over most states, amounting to a population of about 104 million people. This is more than the populations of Australia and the United Kingdom together.

- In the 19th century, anthropologists often described tribes as primitive' or inferior' to civilised people. With deeper studies of tribal communities and their rich and complex cultures, these biased judgments have mostly been rejected.

Interactions Between Belief Systems

- There has been a constant interaction between folk and tribal traditions and major schools of thought. Deities, concepts, legends and rituals have been exchanged freely between these traditions. For example, Jagannath, worshipped in Puri (Odisha), is believed to have been a tribal deity. This is also the case with the mother-goddess worshipped across India.
- Some tribes adopted Hindu deities a long time ago and have their own versions of the Mahabharata and the Ramayana. There have been recorded from India's North-Eastern states to Tamil Nadu.
- Long interactions between these belief systems have led to mixing of ideas. In this way, folk and tribal beliefs and practices also contribute to India's cultural roots.

Similarities between Folk, Tribal and Hindu Belief Systems

- Interactions have occurred among folk, tribal and Hindu belief systems for a long time because they share many similar concepts. In all three, elements of nature such as mountains, rivers, trees, plants, animals, and some stones are regarded as sacred because there is consciousness behind all of them.
- Tribes generally worship many deities associated with these natural elements. For instance, the **Toda** tribes of the Nilgiris in Tamil Nadu consider over thirty peaks of this mountain range as residences of a god or a goddess. These peaks are so sacred to the Todas that they avoid pointing to them with a finger.
- Despite the multiple deities, many tribal groups have a concept of a higher divinity or supreme being, similar to Hinduism. For example, several tribes of Arunachal Pradesh worship **Donyipolo**, a combined form of the Sun and the Moon who later rose to the higher status of a supreme god.
- In parts of central India, the god **Khandoba** holds a similar higher status. In Eastern India, the Munda and Santhal tribals worship Singbonga, a supreme deity who created the world.

Try These

1. **What shared sacred elements are common across folk, tribal, and Hindu belief systems?**
2. **........ is a tribal deity that has become widely worshipped.**
3. **What was the 19th-century anthropological view of tribes?**
4. **........ is a combined form of the Sun and the Moon who later rose to the higher status of a supreme god.**

Glossary

Spiritual It means related to the spirit or soul (atman in Sanskrit and many Indian languages). Spirituality involves seeking a deeper or higher understanding beyond our current personality.

Seeker It refers to a person searching for the truths of the world, such as a sage, saint, yogi or philosopher.

Cosmos The universe as an ordered and harmonious system.

Healer It refers to a person who uses traditional practices to relieve or heal diseases.

Consciousness The state of being aware, for instance of something within oneself.

Ascetic It refers to someone who engages in a strict discipline to achieve a higher consciousness.

Attachment It refers to the condition of having a bond with someone or something, usually through sentiment or habit.

Monk A man who leaves ordinary life to devote himself to religious or spiritual practices.

Nun It refers to the female counterpart to a monk.

Anekantavada It means 'not just one' aspect or perspective. In other words, the truth has many sides and cannot be fully described by any single statement.

Aparigraha It means 'non-possession. It suggests staying away from material possessions and focusing only on what is truly necessary in life.

Rock-cut Caves They are ancient structures carved into natural rocks. They were primarily used for religious, residential or artistic purposes.

Anthropologist Anthropologists are scientists who study human societies, cultures and their development.

Worldview A certain view or understanding of the world, its origin or its workings.

UNESCO It stands for 'United Nations Educational, Scientific and Cultural Organisation. It promotes dialogue between people and nations through education, science and culture.

Refraining It means to stop oneself from doing something.

INDIA's CULTURAL ROOTS

Vedas
- Origin from Sanskrit 'Vid' (Knowledge).
- Four Vedas - Rig, Yajur, Sama and Atharva
- Hymns composed by Rishis in Sanskrit
- Deities-Indra, Varuna and Agni.

Vedic Society Governance
- Organised in clans (janas) like Purus, Kurus and Bharatas.
- Governance-raja (king) sabha, samiti (assemblies)
- Professions-weaver, potter, agriculturist, dancer, etc.

Ancient Indian Culture
- Over thousands of years old.
- Includes art, literature, science, etc.
- Traces back to Indus civilisation.

Vedic Schools of Thought
- Upanishads - Concepts of rebirth, Karma and Atman
- Vedanta-Belief in Brahman (divine essence)
- Yoga-Method to achieve Brahman in consciousness.

Jainism
- Founded by Mahavira in 6th century BCE.
- Focused on Ahimsa, Anekantavada and Aparigraha.
- Highlights interconnectedness of life.

Other Schools
- Charvaka Lokayata-believed only in the material world, no afterlife
- It focused on diversity in beliefs.

Folk and Tribal Traditions
- Tribes-groups with shared culture language, descent, etc.
- Led by chiefs, no private property
- Earlier seen as primitive
- Folk, tribal and Hindu beliefs influence each other, shared respect for nature and deities.

Buddhism
- Founded by Siddhartha Gautama around 560 BC.
- Realised suffering from ignorance and attachment.
- Advocated ahimsa, inner discipline
- Founded Sangha

NCERT FOLDER

Detailed Answers of All NCERT Questions

Let's Explore (Page 109)

Q1. Do you know the term for a society where people select their leaders? How do you think people can benefit from such a situation? What could happen if they live under leaders that they did not choose? (Hint: Think back to what you're learning in the theme 'Governance and Democracy'!) Write your thoughts in a paragraph of 100-150 words.

Ans. The term for a society where people select their leaders is 'democracy'. In a democratic system, individuals have a say in deciding who governs them. This ensures that leaders are accountable and responsive to their needs and interests. This creates a sense of ownership, participation and transparency in governance.

On the other hand, if people live under leaders they did not choose, they may face oppression, lack of representation, and disregard for their rights and needs. Such a situation can lead to dissatisfaction, unrest, and a lack of trust in the governing bodies, ultimately undermining social and political stability.

Let's Explore (Page 115)

Q2.

Discuss the way the Buddha is depicted in the above stone panel. Can you name some states of India or some other countries where Buddhism is a major religion even today? Try to plot these on a world map.

Ans. In the image, Buddha is depicted imparting his teachings to his disciples. Buddhism remains a major religion in several regions and countries.

Some countries and states in India where Buddhism is widely practiced even today are

- **States in India** Sikkim, Arunachal Pradesh, Ladakh and today Himachal Pradesh.
- **Countries** Thailand, Myanmar (Burma) , Sri Lanka and Bhutan.

Let's Explore (Page 118)

Q3.

Observe the above panel (from a Jain temple in New Delhi). What is striking about it? What messages does it carry?

Ans. The panel depicts a lion and a bull sharing water from a common vessel, a striking symbol of peace and coexistence between traditionally opposing forces. This depicts the Jain principle of 'Ahimsa' or non-violence, emphasising respect and harmony for all living beings, even those seen as natural enemies.

Questions, Activities and Projects

Q1. If you were Nachiketa, what questions would you like to ask Yama? Write them down in 100-150 words.

Ans. If I were Nachiketa, I would ask Yama the following questions

- What is the true nature of the soul, and how does it persist beyond physical death?
- How do our actions in this life impact our future lives, and what role does karma play in this process?
- Can you explain the concept of moksha, or liberation, and how one can attain it?
- How does the soul achieve unity with the ultimate reality or brahman?

Q2. Explain a few central ideas of Buddhism. Briefly comment upon them.

Ans. Central ideas of Buddhism are as follows

- **The Four Noble Truths** Buddhism teaches that life is characterised by suffering (dukkha), which is caused by desire and attachment (tanha). The end of suffering is possible through the end of desire, and this can be achieved by following the Eightfold Path.
- **The Eightfold Path** This is a guide for ethical and mental development with the goal of freeing the individual from attachments and delusions. It includes Right Understanding, Right Intent, Right Speech, Right Action, Right Livelihood, Right Effort, Right Mindfulness and Right Concentration.
- **Non-violence** (Ahimsa) Central to Buddhism, it advocates for kindness and compassion towards all living beings as a means to reduce suffering.

Q3. Discuss in class the quotation of the Buddha which begins with "Not by water is one made pure, though many people may bathe here [in sacred rivers" to make sure that its meaning has been understood by all.

Ans. This quotation highlights that physical cleanliness or ritualistic actions, such as bathing in sacred rivers, do not lead to spiritual purity or enlightenment. True purity comes from moral conduct, self-discipline and mental clarity. It emphasises that inner transformation and ethical living are more significant than external rituals.

Q4. Explain a few central ideas of Jainism. Briefly comment upon them.

Ans. Few central ideas of Jainism are as follows

Ahimsa (Non-violence) Jainism teaches that one should avoid causing harm to any living being, emphasising the interconnectedness of all life.

Anekantavada (Non-absolutism) The idea that truth and reality are complex and have multiple aspects. No single perspective can capture the whole truth, and understanding requires recognising different viewpoints.

Aparigraha (Non-possessiveness) It advocates for detachment from material possessions and the limiting of one's needs to what is necessary.

Q5. Consider and discuss in class Andre Beteille's thought

"The thousands of castes and tribes on the Indian sub-continent have influenced each other in their religious beliefs and practices since the beginning of history and before that the tribal religions have been influenced by Hinduism is widely accepted, but it is equally true that Hinduism, not only in its formative phase but throughout its evolution, has been influenced by tribal religions."

Ans. Andre Beteille's thought highlights the reciprocal influence between tribal religions and Hinduism. Tribal religions have impacted Hindu practices and conversely, Hinduism has influenced tribal beliefs. This mutual enrichment shows the fluid nature of cultural and religious exchanges in India.

Q6. Make a list of popular gods and goddesses in your region and the festivals they are associated with.

Ans. Here is a list of popular gods and goddessess in my region and the festivals they are associated with

- **Lord Krishna** Janmashtami
- **Goddess Durga** Durga Puja
- **Lord Ganesh** Ganesh Chaturthi
- **Goddess Lakshmi** Diwali

Q7. As a class activity, list two or three tribal groups from your region or state. Document some of their art and belief systems.

Ans. Here is a list of tribal groups from the state of Tamil Nadu

- **Toda Tribe** They are known for their distinctive traditional shawls and rituals associated with nature worship. They consider mountain peaks sacred.
- **Irula Tribe** They are famous for their traditional weaving skills and snake-catching techniques. They practice animistic beliefs centered around natural elements.

True or False

1. The Vedic hymns were written on palm-leaf manuscripts.
2. The Vedas are India's oldest texts.
3. The Vedic statement *ekam sat vipra bahudha vadanti* reflects a belief in the unity of cosmic powers.
4. Buddhism is older than the Vedas.
5. Jainism emerged as a branch of Buddhism.
6. Both Buddhism and Jainism advocated for peaceful coexistence and the avoidance of harm to all living beings.
7. Tribal belief systems are limited to belief in spirits and minor deities.

Ans. 1. False 2. True 3. True 4. False 5. False 6. True 7. False

Class Activity

1. **Stage a small play with Yama, god of death, surrounded by several Nachiketas asking him questions about life.**

Ans. Here is a role-play example consisting of Yama, god of death, surrounded by several Nachiketas asking him questions about life.

- **Characters** Nachiketa, Yama and other actors as onlookers.
- **Scene** Nachiketa approaches Yama and asks profound questions about life, death and the nature of the soul.
- **Dialogues** Yama provides answers that reveal the nature of existence and spiritual truths.

REVIEW EXERCISE

Including Competency Based Questions

Part I

Very Short Answer Type Questions

1. What was Siddhartha Gautama known as after attaining enlightenment?

Ans. He was known as the Buddha.

2. How many tribes were officially recorded in India in 2011?

Ans. There were 705 tribes recorded in India in 2011.

3. What does the term "Vedanta" refer to in Vedic thought?

Ans. Vedanta refers to the concept that everything is one divine essence called brahman.

4. What is the term for the practice of not owning material possessions in certain Indian philosophies?

Ans. Aparigraha refers to the practice of not owning material possessions in certain Indian philosophies.

5. Indian culture is thousands of years old, and has many parts that are all connected. Which ancient civilisation is connected to India's cultural roots?

Ans. Harappan civilisation is connected to India's cultural roots.

Short Answer Type Questions

1. How do folk and tribal traditions interact with leading philosophical schools in India?

Ans. Folk and tribal traditions in India have interacted with major philosophical schools through the exchange of deities, rituals and concepts. For instance, tribal deities and mother-goddess worship have influenced mainstream religions. Similarly, Hindu deities have been incorporated into tribal beliefs, creating unique versions of epics like the Mahabharata and the Ramayana. This interaction has enriched both folk and philosophical traditions, reflecting a dynamic cultural exchange.

2. What was the Charvaka school of thought and its primary belief?

Ans. The Charvaka school, also known as Lokayata, held that the material world is the only reality and denied the existence of life after death.It did not gain widespread popularity and eventually faded away. It was overshadowed by other philosophical traditions that offered broader spiritual and ethical perspectives.

Long Answer Type Questions

1. Discuss the similarities and differences between Buddhism and Jainism, focusing on their core teachings.

Ans. Buddhism was founded by Siddhartha Gautama (the Buddha) and Jainism was founded by Mahavira. Both religions emerged around the same time and share some core ideas, but differ in their approaches.

Similarities between Buddhism and Jainism include non-violence (ahimsa), karma (the principle of cause and effect) and rebirth, aiming to overcome suffering and ignorance. Buddhism teaches that following the Four Noble Truths and the Eightfold Path leads to Nirvana, or enlightenment. It emphasises a balanced approach known as the middle way, avoiding extremes. Whereas Jainism focusess on strict ascetic practices and renouncing material possessions. It introduced ideas like anekantavada (the belief that reality is complex and cannot be captured by a single perspective) and aparigraha (non-possessiveness), which are less emphasised in Buddhism.

2. How did early Vedic society organise itself, and what does this reveal about its governance and social structure?

Ans. Early Vedic society was organised into different janas or clans, which were larger groups of people associated with specific regions. The Rig Veda lists over 30 such janas, including the Bharatas, Purus and Kurus. Each jana had its own social and territorial identity.

Although the Vedic texts provide limited information on governance, terms like raja (king), sabha (assembly), and samiti (gathering) suggest that early Vedic society was organised around collective decision-making and leadership roles.

The mention of various professions in the Vedic texts also indicates a complex social structure with specialised roles and occupations, reflecting the organised and hierarchical nature of Vedic society.

3. A group of texts known as 'Upanishads' expanded the Vedic concepts. What are the main concepts introduced in the Upanishads?

Ans. The Upanishads, a collection of texts emerging from Vedic tradition, introduced several concepts.

Important among them are the ideas of rebirth (the cycle of repeated births and deaths) and karma (the law of actions and their consequences).

The Upanishads also elaborate on the concept of brahman, the ultimate, unchanging reality that underpins the universe, and atman, the true self that resides within every being. These texts suggest that the essence of existence is interconnected and that realising the unity between atman and brahman leads to spiritual enlightenment. These philosophical ideas form the basis for Vedanta, one of the major schools of thought in Hinduism.

Part II

Multiple Choice Questions (MCQs)

1. In the context of Vedic society, what does the term 'jana' refer to?

(a) A specific profession or occupation.
(b) A type of ritual or prayer.
(c) A clan or larger group of people associated with a particular region.
(d) A sacred hymn recited during rituals.

2. Which of the following correctly describes the origins of Indian culture?

(a) Indian culture is solely based on Vedic traditions.
(b) Indian culture has multiple roots including the Indus, Harappan and Sindhu-Sarasvati civilisations.
(c) Indian culture only began with the arrival of the Aryans.
(d) Indian culture started with the rise of Buddhism and Jainism.

3. Which of the following is recognised by UNESCO as 'a masterpiece of the oral and intangible heritage of humanity'?

(a) The Upanishads (b) Vedic chanting
(c) Mahabharata (d) The Ramayana

4. Which of the following terms refers to a collective gathering or assembly in Vedic society?

(a) Raja (b) Sabha (c) Samiti (d) Both (b) and (c)

5. According to Buddhism, what are the sources of human suffering?

(a) Ignorance and attachment (b) Karma and dharma
(c) Rebirth and sacrifice (d) Desire and duty

6. The Charvaka school of thought is known for what belief?

(a) The material world is the only thing that exists
(b) Life after death is certain
(c) The importance of rituals
(d) The concept of rebirth

7. Which concept is central to the Upanishads?

(a) The importance of animal sacrifice.
(b) The concept of 'Atman' or the self.
(c) The denial of the existence of the soul.
(d) The promotion of polytheism.

8. Which of the following is not a characteristic of Jainism?

(a) Belief in the concept of karma.
(b) Emphasis on non-violence (ahimsa).
(c) Worship of multiple gods.
(d) Practice of asceticism.

9. Which of the following is true about tribes in ancient India?

(a) They lived under a chief
(b) They held private property
(c) They were considered inferior to civilised people
(d) Both (a) and (c)

10. What is the significance of the Sangha in Buddhism?

(a) It is a sacred text.
(b) It is a place of worship.
(c) It is a community of monks and nuns.
(d) It is a philosophical concept.

11. The Vedic texts were primarily transmitted through which method?

(a) Written manuscripts (b) Oral recitation
(c) Carvings on stones (d) Illustrated scrolls

12. Which deity is associated with fire in the Vedic rituals?

(a) Indra (b) Agni
(c) Varuna (d) Sarasvati

13. The Vedic hymns were composed by which of the following groups?

(a) Rishis (male seers) (b) Rishikas (female seers)
(c) Both (a) and (b) (d) Neither (a) nor (b)

14. Consider the following statements. Choose the option that correctly describes the interaction between folk, tribal traditions, and leading schools of thought in Indian culture.

(i) Folk and tribal traditions were isolated and did not influence mainstream beliefs.
(ii) There was constant interaction, with deities, concepts, and rituals being exchanged freely.
(iii) Tribal beliefs were eradicated by the leading schools of thought.
(iv) Leading schools of thought rejected any influence from folk and tribal traditions.

Options

(a) Only (i) and (ii) (b) Only (ii)
(c) Only (iv) (d) None of these

Answers

1. (c) **2.** (b) **3.** (b) **4.** (d) **5.** (a)
6. (a) **7.** (b) **8.** (c) **9.** (d) **10.** (c)
11. (b) **12.** (b) **13.** (c) **14.** (b)

Fill in the Blanks

1. The idea of .... in Buddhism is generally translated as 'non-violence' but originally means 'non-hurting' or 'non-injuring'.
2. The Charvaka school, also known as ...., believed that the material world is the only thing that exists.
3. A .... is a group of families or clans sharing a tradition of common descent, culture and language.
4. The .... is considered the most ancient of the four Vedas.
5. Siddhartha Gautama, who became known as the Buddha, was born in ....

Ans. 1. ahimsa 2. Lokayata 3. tribe 4. Rig Veda 5. Lumbini

True or False

1. The word "Veda" comes from the Sanskrit word "vid" which means "truth."
2. According to Vedanta, everything ranging from human life, nature, and the universe is one divine essence called brahman.
3. The word 'Jain' comes from jina, meaning 'conqueror,' referring to the conquest of territory.
4. Buddhism emerged as a distinct school of thought that accepted Vedic authority.
5. There are five Vedas, namely, the Rig Veda, the Yajur Veda, the Sama Veda, the Atharva Veda and the Agni Veda.

Ans. 1. False 2. True 3. False 4. False 5. False

Assertion-Reason

1. **Assertion** (A) Tribal and Hindu belief systems have enriched each other through interactions.

   Reason (R) They share many similar concepts, including the worship of natural elements and deities.

   Codes
   (a) Both A and R are true and R is the correct explanation of A
   (b) Both A and R are true, but R is not the correct explanation of A
   (c) A is false, but R is true
   (d) A is true, but R is false

2. **Assertion** (A) The Todas of the Nilgiris avoid pointing to their sacred peaks with a finger.

   Reason (R) They consider these peaks as residences of gods or goddesses.

   Codes
   (a) Both A and R are true, and R is the correct explanation of A
   (b) Both A and R are true, but R is not the correct explanation of A
   (c) A is false, but R is true
   (d) A is true, but R is false

3. **Assertion** (A) The Charvaka school believed in life after death.

   Reason (R) Charvaka taught that the material world is the only thing that exists.

   Codes
   (a) Both A and R are true and R is the correct explanation of A
   (b) Both A and R are true, but R is not the correct explanation of A
   (c) A is false, but R is true
   (d) A is true but R is false

Ans. 1. (a) 2. (a) 3. (c)

Case Based Questions

1. There has been a constant interaction between folk and tribal traditions, and the leading schools of thought. Deities, concepts, legends and rituals have been freely exchanged in both directions. For instance, according to tradition, Jagannath, worshipped at Puri (Odisha), was originally a tribal deity; this is also the case with various forms of the mother-goddess worshipped across India.Some tribes, on the other hand, adopted Hindu deities long ago, and possess their own versions of the Mahabharata and the Ramayana – this has been well documented from India's North-Eastern states, all the way to Tamil Nadu.

   (i) What is the significance of the interaction between folk and tribal traditions with leading schools of thought?

   (ii) Which Indian region is mentioned as having tribes that possess their own versions of the Mahabharata and the Ramayana?

   (iii) What is one example of a deity that was originally tribal but became integrated into mainstream Hindu worship?

Ans. (i) The interaction between folk and tribal traditions with leading schools of thought have led to an exchange between deities, concepts, legends, and rituals.

(ii) India's North-Eastern states and Tamil Nadu are the regions having tribes that possess their own versions of the Mahabharata and the Ramayana.

(iii) Lord Jagannath is a deity that was originally tribal but became integrated into mainstream Hindu worship.

2. There were yet other schools of thought at the time. For example, one of them, known as the 'Charvaka' school (sometimes also 'Lokayata'), believed that this material world is the only thing that exists, and therefore there can be no life after death. This school does not seem to have gained much popularity and it disappeared with time. We mention it to show that there was a wide diversity of intellectual or spiritual belief systems; people were free to choose what suited them. Although the Vedic, Buddhist and Jain schools had important differences, they also shared some common concepts, such as dharma, karma, rebirth, the search for an end to suffering and ignorance, and many important values.

(i) What did the Charvaka school of thought believe in?

(a) The existence of multiple deities
(b) Rebirth and karma
(c) The material world is the only reality and no life after death
(d) The importance of ritual sacrifices

(ii) Which of the following is true about the Charvaka school?

(a) It was highly popular and widely accepted
(b) It disappeared with time due to lack of popularity
(c) It merged with the buddhist school of thought
(d) It was primarily focused on ritual sacrifices

(iii) Which concepts were shared by the Vedic, Buddhist and Jain schools despite their differences?

(a) Worship of a single god
(b) Materialism and skepticism
(c) Dharma, karma, rebirth, the search for an end to suffering and ignorance
(d) Exclusivity of their own spiritual paths

(iv) What does the diversity of intellectual and spiritual belief systems in ancient India indicate?

(a) Strict adherence to a single religion
(b) People were free to choose what suited them
(c) Absence of philosophical debates
(d) Uniformity in spiritual beliefs.

Ans. (i) (c) (ii) (b) (iii) (c) (iv) (b)

Competency Based Questions

1. Tribes generally worship many deities associated with these natural elements. What is the role of nature in tribal and folk belief systems in India?

Ans. In tribal and folk belief systems, elements of nature such as mountains, rivers and trees are considered sacred. Tribes often worship natural deities associated with these elements, reflecting a deep connection with the environment. For example, the Toda tribals view certain mountain peaks as divine residences. These beliefs highlight the integral role of nature in spiritual and cultural practices.

2. Buddhism emerged as a distinct school of thought rejecting Vedic authority. What distinguishes Buddhism from Vedic tradition?

Ans. Buddhism differs from Vedic tradition as it rejects Vedic authority. It was founded by Siddhartha Gautama, who became the Buddha; it focused on overcoming suffering through enlightenment. Buddha's teachings include the concepts of 'ahimsa' (non-hurting) and the Four Noble Truths. Unlike Vedic traditions that emphasise rituals and deities, Buddhism centers on personal spiritual awakening and the path to Nirvana.

3. Jainism is another important school of thought that became widespread at the same time as Buddhism. Briefly explain some key beliefs in Jainism.

Ans. Jainism, an ancient school of thought, emphasises key principles such as ahimsa (non-violence), anekantavada (non-absolutism), and aparigraha (non-possessiveness). Some of its key beliefs are

- Ahimsa is central to Jain practice and involves avoiding harm to any living being, including insects and microorganisms.
- Anekantavada advocates for the understanding that truth and reality are complex and multi-faceted, encouraging openness to different perspectives.
- Aparigraha involves minimising material possessions and desires to achieve spiritual liberation. Jainism highlights the interconnectedness and interdependence of all life forms, advocating for harmony with nature and all living beings. These principles are essential for achieving liberation (moksha) from the cycle of birth and rebirth.

Skill Based Questions as per NEP 2020

1. Create a list of modern situations or problems where the principles of non-violence and interconnectedness could be beneficial. Discuss or present your ideas with the class.

Ans. Here is a list of modern situations or problems where the principles of non-violence and interconnectedness could be beneficial

(a) **Conflict Resolution** In global or community conflicts, using non-violent communication and recognising shared human needs can lead to peaceful solutions.

(b) **Environmental Issues** Addressing climate change and environmental degradation through collaborative efforts and recognising the interconnectedness of ecosystems and human activities can promote sustainable practices.

(c) **Social Injustice** Fighting against racism, sexism, and other forms of discrimination by fostering empathy, solidarity, and non-violent activism can create a more equitable society.

2. Research a specific tribe in India. What are their unique traditions, beliefs and ways of life? How have they interacted with mainstream culture?

Ans. The Gond tribe is one of India's largest tribal groups. They live mainly in Madhya Pradesh, Chhattisgarh, Maharashtra, Andhra Pradesh and Odisha. They practice animism, worshipping nature and deities like Pharsa Pen, the god of hunting.

They have a rich oral tradition, vibrant art, and tattooing practices. Agriculture, hunting, and fishing are their main occupation of Gonds, with a strong emphasis on community living and collective decision-making. Interaction with mainstream Hindu culture has led to the adoption of festivals like Diwali and Holi.

Despite modern influences, the Gonds strive to preserve their unique cultural identity.

ASSESSMENT EXERCISE

Objective Type Questions

1. What is the approximate range of years proposed by experts for the composition of the Rig Veda?

(a) 1st to 5th century BCE (b) 7nd to 4th millennium BCE
(c) 5th to 2nd millennium BCE (d) 6th to 1st millennium CE

2. What is the term for the ritual sacrifices mentioned in Vedic culture?

(a) Yajna (b) Puja
(c) Homa (d) Tarpan

3. Which text introduced the concept of the divine essence called brahman?

(a) Mahabharata (b) Upanishads
(c) Bhagavad Gita (d) Rig Veda

4. In which region were the hymns of the Vedas primarily composed?

(a) Ganges Valley (b) Deccan Plateau
(c) Sapta Sindhava region (d) Indo-Gangetic Plain

5. Assertion (A) The Vedas are among the most ancient texts in the world.

Reason (R) The Vedas were composed in an early form of the Sanskrit language.

Codes

(a) Both A and R are true and R is the correct explanation of A
(b) Both A and R are true, but R is not the correct explanation of A
(c) A is false, but R is true
(d) A is true, but R is false

6. Assertion (A) Mahavira is known as the "great hero."

Reason (R) Mahavira achieved 'infinite knowledge' or supreme wisdom after 12 years of ascetic practice.

Codes

(a) Both A and R are true and R is the correct explanation of A
(b) Both A and R are true, but R is not the correct explanation of A
(c) A is false, but R is true
(d) A is true, but R is false

7. The common prayer '*Sarve Bhavantu Sukhinah*' translates to "................."

8. Siddhartha Gautama attained enlightenment under a .... tree at Bodh Gaya.

9. Tribal beliefs and practices have enriched Indian cultural roots through mutual exchange with leading schools of thought. (True/False)

10. Jainism, like Buddhism, emphasises the idea of ahimsa. (True/False)

Subjective Questions (VSA, SA & LA)

1. What term is used to describe the interconnectedness of all creatures in Jainism?

2. What is the name given to the divine essence that resides in every being according to Vedanta?

3. Name a few important clans mentioned in the Rig Veda. Where were these clans primarily located?

4. Explain the role of rishis and rishikas in the Vedic tradition and how their hymns were preserved.

5. Explain the significance of the Vedas in Indian culture and their method of transmission.

6. Describe the concept of '*Sarve Bhavantu Sukhinah*' and its significance in the Vedic worldview.

CHAPTER 8

Unity in Diversity, or 'Many in the One'

India has a rich diversity which attracts many visitors across the world to it. Travelling through India by train shows different landscapes, diverse dresses and foods, various languages and different scripts. Even within the same region, people from other parts of India with different customs and traditions are seen. This accommodation of people with different backgrounds reflects the principle of unity in diversity in India.

8.1 A Rich Diversity

- India has over 1.4 billion inhabitants (about 18 per cent of the world's population). In the late 20th century, the **Anthropological Survey of India** (ASI) which is a national organisation conducted the **'People of India Project.'**
- According to this project, there were 4,635 communities across all states and 325 languages using 25 scripts.The organisation observed that there are many Indians who could be considered migrants i.e., those who live far from their birthplace or original community.
- Diversity is beautiful, but it can be challenging to understand it. More than a hundred years ago, British historian **Vincent Smith** questioned the possibility of writing the history of India because of its great diversity. He discovered the answer in the concept of India's **unity in diversity**. This means that despite the vast differences, there is a sense of unity.

8.2 Food for All

- India has a rich diversity. There are many varieties of dishes and preparations available in India, possibly thousands or even lakhs.
  However, certain food grains are common to almost every part of the country. This includes cereals like rice, barley and wheat; millets like bajra, jowar and ragi; and pulses like various dals and grams. These are called **staple grains** because they are the basic food for most Indians.
- Common spices like turmeric, cumin, cardamom and ginger are also used nationwide. Common vegetables and oils are also widely used across the country.
- These common ingredients (unity) can be used in a number of combinations (diversity) to prepare many varieties of dishes.

8.3 Textiles and Clothing

- There is also a diversity in style of clothing in India. Every region and community has developed its own styles of clothing and dresses. However, there is commonality in some traditional Indian dresses, regardless of the material used.
- A clear example of commonality in traditional dresses is the **sari**. It is a type of clothing worn in most parts of India.
- Sari is an unstitched piece of cloth that comes in hundreds of varieties. It is made from various fabrics and mainly includes cotton and silk.
- Nowadays, **synthetic fabrics** are also commonly used. Famous types of silk saris include Banarasi, Kanjivaram, Paithani, Patan Patola, Muga and Mysore. There are also many kinds of cotton saris.
- It is produced by different methods of weaving and designing. Some designs are part of the cloth, while others are printed after weaving. There are great differences in colours. These colours are produced from various types of pigments.
- The sari has a long history. A stone relief which is hundreds of years old has been found from Vaishali, which is now in Bihar. It shows a woman wearing a sari.
- There are many ways of wearing the sari, as they vary from one region to another or from one community to another. New draping methods for the sari are still being invented. Despite changes over time, sari remains the same dress.

- In past centuries, many travellers to India praised the sari for its simplicity, affordability and the various ways it can be worn. Apart from wearing it as a dress, women also use saris in many different ways.

Stone relief of a woman in a sari from Vaishali (today in Bihar)

Must Know !

For a very long time, India produced the finest cotton in the world. Indian textiles were exported as far away as Europe. A beautiful type of printed cotton called Chintz became very popular in 17th-century Europe. This caused the sale of some European dresses to decrease. Thus, to protect their own products, England and France decided to ban the import of chintz from India.

Try These

1. **What did Vincent Smith question about Indian history?**
2. **Name two millets common in India.**
3. **The sari has been admired for its .... and diverse ways it is worn.**
4. **What happened to European sales due to the popularity of Chintz?**

8.4 Celebrating Festivals

- People of India celebrate a variety of festivals.
- Some common festivals are celebrated across the country around the same time but have different names.

  For example, Makar Sankranti marks the beginning of the harvest season in many parts of India on or around 14th January. It is known as **Pongal** in Tamil Nadu, **Uttarayan** in Gujarat and **Khichdi Parv** in Uttar Pradesh.

Literary Diversity and Influence

- Literature provides another example of unity in diversity in India. Indian literature is extremely diverse and abundant.
- Over the centuries, despite different languages and styles, common themes and issues have been present. Both the **Panchatantra** and the **Mahabharata** show how Indian literature has spread across different languages and cultures over time.

Panchatantra

- The Panchatantra is a collection of stories which features animals as the main characters. It teaches important life skills.
- The original Sanskrit text of Panchatantra is over 2,200 years old. Its stories have been translated in almost every Indian language. In fact, they have travelled beyond India, to South-East Asia, the Arab world and Europe.
- Panchatantra has also inspired new collections of stories. There are about 200 adaptations of the Panchatantra in more than 50 languages.
- This shows how one set of stories has turned into many different versions in various cultures and languages.

Ramayana and Mahabharata

- For over two thousand years, the Ramayana and Mahabharata have been translated into many regional languages. They have also been adapted into various cultures both within India and abroad.
- In addition, there are countless **folk** versions of them. A survey in Tamil Nadu identified approximately one hundred folk versions of the Mahabharata.
- These two large Sanskrit epics cover about 7,000 pages each. They tell the stories of heroes fighting to restore justice.
- In the Mahabharata, the Pandavas, with Krishna's help, fight their cousins, the Kauravas, to get back their kingdom.
- In the Ramayana, Rama, with Lakshmana and Hanuman, defeats the demon Ravana, who kidnapped his wife Sita.
- Both epics also have many short stories about values and what is right and wrong.
- Many communities have their own versions of these epics. They have also preserved stories that link their own histories to these epics. These include tribal communities in many parts of India, such as the Bhils, Gonds, Mundas and others.

- Tribes in India's North-East and Himalayan regions, including Kashmir, have their own versions of the Ramayana and the Mahabharata.
- These stories and versions of the epics were shared orally. They include legends about how the heroes of the Ramayana and the Mahabharata visited the tribal regions. Anthropologist **KS Singh** observed that epic heroes like the Pandavas visited almost every part of India.
- The Mahabharata and Ramayana have connected cultures across India and Asia. It shows how diverse cultures can be united.

'Pancha Pandavar', a carved stone in a forest of the Nilgiris, Tamil Nadu, depicting the five Pandava brothers. The shrine containing this stone is maintained by Irula tribals to commemorate the Pandava's passing through the area.

Try These

1. **Makar Sankranti is typically celebrated on ....**
2. **Who helps the Pandavas fight the Kauravas in the Mahabharata?**
3. **What did anthropologist KS Singh observe about the epic heroes?**
4. **Which tribal communities have their own versions of the Ramayana and Mahabharata?**

Glossary

Inhabitants It refers to people or animals that live in a particular place.

Epic It is a long poem generally narrating the adventures of heroes and other great figures of the past.

Pigments It refers to substances used for colouring, such as dyes or paints.

Folk It refers to the traditional stories, culture and practices of ordinary people, often passed down orally through generations.

Legends It is a traditional story passed down through generations. It often involves historical or mythical characters and events.

Relief It is a design that stands out from the surface of a panel (which may be of stone, wood, ceramic or another material).

UNITY IN DIVERSITY, OR 'MANY IN THE ONE'

India's Diversity

- Varied landscapes, dresses, foods, etc.
- Population-1.4 billion people, 18% of the world's total.
- 'People of India project' - found 325 languages and 25 scripts.

Food Diversity

- Staple grains- rice, barley, wheat, bajra, etc are common.
- Common spices cumin, turmeric, cardamom and ginger are widely used.
- Common ingredients create many dishes.

India's Epic Literature

- Diverse but shared key themes.
- The Panchatantra (2200 years old) has many adaptations.
- Ramayana and Mahabharata contains many regional versions.
- Tribals have their own versions.
- Epics connect cultures across, India and Asia.

Textiles and Clothing

- Unique clothing styles across regions.
- Sari is a common garment.
- Made from silk, cotton, etc.
- Famous : Banarasi, Patan Patola and Muga
- Sari-used in various ways.
- Has ancient roots.

Festivals

- India celebrates many festivals.
- Some festivals celebrated nationwide (under different names).
- Makar Sankranti-marks harvest season around 14th January.

NCERT FOLDER

Detailed Answers of All NCERT Questions

Let's Explore (Page 126)

Q1. As a class activity, make lists of (1) the birthplaces of at least 5 classmates and the birthplaces of their parents; (2) the students' mother tongues and other languages known to them. Discuss the results in terms of diversity.

Ans. Here is a list of (1) the birthplaces of at least 5 classmates and the birthplaces of their parents; (2) the students' mother tongues and other languages known to them.

Classmate 1

- **Birthplace** Mumbai, Maharashtra
- **Parent 1 Birthplace** Kolkata, West Bengal
- **Parent 2 Birthplace** Chennai, Tamil Nadu
- **Mother Tongue** Marathi
- **Other Languages** Hindi, English, Bengali, Tamil

Classmate 2

- **Birthplace** Bangalore, Karnataka
- **Parent 1 Birthplace** Hyderabad, Telangana
- **Parent 2 Birthplace** Kochi, Kerala
- **Mother Tongue** Kannada
- **Other Languages** Telugu, English, Malayalam, Hindi

Classmate 3

- **Birthplace** Delhi
- **Parent 1 Birthplace** Amritsar, Punjab
- **Parent 2 Birthplace** Jaipur, Rajasthan
- **Mother Tongue** Hindi
- **Other Languages** Punjabi, English, Rajasthani

Classmate 4

- **Birthplace** Ahmedabad, Gujarat
- **Parent 1 Birthplace** Bhopal, Madhya Pradesh
- **Parent 2 Birthplace** Surat, Gujarat
- **Mother Tongue** Gujarati
- **Other Languages** Hindi, English, Marathi

Classmate 5

- **Birthplace** Pune, Maharashtra
- **Parent 1 Birthplace** Nagpur, Maharashtra
- **Parent 2 Birthplace** Patna, Bihar
- **Mother Tongue** Marathi
- **Other Languages** Hindi, English, Bhojpuri

Discussion on Diversity The results of this class activity highlight the rich diversity within our own classroom.

The variety of birthplaces of classmates and their parents illustrates the geographic spread and mobility of families across India. This movement contributes to the mixing of cultures and traditions.

The range of mother tongues and additional languages known by students further highlights linguistic diversity. The ability to speak multiple languages reflects India's multicultural environment, where exposure to different languages is common. This linguistic capability also leads to better communication and understanding among people from different backgrounds.

Such diversity in birthplaces and languages enriches our classroom experience, providing a picture of India's vast cultural heritage. It demonstrates how diverse backgrounds contribute to a shared learning environment, promoting mutual respect and cultural appreciation.

Let's Explore (Page 128)

Q2. As a class activity, make a list of ingredients (grains, spices, etc) that are used in your home. Take any one vegetable and think of the number of different dishes you can prepare with it.

Ans. Here is a list of ingredients used at home

- **Grains** Rice, Wheat, Barley
- **Millets** Bajra, Jowar, Ragi
- **Pulses** Moong Dal, Chana Dal, Urad Dal
- **Spices** Turmeric, Cumin, Cardamom, Ginger, Coriander, Red Chili Powder, Mustard Seeds
- **Oils** Mustard Oil, Sunflower Oil, Coconut Oil

Different Dishes with One Vegetable (Potato) Aloo Sabzi (Potato Curry), Aloo Paratha (Potato-stuffed Flatbread), Aloo Tikki (Potato Patties) and French Fries, etc.

Let's Explore (Page 129)

Q3. Explain how the example of the sari reflects both unity and diversity (in 100-150 words).

Ans. The sari exemplifies both unity and diversity in Indian culture. As a traditional garment worn by women across India, the sari represents unity. Regardless of the region, the basic form of the sari, i.e.,a long piece of cloth draped around the body remains consistent. This unstitched fabric is a common element that connects women from different backgrounds.

However, the diversity of the sari is evident in its many regional variations. Saris are made from various fabrics such as cotton, silk and synthetics and feature different weaving techniques and designs. For instance, the Banarasi silk sari from Varanasi, the Kanjivaram from Tamil Nadu and the Paithani from Maharashtra each have distinct patterns and cultural significance. Additionally, there are numerous ways to drape a sari, reflecting local customs and traditions. Thus, the sari embodies the concept of "unity in diversity," highlighting a shared cultural heritage enriched by regional differences.

Let's Explore (Page 130)

Q4. In the given pictures, can you recognise what a sari has been used for? Are you aware of, or can you imagine, more uses for the sari? Following the example of the sari, make a list of different styles you have seen for the dhoti-both as regards the fabric and the uses the dhoti can be put to. What conclusion can you draw?

Ans. In these images, the sari is being used in several practical ways beyond its role as a garment are as follows

(i) **Hammock for a Baby** In the top left image, a sari is tied to a tree and used as a hammock or cradle to hold a baby.

(ii) **Carrying Grains** In the bottom left image, a woman is using a sari to hold grains as a man pours them in.

(iii) **Veiling** In the bottom right image, a woman is using a sari to cover her head and face.

Other uses of sari can involve

(i) **Curtain or room divider** The sari can be hung as a curtain or used as a room divider.

(ii) **Tablecloth or bedspread** The sari can be used as a tablecloth or bedspread.

Common Styles of the Dhoti include

(i) **Nivi Dhoti** This style is common in South India. The dhoti is pleated at the waist and draped around the legs, often with a portion of the fabric tucked between the legs for ease of movement.

(ii) **Angarkha Dhoti** This style is common in North India. The dhoti is pleated at the waist and draped around the legs. The upper part of the dhoti, known as the angarkha, is gathered and tied at the waist, resembling a shirt-like top.

(iii) **Lungi** This style is common in South India and Sri Lanka. The lungi is a long piece of cloth wrapped around the waist and tied at the front. It is usually worn casually and is often used as everyday attire.

These descriptions depict the regional variations and specific ways dhoti is worn in different regions of India.

Let's Explore (Page 132)

Q5. I. What is your favourite festival and how is it celebrated in your region? Do you know whether it is celebrated in any other part of India, maybe under a different name?

II. During October-November, many major festivals take place in India. Make a list of the few main ones and their various names in different parts of the country.

Ans. My favourite festival is Diwali, which is also known as the Festival of Lights. In my region, Diwali is celebrated with great enthusiasm and joy. Homes are cleaned and decorated with oil lamps, candles and colourful rangoli designs. People wear new clothes and prepare special sweets and savoury dishes. In the evening, families gather to perform a puja (worship) to Goddess Lakshmi, the deity of wealth and prosperity.

After the puja, fireworks light up the night sky as people celebrate the victory of light over darkness and good over evil.

Diwali is celebrated throughout India, but it goes by different names in various regions.

Major festivals during October-November are

(i) **Diwali** (Deepavali)
- **North India** Diwali
- **South India** Deepavali
- **West Bengal** Kali Puja

(ii) **Durga Puja**

(iii) **Navratri**
- **Gujarat** Navratri (with Garba and Dandiya Raas dances)
- **Maharashtra** Navratri
- **West Bengal** Sharad Navratri, leading to Durga Puja

(iv) **Dussehra** (Vijayadashami)
- **North India** Dussehra
- **South India** Vijayadashami
- **West Bengal** Bijoya Dashami (Culmination of Durga Puja)

(v) **Karva Chauth** (celebrated primarily in North India).

Let's Explore (Page 134)

Q6. In a class discussion, try to identify the episode depicted in the painting shown in the figure and important details associated with it.

Ans. The painting depicts an important episode from the Ramayana, illustrating the abduction of Sita by Ravana, the demon king of Lanka. In this scene, Sita, the wife of Rama, is forcibly taken away by Ravana, who is depicted in his chariot. Jatayu, the noble vulture and devoted follower of Rama, is shown bravely attacking Ravana in an attempt to save Sita.

Jatayu plays a heroic but tragic role, trying to rescue Sita by attacking Ravana. Despite his bravery, Jatayu is ultimately overpowered and defeated by Ravana, who cuts off his wings. This moment is important as it sets off a chain of events leading to the epic battle between Rama and Ravana and the eventual rescue of Sita.

Questions, Activities and Projects

Q1. Conduct a class discussion on the two quotations

Quotation 1: Rabindranath Tagore

"Oh, grant me my prayer, that I may never lose the bliss of the touch of the one in the play of the many."

Ans. Tagore is asking for the joy of feeling connected to a single presence or essence even while interacting with many different people or things.

Interpretation This can be seen as a wish to maintain a sense of unity or a deep connection amidst the diversity of life.

Application How can we stay connected to what is most important to us while experiencing different things in life?

Quotation 2: Sri Aurobindo

"... The principle of unity in diversity which has always been normal to [India] and its fulfilment the fundamental course of her being and its very nature, the many in the one, would place her on the sure foundation of her Swabhava and Swadharma."

Ans. Aurobindo is talking about India's strength in embracing unity in diversity. He believes this principle is essential to India's true nature (Swabhava) and duty (Swadharma).

Interpretation The idea is that India can thrive by recognising and honouring its diverse cultures, beliefs and traditions as part of a unified whole.

Application How does embracing diversity strengthen a community or nation? What can we learn from India's example?

Q2. Read the National Anthem and its translation in the preliminary pages of this textbook. Where do you see the diversity? And where is the unity? Write two or three paragraphs on this.

National Anthem of India

Jana-gana-mana-adhinayaka jaya he
Bharata-bhagya-vidhata.

Punjaba-Sindhu-Gujarata-Maratha
Dravida-Utkala-Banga.
Vindhya-Himachala-Yamuna-Ganga
uchchala-jaladhi-taranga.

Tava shubha name jage, tava shubha asisa mage, gahe
tava jaya-gatha.
Jana-gana-mangala-dayaka jaya he
Bharata-bhagya-vidhata.
Jaya he, jaya he, jaya he, jaya jaya jaya jaya he!

Translation of the National Anthem

Thou art the ruler of the minds of all people, dispenser of India's destiny. Thy name rouses the hearts of the Punjab, Sindh, Gujarat and Maratha, of the Dravida and Odisha and Bengal. It echoes in the hills of the Vindhyas and Himalayas, mingles in the music of Yamuna and Ganga and is chanted by the waves of the Indian Sea. They pray for thy blessings and sing thy praise. The saving of all people waits in thy hand, thou dispenser of India's destiny. Victory, Victory, Victory to thee!

Ans. In the Indian National Anthem, Jana Gana Mana both diversity and unity are highlighted in the lyrics. The anthem mentions different regions and rivers of India, showing the country's wide and varied landscape. Names like Punjab, Sindh, Gujarat, Maratha, Dravida, Utkala and Banga represent different states and cultures, showcasing India's rich cultural heritage. Natural landmarks like the Vindhya and Himachala mountains and the Yamuna and Ganga rivers, reflect the diverse natural beauty of the nation.

Despite this diversity, the anthem also emphasises unity. The phrase "Bharata-Bhagya-Vidhata" meaning "dispenser of India's destiny" brings all these diverse elements together under one identity—India. The anthem calls for blessings and good fortune for the entire nation, creating a sense of collective pride and destiny. By mentioning various regions and cultures, it shows that although India is diverse, there is a strong bond that unites the country.

Q3. Select a few stories from the Pañchatantra and discuss how their message is still valid today. Do you know of any similar stories from your region?

Ans. Stories from the Panchatantra and their modern relevance are as follows

(i) **The Monkey and the Crocodile**

Story A crocodile befriends a monkey and plans to kill him to take his heart to his wife. The monkey, realising the danger, cleverly convinces the crocodile that he left his heart on a tree. The crocodile swims back to the tree and the monkey escapes.

Message Intelligence and quick thinking can help overcome dangerous situations.

Relevance Today This story teaches the importance of wit and presence of mind, which are crucial in modern problem-solving and conflict resolution.

(ii) **The Tortoise and the Geese**

Story A tortoise, wanting to fly, holds onto a stick carried by two geese. Despite warnings to remain silent, he speaks and falls to his death.

Message Listening to advice and controlling one's urges are essential.

Relevance Today This tale highlights the importance of listening to good advice and the dangers of acting without thinking carefully, which is relevant in both professional and personal life.

(iii) Similar stories from my regions are as follows

The Fox and the Grapes

Story A fox tries to reach grapes hanging high but fails and then dismisses them as sour.

Message It's easy to say bad things about something you can't have.

Relevance Today This story teaches us how to deal with disappointment and the need to keep trying.

Q4. Collect a few folk tales from your region and discuss their message.

Ans. Folk tales from my region and their messages are as follows

(i) **The Boy Who Cried Wolf**

Story A shepherd boy repeatedly tricks villagers into thinking a wolf is attacking his flock. When a wolf actually appears, the villagers don't believe him and the sheep are eaten.

Message Honesty is crucial, and habitual lying can lead to serious consequences.

(ii) **The Thirsty Crow**

Story A crow finds a pitcher with water at the bottom. Unable to reach the water, it drops pebbles into the pitcher until the water rises high enough to drink.

Message Being clever and persistent can solve difficult problems.

Q5. Is there any ancient story that you have seen being depicted through a form of art? It could be a sculpture, a painting, a dance performance, a movie. Discuss with your classmates.

Ans. Yes, the ancient story of the 'Ramayana' is often depicted through various forms of art. For example, 'Ram Leela' is a traditional dance and drama performance that tells the story of Lord Rama. Additionally, there are many beautiful paintings and sculptures showing scenes from the Ramayana in temples and museums. Modern movies and TV shows also retell this epic story.

Q6. Discuss in class the following quotation by India's first Prime Minister, Jawaharlal Nehru, when he travelled to many parts of India before Independence.

"Everywhere I found a cultural background which had exerted a powerful influence on their lives. The old epics of India, the Ramayana and the Mahabharata and other books, in popular translations and paraphrases, were widely known among the masses and every incident and story and moral in them was engraved on the popular mind and gave a richness and content to it. Illiterate villagers would know hundreds of verses by heart and their conversation would be full of references to them or to some story with a moral, enshrined in some old classic."

Ans. Jawaharlal Nehru's quotation highlights how deeply the ancient Indian epics, like the Ramayana and Mahabharata, have influenced the lives of people across India. He observed that these stories and their lessons were well-known, even among those who couldn't read. Villagers would often memorise and recite verses from these epics and their daily conversations were filled with references to these ancient texts.

The discussion can be continued on the following points

- **Cultural Impact** These stories have shaped the values and thoughts of people across generations.
- **Education and Oral Tradition** Even without formal education, people learned important life lessons from these epics.
- **Relevance** How do ancient stories continue to influence modern life and culture?

REVIEW EXERCISE

Including Competency Based Questions

Part I

Very Short Answer Type Questions

1. In the late 20th century, the Anthropological Survey of India conducted the 'People of India project'. How many languages and scripts were counted in this project?

Ans. 325 languages using 25 scripts were counted by the ASI in the 'People of India' project.

2. Which two long Sanskrit poems narrate stories of heroes re-establishing Dharma?

Ans. The Ramayana and the Mahabharata are the two long Sanskrit poems which narrate stories of heroes re-establishing Dharma.

3. Which communities have their own versions of the Ramayana and the Mahabharata?

Ans. Tribal communities such as the Bhils, Gonds and Mundas have their own versions of the Ramayana and the Mahabharata.

4. What are some staple grains common to almost every part of India?

Ans. Rice, barley and wheat are some staple grains common to almost every part of India.

5. Who observed that epic heroes visited almost every place in India according to folklore?

Ans. The anthropologist KS Singh observed that epic heroes visited almost every place in India according to folklore.

6. How did European countries react to the popularity of chintz?

Ans. European countries reacted to the popularity of chintz by banning its import to protect their own textile industries.

Short Answer Type Questions

1. What was Vincent Smith's view regarding India's diversity and unity?

Ans. British historian Vincent Smith questioned how the history of India could be written given its great diversity. He found the answer in India's "unity in diversity." This concept means that despite the vast differences in cultures, languages and traditions, there is an underlying sense of unity that binds the country together, making its diversity manageable.

2. What was the purpose of the 'People of India' project conducted by the Anthropological Survey of India (ASI)?

Ans. The 'People of India' project aimed to document the diversity within India by surveying 4,635 communities across all states. It found that India has 325 languages using 25 scripts and highlighted the significant number of Indians living away from their birthplace or original community. This project illustrated the country's rich cultural and linguistic diversity and provided insights into the various communities and their unique identities.

3. How does the celebration of festivals like Makar Sankranti exemplify India's cultural unity?

Ans. Festivals like Makar Sankranti exemplify India's cultural unity by being celebrated across the country, under different names and customs. This festival marks the harvest season and is observed with various regional traditions.

The shared timing and underlying significance of the festival highlight a common cultural thread, despite the diverse ways it is celebrated. This reflects the unity in diversity that characterises Indian culture.

Long Answer Type Questions

1. How does the Panchatantra exemplify the concept of "unity in diversity" within Indian literature and beyond?

Ans. The Panchatantra, a collection of ancient Indian stories, exemplifies "unity in diversity" through its widespread adaptation and translation across various cultures and languages. Originally written in Sanskrit over 2,200 years ago, the Panchatantra features animal characters to teach important life skills and moral lessons. Despite linguistic and cultural differences, its universal themes have connected people globally.

This has led to approximately 200 adaptations in more than 50 languages. This widespread acceptance and adaptation show how a single literary work can unify large audiences. Panchatantra's journey from India to South-East Asia, the Arab world and Europe showcases the ability of literature to cross cultural boundaries, illustrating the inter-connectedness of human societies.

2. What role do tribal communities play in preserving the Ramayana and Mahabharata?

Ans. Tribal communities play a crucial role in preserving the Ramayana and Mahabharata through their unique adaptations and oral traditions.

For over two thousand years, these epics have been translated into many regional languages. They have also been adapted into various cultures both within India and abroad. Tribal communities, such as the Bhils, Gonds and Mundas, have their own versions of these epics. They include local folklore and cultural elements, which makes the stories relevant to their own histories and values.

In many parts of India, including the North-East and Himalayan regions like Kashmir, tribes have preserved and transmitted these epics through oral storytelling. These versions often include local legends about how the epic heroes, such as the Pandavas, visited their regions, as observed by anthropologist KS Singh.

3. How does travelling through different regions of India highlight the country's diversity in landscapes, clothing, foods and languages?

Ans. Travelling through different regions of India showcases the country's remarkable diversity. Each area presents a new landscape, from mountains and rivers to deserts and coastal plains. The clothing styles vary widely, with different fabrics, colours and patterns reflecting the region's climate and culture. India has a great variety of food.

Each region offers its own unique dishes and flavours that reflect local ingredients and culinary traditions. There are many different languages and scripts used across India. This highlights the country's linguistic diversity, as each language carries its own rich history and cultural significance. Even within the same region people from various parts of India bring their own customs and traditions. This adds to the rich Indian culture. This incredible diversity is often what first attracts visitors to India.

Part II

Multiple Choice Questions (MCQs)

1. How is the sari described in terms of its diversity and unity?

(a) It is worn in only one way across India.
(b) It is made of the same fabric throughout India.
(c) It has many styles and fabrics but remains a single type of clothing.
(d) It is worn only in formal settings.

2. Which epic stories are mentioned as examples of unity in diversity in Indian literature?

(a) The Ramayana and the Mahabharata
(b) The Jataka Tales and the Panchatantra
(c) The Bhagavad Gita and the Upanishads
(d) The Vedas and the Puranas

3. How do the Ramayana and Mahabharata illustrate cultural unity across India?

(a) They are adapted and translated into various regional languages.
(b) They are not recognised outside India.
(c) They are ignored by tribal communities.
(d) They have no influence on Indian culture.

4. Which of the following is not a staple grain used in India?

(a) Rice (b) Barley (c) Quinoa (d) Bajra

5. What is the significance of the Panchatantra in Indian literature?

(a) It is the only ancient text in Sanskrit.
(b) It consists of stories that teach important life skills.
(c) It is only known in India.
(d) It is a modern collection of short stories.

6. What role do food grains like rice and wheat play in Indian cuisine?

(a) They are used only in specific regions.
(b) They are not commonly found in Indian dishes.
(c) They are staple ingredients used throughout India.
(d) They are exclusively used in desserts.

7. The sari is traditionally worn in most parts of India. Which of the following is not a type of sari mentioned?

(a) Banarasi (b) Kanjivaram
(c) Chintz (d) Paithani

8. Which common festival is celebrated across India on 14th January?

(a) Diwali (b) Holi
(c) Makar Sankranti (d) Eid

9. According to KS Singh, which heroes are mentioned as visiting various regions of India in folklore?

(a) The Pandavas (b) The Ten Avatars
(c) The Chakravartins (d) The Asuras

10. What is a notable characteristic of Indian festivals?

(a) They are celebrated in the same way across the country.
(b) They are limited to only one religion.
(c) They vary by region but often occur around the same time.
(d) They are all celebrated in October.

11. Which statement best describes the sari?

(i) It is a uniform dress style worn by all Indian women.

(ii) It has multiple variations and ways of draping across regions.

(iii) It is no longer worn in modern India.

(iv) It is exclusively made from silk.

Options

(a) Only (i) and (ii) (b) Only (ii)

(c) Only (iii) (d) Only (iv)

12. Which of the following are types of silk saris?

(i) Banarasi (ii) Kanjivaram

(iii) Khadi (iv) Kota Doria

Codes

(a) (i) and (ii) (b) (i) and (iii)

(c) (ii) and (iv) (d) All of these

Answers

1. (c)	2. (a)	3. (a)	4. (c)	5. (b)
6. (c)	7. (c)	8. (c)	9. (a)	10. (c)
11. (b)	12. (a)			

Fill in the Blanks

1. India has over 1.4 billion inhabitants, which is about .... per cent of the world's population.
2. Many Indians, sometimes called .... , live away from their birthplace or original community.
3. Festivals like Makar Sankranti mark the beginning of the .... season in many parts of India.
4. The original Sanskrit text of the Panchatantra is over .... years old.
5. The Mahabharata narrates the story of the Pandavas fighting their cousins, the ...., to recover their kingdom.
6. In the Ramayana, Rama defeats the demon ...., who had kidnapped his wife Sita.

Ans. 1. 18 2. migrants 3. harvest
4. 2200 5. Kauravas 6. Ravana

True or False

1. The ASI survey covered only 1,000 communities across India.
2. The Panchatantra is a collection of stories featuring human characters.
3. Tribal communities in India have their own versions of the Ramayana and Mahabharata.
4. Indian classical arts and architecture display both diversity and unity.
5. The sari is a traditional dress worn only in Southern India.
6. Common ingredients used in Indian cooking include rice, barley and wheat.

Ans. 1. False 2. False 3. True
4. True 5. False 6. True

Assertion-Reason

1. **Assertion** (A) Many Indians are considered migrants because they do not live near their birthplace.

   Reason (R) Migration in India is solely due to economic reasons.

   Codes

   (a) Both A and R are true and R is the correct explanation of A
   (b) Both A and R are true, but R is not the correct explanation of A
   (c) A is false, but R is true
   (d) A is true, but R is false

2. **Assertion** (A) The concept of 'unity in diversity' means that despite differences, there is a common bond.

   Reason (R) India's historical and cultural diversity is unified by a shared sense of identity and values.

   Codes

   (a) Both A and R are true and R is the correct explanation of A
   (b) Both A and R are true, but R is not the correct explanation of A
   (c) A is false, but R is true
   (d) A is true, but R is false

3. **Assertion** (A) Folk versions of the Mahabharata are found in many Indian states.

   Reason (R) These folk versions have been preserved by various communities, including tribal ones.

   Codes

   (a) Both A and R are true and R is the correct explanation of A
   (b) Both A and R are true, but R is not the correct explanation of A
   (c) A is false, but R is true
   (d) A is true, but R is false

4. **Assertion** (A) The diversity in Indian festivals reflects the country's varied cultural practices.

   Reason (R) Many festivals share similar themes but are celebrated differently in different regions.

   Codes

   (a) Both A and R are true and R is the correct explanation of A
   (b) Both A and R are true, but R is not the correct explanation of A
   (c) A is false, but R is true
   (d) A is true, but R is false

5. **Assertion** (A) The National Anthem of India represents the unity of the nation.

   Reason (R) The National Anthem mentions different regions and states of India, showcasing diversity.

Codes

(a) Both A and R are true and R is the correct explanation of A

(b) Both A and R are true, but R is not the correct explanation of A

(c) A is false, but R is true

(d) A is true, but R is false

Ans. 1. (c) 2. (a) 3. (a) 4. (a) 5. (a)

Case Based Questions

1. Read the paragraph given below and answer the following questions.

Every region and community in India has developed its own styles of clothing and dresses. Yet, we notice a commonality in some traditional Indian dresses, irrespective of the material used.

An obvious example is the plain length of cloth called the sari, a type of clothing worn in most parts of India and made from different fabrics-mostly cotton or silk, but nowadays synthetic fabrics too. Banarasi, Kanjivaram, Paithani, Patan Patola, Muga or Mysore are some of the famous types of silk saris. There are many more kinds of cotton saris. Altogether, this unstitched piece of cloth comes in hundreds of varieties. They are produced by different methods of weaving and designing. Some designs are part of the cloth, while others are printed after the cloth is woven. Finally, there are endless variations in the colours, which are produced from many kinds of pigments. The sari has a long history. The stone relief from Vaishali (today in Bihar) goes back a few centuries BCE. There are many ways of wearing the sari, as they vary from one region to another or from one community to another. In fact, new ways of draping it are still being invented. But in the end, it is a single dress-the sari.

(i) Which of the following fabrics is not mentioned as a material used for making saris?

(a) Cotton (b) Silk (c) Synthetic fabrics (d) Wool

(ii) How are the colours of saris produced?

(a) Using only natural dyes

(b) Using various pigments

(c) Using embroidery

(d) Using digital printing

(iii) Which statement about the sari is true?

(a) It is only worn in specific regions of India.

(b) It has a single standard method of draping.

(c) It has a long history and various regional draping styles.

(d) It was invented in the 20th century.

(iv) What aspect of the sari is still evolving?

(a) The types of fabric used

(b) The ways of draping it

(c) The number of colours available

(d) The history of the garment

Ans. (i) (d) (ii) (b) (iii) (c) (iv) (b)

2. Read the paragraph given below and answer the following questions.

Literature offers us another fine illustration of unity in diversity. Indian literatures are extremely diverse (and among the most abundant in the world). Over centuries, despite differences in language, technique, etc., they have shared important themes and concerns. Who has not heard of the Panchatantra, for example–

This collection of delightful stories, with animals as the main characters, teaches us important life skills. The original Sanskrit text is at least 2,200 years old, but its stories have been adapted in almost every Indian language. In fact, they have travelled well beyond India, all the way to South-East Asia, the Arab world and Europe, inspiring new collections of stories on the way–it is estimated that about 200 adaptations of the Panchatantra exist in more than 50 languages! This 'illustrates how 'one' collection of stories has become 'many'.

(i) How has the Panchatantra influenced regions outside of India?

(ii) What does the adaptation of the Panchatantra into various languages illustrate?

(iii) What is a significant feature of the Panchatantra stories?

Ans. (i) The Panchatantra's influence extends beyond India, reaching South-East Asia, the Arab world and Europe. It has inspired new collections of stories and has been adapted into approximately 200 versions in over 50 languages.

(ii) The wide range of adaptations of the Panchatantra shows how one set of stories can become many different versions but still keep the same main ideas.

(iii) A significant feature of the Panchatantra stories is that they teach important life skills.

Competency Based Questions

1. For a very long time India produced the finest cotton in the world. This led to the export of Indian textiles as far away as Europe. How did Indian textiles impact 17th-century Europe?

Ans. Indian textiles, particularly the printed cotton called 'chintz,' was highly popular in 17th-century Europe. They were so popular that they affected the sale of European dresses. This led England and France to ban the import of chintz to protect their own textile industries. This historical example highlights the global influence of Indian craftsmanship and the far-reaching impact of India's cultural products.

2. **The common ingredients (unity) can be used in a number of combinations (diversity) to prepare an endless variety of dishes. How does the variety of food in India illustrate the concept of unity in diversity?**

Ans. India's food diversity shows unity in diversity. Even though different regions have their own unique dishes, they all use common ingredients. Staples like rice, wheat and millets are common across India. Spices like turmeric, cumin and coriander are essential in many recipes. These shared ingredients help create a wide range of dishes. For instance, rice can be a simple steamed dish or a flavourful biryani.

3. **How have the Ramayana and the Mahabharata maintained their significance and adaptability in Indian literature and culture over the centuries? Also, discuss their themes.**

Ans. The Ramayana and the Mahabharata have demonstrated their enduring significance and adaptability in Indian literature and culture through their numerous translations and adaptations for over two thousand years. These two epics have been transformed into regional literatures across India and beyond, showcasing their wide-reaching influence.

In Tamil Nadu alone, a survey revealed about a hundred folk versions of the Mahabharata. Together, these epics contain approximately 7,000 pages in their original Sanskrit versions and narrate the heroic efforts to re-establish dharma.

The Mahabharata tells the story of the Pandavas, who, with the help of Krishna, fought with their cousins, the Kauravas, to get their kingdom back. The Ramayana tells how Rama, helped by his brother Lakshmana and Hanuman, defeats the demon Ravana to save his wife Sita. These stories explore values and ethical questions, making them timeless and important in culture.

Skill Based Questions as per NEP 2020

1. **Research the different types of saris mentioned in the text (e.g., Banarasi, Kanjivaram). Create a presentation or poster showcasing their unique features, materials and weaving techniques.**

Ans. Do it yourself.

2. **Select a common vegetable like potato or spinach. Research and list at least five different dishes from various Indian regions that use this vegetable.**

Ans. Five different dishes from various Indian regions using potato are as follows

Region	Dish
Maharashtra	Pao bhaji
Delhi	Chhole bhature
Kerala	Masala dosa
Kashmir	Dum aloo
Punjab	Aloo paratha

3. **Choose a character from either the Ramayana or the Mahabharata and research how their story is adapted in different regional or tribal versions.**

Ans. Character: Rama from Ramayana

Adaptations of Rama's story in different regional or tribal versions are given below

- **Rama in the Tamil Version** The Tamil adaptation is written by poet Kamban. The Kamba Ramayanam, while retaining the core elements of the story, places a stronger focus on the emotional and devotional aspects of Rama's life.
- **Rama in the Bengali Version** The Bengali adaptation features a narrative style that reflects Bengali cultural and religious practices. It often focuses on Rama's role as a deity and his divine attributes, reflecting the regional devotional practices and local legends.
- **Rama in Tribal Versions** In tribal communities such as Bhil and Gond, the story of Rama is adapted to fit local myths and cultural contexts.

ASSESSMENT EXERCISE

Objective Type Questions

1. Which of the following is not a common spice used in Indian cuisine?
   (a) Turmeric (b) Cumin
   (c) Oregano (d) Cardamom
2. Why did England and France ban the import of chintz from India?
   (a) Chintz was not popular in Europe
   (b) It was too expensive
   (c) It caused a drop in European textile sales
   (d) It was considered inferior quality
3. The Panchatantra stories are originally written in which language?
   (a) Tami (b) Sanskrit (c) Hindi (d) Telugu
4. What is the primary theme of the Ramayana and Mahabharata?
   (a) History of kingdoms
   (b) Stories of gods
   (c) Heroes fighting to re-establish dharma
   (d) Daily life of ancient people
5. **Assertion** (A) Indian epics like the Ramayana and Mahabharata have influenced literature beyond India.
   Reason (R) These epics have inspired adaptations and translations in many other countries.
   Codes
   (a) Both A and R are true and R is the correct explanation of A
   (b) Both A and R are true, but R is not the correct explanation of A
   (c) A is false, but R is true
   (d) A is true, but R is false
6. These tribal adaptations of the epics are transmitted ...., along with legends on how the heroes visited the tribes' regions.
7. In the past, Indian textiles were exported as far away as ....
8. The Mahabharata is a story about the Pandavas' struggle for their kingdom. (True/False)
9. Vincent Smith questioned how to write India's history due to its diversity. (True/False)

Subjective Questions (VSA, SA & LA)

1. What are some materials from which saris can be made?
2. What is an example of a popular Indian textile in Europe?
3. What concept describes India's unity despite its vast differences?
4. Which festival is known as Pongal in Tamil Nadu?
5. Which Indian epic involves heroes like the Pandavas and Krishna?
6. What role do festivals play in showcasing India's unity in diversity?
7. Why has the sari been admired by travellers to India over the centuries?
8. How are the stories of the Panchatantra shared?
9. What does 'unity in diversity' mean in the context of Indian history?
10. The same ingredients (unity) can be used in a number of combinations (diversity) to prepare an endless variety of dishes. Comment.

CHAPTER 9

Family and Community

Families are the fundamental units of society, shaping our daily lives and values. In India, families range from large joint families to smaller nuclear families. Each type has unique characteristics and roles. Beyond individual families, communities form through shared activities and mutual support. This interconnectedness extends from rural villages to urban neighbourhoods, reflecting the diverse ways people live and work together across different contexts.

Family plays a crucial role in shaping our identities, values and overall well-being. It provides emotional support and helps in proper development of a person. Families also play an important role in imparting values, offering security and fostering a sense of belonging.

9.1 Types of Family

- The family is the fundamental and most ancient unit of any society. In Indian society there are several types of families today. Two broad types are the **joint family** and the **nuclear family**.
- In a joint family, individuals of several generations such as the grandparents, parents, uncles, aunts, brothers, sisters and cousins live together.
- In the nuclear family, only a couple and their children, and sometimes one parent and children live together.
- In the English language, there are limited terms to describe relationships in a family whereas in Indian languages there are many terms.

  For example, in the Hindi language bua, tau, tai, chacha, mausi, nana, nani and many more terms exist. Tamil language even has different terms for elder brother/sister or younger brother/sister.
- There is no such term for the word 'cousin' in most of the Indian languages because they are considered as 'brothers' and 'sisters' only. This signifies the deep bond among all the children in the family.

Roles and Responsibilities of Family Members

Relationships among the members of a family are based on love, care, cooperation and interdependence. 'Cooperation' signifies doing work together.

- Every member in a family has a role and responsibility towards each other. For example, parents are responsible for raising their children to become happy individuals and responsible members of society. Children take part in more responsibilities at home as they grow up.
- In many homes, children also learn the traditions and practices which their family has been following for generations.
- An important principle of Indian culture is to follow our dharma or doing our duty. The family as a 'school' teaches children the important values of ahimsa, **dana** (giving), **seva** (service) and **tyaga** (sacrifice).
- Individuals in the family often give up their own needs to take care of the family's needs.

9.2 Community

- A community is the group of people and many other families that are connected with each other.
- Families are connected not only within themselves, but also with other families and people around them.
- The members of the community come together for various reasons like celebrating festivals and organising other events such as feasts, weddings, etc. In some villages, people come together to help each other in agricultural operations such as preparation of land, sowing and harvesting.
- Communities have commonly agreed upon some practices or rules regarding the use of shared natural wealth. This includes resources such as water, grazing lands and forest produce. Such rules are followed in many tribal communities as well as village communities in rural India at present.

- These 'rules' are rarely written down but they ensure a secure access to resources for communities. This system also assigns specific duties to all families and individuals within the community. Otherwise, the community will not function smoothly.
- Community is a **flexible concept**. This can be understood through following examples
  - A **Jati** or a sub-division of it, is also called a community.
  - A group of people belonging to a particular religion, region, common work or interest, especially a smaller group may also be called a community. For example, the Parsi community of Mumbai, Sikh community of Chennai, Indian community of America, etc.
  - A student is a part of many communities in the school such as the sports community, science or drama club, etc.

Types of Community

Communities may be rural or urban. An example of the rural community is **Bhil community** and an example of urban community is **Resident's Welfare Association**.

Bhil Community

- The Bhil community in the town of Jhabua in Madhya Pradesh followed their halma tradition during an acute water crisis.
- Halma tradition involves coming together with community people to support any individual or family in times of crisis. The objective of this tradition is to serve mother Earth.
- The Bhil community planted thousands of trees in hundreds of villages, dug trenches to conserve rainwater and created other water harvesting structures. They did this work as their duty towards their community and the environment without any payment.
- **Shri Mahesh Sharma** of the Shivganga Movement received the **Padma Shri award** in 2019 for his transformational work with the Bhil community.

Must Know!

In the year 2015, Chennai was hit by a severe flood. The roads were filled with water and people could not move. Almost all the shops were closed and services hindered. At that time, many private spiritual and religious organisations cooked and distributed large quantities of food to the people in need.

Residents' Welfare Associations

- Residents' Welfare Associations in many urban areas are a kind of community that make their own rules and regulations related to several issues such as waste management, cleanliness, taking care of pets, etc.
- People living in the community participate in making such rules and regulations.

Interdependence of Communities

- The communities are ultimately interdependent. One community depends on the other for their different works. For example, the Residents' Welfare Associations are dependent on the trading community for the supply of different products and on municipal workers to handle waste.
- Everyone is dependent on so many other people and communities in our complex society.

Try These

1. **What terms are used for maternal grandfather and grandmother in Hindi language?**
2. **There is a family in which children live with their parents, grandparents, uncle, aunts and cousins in the same house. Which kind of family is this?**
3. **What are some examples of community?**
4. **A number of people are served with food in *langar* free of cost. Name the community which organises these *langars*.**

Glossary

Family A family is a group of people related by blood, marriage and other factors who support, care and take responsibilities for each other.

Cooperation Cooperation means working together with others to achieve a common goal or task.

Interdependence Interdependence means reliance of people or groups on each other to perform various functions.

Dharma Dharma means doing the right thing and following good rules to be a good person.

Community A community is a group of people who live in the same area or share common interests and work together.

Water Harvesting Water harvesting means collecting and storing rainwater for future use, instead of letting it flow away.

FAMILY AND COMMUNITY

Family
- Family is the fundamental and most ancient unit of any society.
- Family members performs duties and tasks.
- Divided into two main types.

Roles and Responsibilities
- Relationship between family members is based on love, care, cooperation and interdependence.
- Family functions as a school and teaches the important values of ahimsa, dana, seva and tyaga.

Joint Family
- Consists of many members from several generations.

Nuclear Family
- Consists of few closely connected members.
- Usually, parents and children.

Community
- Usually a group of individuals or families that are connected with each other.
- Perform several tasks and activities together. e.g, celebrating festivals, organising events, etc.
- Use natural resource of their community as per their mutually agreed rules.

Types
- May be rural or urban.
- New types of communities have emerged in recent years. e.g., Resident's Welfare Association.

Interdependence
- Members of a community in a society depend on each other for several reasons.
- Community is a flexible concept.
- Jati or a subdivision of it, group of people belonging to a particular religion, region and other such smaller groups are also communities.

NCERT FOLDER

Detailed Answers of All NCERT Questions

Let's Explore (Page 138)

Q.1 What types of families do you see in your neighbourhood? List the type with the number of households for each type.

Ans. I see the following types of families in my neighbourhood

- Children living with their parents
- Children living with a single parent
- Children living with their grandparents and parents
- Children living with their grandparents, parents, uncles, aunts and cousins

Type of families in my neighbourhood	Number of households
1. Children living with both parents	5
2. Children living with a single parent	1
3. Children living with their grandparents and parents	3
4. Children living with grandparents, parents, uncles, aunts and cousins	2

Q.2 What types are more frequent? Why do you think this is so?

Ans. The families in which children live with both of their parents are more frequent. I think this is because nowadays most people move out from their native places in search of better work opportunities. So, it is often difficult to maintain a big family.

Let's Explore (Page 139)

Q.3 Make a list of all the members of your family you can think of, including a few distant relatives. List their terms in your mother tongue or regional language and try to find the equivalent in English. Two examples are below for Hindi.

Name	Term in Hindi	Description / Term in English
Rani	बहन	Mother's brother's daughter (cousin) (among other possible meanings)
Sameer	चाचा	Father's younger brother (uncle)

Notice how, quite often, a single word in your mother tongue or regional language, requires several words in English to give a precise definition.

Ans. The list of all the members of my family that I can think of India my mother tongue (Hindi) with their English equivalent are as follows

Name	Term in Hindi	Description / Term in English
Shalini	मम्मी	Mother/Mummy
Vinay	पापा	Father / Papa
Tushar	भईया	Brother
Reena	मौसी	Mother's sister (aunt)
Ritu	मौसी	Maternal grandmother' sister's daughter (aunt)
Taru	भईया	Father's sister's son (cousin)
Kriti	दादा	Mother's sister's daughter (cousin)
Ram	ताऊ जी	Father's elder brother (uncle)
Dheeraj	भईया	Maternal grandfather's brother's son's eldest son (cousin)
Amar	ताऊ जी	Grandfather's brother's son
Sunil	फूफा जी	Father's sister's husband

Let's Explore (Page 140)

Q.4 Answer these questions and compare your answers with a few classmates

A. Who in your family decides what is to be bought from the market?

Ans. My mother decides what is to be bought from the market as she manages the home.

B. Who cooks food in your home?

Ans. My mother usually cooks food in my home but sometimes my sister cooks food too.

C. Who is the oldest person in your family?

Ans. My grandfather is the oldest person in my family.

D. Who cleans the floor in your home?

Ans. Our maid cleans the floor in our home and in her absence, my mother sometimes cleans the floor.

E. Who washes utensils in your house?

Ans. My mother and my sister wash utensils in my house.

F. Who helps you to do your homework?

Ans. My elder sister and sometimes my father help me to do my homework.

Let's Explore (Page 41)

Shalini lives with her family in a town in Kerala. Her father runs a small business and her mother is a teacher in a nearby school. Shalini has a younger brother. Her grandmother, Acchamma (father's mother), Chittappa (father's brother or paternal uncle) and her Chitti (aunt or uncle's wife) live with them. They have a daughter, Shalini's cousin, who she calls Chinni. Shalini's uncle has just lost his job and her aunt is a homemaker. The whole family was preparing for the festival of Onam. Acchamma told Shalini's father that his brother was having financial difficulties, so they were not able to buy new clothes for the festival. When Shalini's parents took her and her brother shopping, they bought new clothes not only for themselves, but also for Chithappa, Chitti and Chinni. As a result, Shalini did not get the silk dress she had expected; she had to settle for a simple cotton one. Achamma explained to Shalini that this is how families support each other and share what they have. Shalini did not mind her simpler dress. She was happy that everyone could get some new clothes.

Q.5 Draw a simple tree of this family of seven members.

Ans. Do it yourself.

Q.6 Why do you think Shalini's parents bought clothes for everyone?

Ans. Shalini's parents bought clothes for everyone as Chittappa (Shalini's paternal uncle) was facing financial difficulties and could not buy clothes. Families are expected to help each other and share what they have so they all can celebrate the festival happily.

Q.7 What would you have done if you were in Shalini's place?

Ans. If I were in Shalini's place I would have felt happy that my father bought clothes for everyone and at the same time I would not mind my simple dress instead of silk one.

Think About It (Page 142)

My name is Tenzing. I love the mountains we live in, though life is sometimes hard. My father runs a small grocery store. After my mother became busy in a local handicraft cooperative, making our beautiful traditional fabrics, wood carvings and other items for sale to tourists, my father joined in cleaning the house, taking care of our small vegetable garden and other household chores. Often, he helps my grandmother prepare food for us all. Grandmother always has all sorts of interesting stories to tell me, with humour and wisdom; no one seems to understand people better than her! Grandfather helps me with my homework and takes me to the school bus stop. He is also actively involved in social work in our colony and is always offering his help to others. For example, when there is a power failure in our area, he goes and registers a complaint at the nearby office. When our neighbours' house got damaged in a storm, he collected some money from the whole neighbourhood to help with repairs. We are lucky that my parents can take care of our basic necessities like food and clothing. When any special expenses come up, I have often seen that they discuss them together. Mother says that we should always try to save some money for any unexpected needs that may arise in the future.

Q.8 Why does Tenzing's father consult his wife for special expenses?

Ans. Tenzing's father consulted his wife for special expenses because they both earn and discussion makes it easier to manage the expenses efficiently as well as save some money for any unexpected needs in future.

Q.9 How do you feel about his participation in household chores?

Ans. His participation in the household chores shows that he does not hesitate in doing household work if his wife is busy at work. His support to his wife enables the family to take care of the basic necessities of the family.

Q.10 What roles do the grandparents fulfil?

Ans. The grandparents fulfil the following important roles in Tenzing's family

- The grandmother cooks food for the family in the absence of Tenzing's mother.
- She tells stories to Tenzing which have humour as well as wisdom.
- Tenzing's grandfather helps him in his homework as well as takes him to the school bus stop.
- The grandfather is also involved in social work by helping other families in the colony.

Let's Explore (Page 143)

Q.11 Create a story of a family somewhere in India, where we see some family values practised. Share it with your class either through writing or drawing.

Ans. Ramesh, his wife, Sita and their two children, Ravi and Priya, lived in a small village in India. One day, Ramesh's mother, who lived with them, fell ill. Everyone became concerned about her health. Sita took care of her by looking after her needs, cooking her favourite food and giving her medicine. Ravi and Priya helped their mother in the household chores. Ramesh worked hard in a nearby construction site to earn money for her treatment.

When Ramesh's mother recovered, the family was happy. They sat together, shared food, and thanked each other for their support. Ramesh said, "We are strong because we are together." Sita added, "We help each other, that's what family is for." Ravi and Priya learned that family values like love, care and support are important.

This family showed values like

- Respect for elders
- Care for each other
- Teamwork
- Gratitude

They proved that simple acts of love and kindness make a family strong.

Q.12 Stage a small drama with all your classmates around two or three families. The play you write could include some challenging situations that the families faced and show how they are resolved.

Ans. Title of the drama : "Together We Stand"

Characters

- Family 1: Mr. Kumar, Mrs. Kumar and their son, Rohan
- Family 2: Mr. Patel, Mrs. Patel and their daughter, Kiara
- Family 3: Mrs. Sharma (a widow) and her son, Aryan

Act 1: (The scene opens with the three families living in the same neighbourhood. Mr. Kumar loses his job and Mrs. Patel falls ill.)

Mr. Kumar: (worried) I don't know how I'll take care of my family now.

Mrs. Kumar: (supportively) We"ll face this together.

Mrs. Patel: (weakly) I'm sorry, I can't cook for my family today.

Kiara: (helpfully) I'll cook, mom.

Act 2: (Mrs. Sharma's son, Aryan, makes friends with Rohan and Kiara. They decide to help each other's families.)

Rohan: (kindly) My mom can cook for your family, Kiara.

Kiara: (gratefully) Thanks, Rohan!

Aryan: (helpfully) I can help Mr. Kumar find a new job.

Act 3: (The families come together to support each other. Mr. Kumar finds a new job and Mrs. Patel recovers.)

Mr. Kumar: (gratefully) Thanks, friends, we did it together!

Mrs. Patel: (happily) We're strong because we have each other!

Mrs. Sharma: (proudly) Our children showed us the power of unity!

(All families come together, hold hands and smile.)

Values shown by this drama

- Support and encouragement
- Kindness and help
- Unity and togetherness

This drama shows how families can come together to face challenges and support each other in times of need.

Q.13 In the stories of Shalini and Tenzing, we see examples of joint families. What do you think are the aspects of modern living that make some couples opt for a nuclear family (i.e. living apart from older generations or other relatives)? What could be some advantages as well as disadvantages of the two kinds of families?

Ans. The aspects of modern living that makes some couples opt for a nuclear family are as follows

- Nuclear family allows greater freedom and privacy.
- Nuclear family makes it easy to move to other places for work and study.
- Nuclear families put less financial burden on the earning individual.
- It is easier to make decisions in a nuclear family without multiple opinions.

Advantages and disadvantages of a nuclear family are as follows

Advantages	Disadvantages
More space and privacy	Feeling of isolation and loneliness.
Less financial burden on the family.	Fewer members means lesser help when needed.
Easier to move for work or education.	Children miss out on learning from grandparents and other relatives.
More deeper bonding of parents with children.	If parent lose their job it is hard to manage the family.

Advantages and disadvantages of joint family are as follows

Advantages	Disadvantages
More members to take care of the children.	Less privacy and space.
Finance or the family may be divided between the members.	Supporting a large family is difficult financially.
All the members celebrate festivals together.	More conflicts because of multiple opinions.
More people to look after children if both of the parents work.	More household responsibilities on females.

Questions Based on Story (Page 146-147)

More than 20 years ago, in an area of Ahmedabad (Gujarat), Kamal Parmar, owner of a small auto-fabrication workshop, noticed a group of underprivileged children on the street. Some had dropped out of school, while others had never been to school. Kamal started giving them tuition from 5:30 to 9:30 pm every day, after his regular work hours. He also provided the kids with a free dinner. Soon, 150 children were attending those classes regularly and were deeply interested in the lessons! A few teachers from a local school noticed the classes and joined the teaching for a while. One of them observed, "These children don't get proper benches to sit on, have no 'silence zone' classrooms and the vehicles passing by make lots of noise, yet they pay all their attention to what the teachers tell them. This touched my heart. The love and affection I got from them was unbelievable." Some older children who were attending regular schools also joined as volunteers to teach in Kamal's classes. One of them remarked, "We went there to teach, instead we learnt a lot from them."

Q.14 Discuss this story in your class. What kind of attitude towards the community does it reveal?

Ans. This story revealed the empathetic and supportive attitude of the people towards this community.

Q.15 What values get reflected in Kamal Parmar's initiative?

Ans. Values of empathy, kindness, responsibility, compassion, inclusivity, supportiveness and volunteerism are reflected in Kamal Parmar's initiative.

Q.16 Think about those underprivileged children. Do you think society has been unfair to them?

Ans. Yes, society has been unfair to underprivileged children in many ways. They often face

- Limited access to quality education and resources.
- Poverty and economic instability.
- Lack of healthcare and nutrition.
- Discrimination and stigma.

Despite having the ability to succeed in life, this unfairness makes it difficult for them to achieve their goals.

Q.17 What should society do to make sure that all children get access to education?

Ans. A society can do the following to make sure that all children get access to education

- By building more schools.
- By providing an opportunity for free education.
- By helping families to educate their children as per our capabilities.
- By raising awareness among people about the importance of education.
- By volunteering to provide free tuition classes to poor children.

Let's Explore (Page 147)

Q.18 Make a list of all people outside your family that are supporting you through their work in one way or another.

Ans. People outside my family that support us through their work in one way or another are as follows

Farmers They support us by growing crops on the farm.

Teachers They support us by providing education.

Doctors They support us by providing treatment to us when we are sick.

Police They support us by providing safety.

Let's Explore (Page 148)

Q.19 What types of communities are you part of?

Ans. I am a part of the following communities

- Hindu community
- Hindi speaking community
- North Indian community
- Student's community

Q.20 Is there a club that you are a part of in school? How does it function?

Ans. Yes, I am a part of the eco club at my school. This club functions by organising eco-friendly events and functions such as the following

- Organising campaigns such as tree planting and cleanliness drives.
- Create garden or green spaces at school.
- Promoting recycling of school waste.
- Conducting workshops and seminars.

Questions, Activities and Projects

Q.1 What are some of the rules you follow in your family and neighbourhood? Why are they important?

Ans. Some of the rules that I follow in my family are as follows

- Share household chores and responsibilities.
- Respect elders and maintain a healthy relationship with everyone.
- Wake up early and sleep early.
- Keep the house clean.

Some of the rules that I follow in my neighbourhood are as follows

- Throw garbage at designated places.
- Avoid creating unnecessary noise.
- Respect elders and help them.
- Follow parking and traffic rules.

These rules are important to maintain a harmonious relationship in the family and neighbourhood.

Q.2 Do you think some rules are unfair to a few people in the family or community? Why?

Ans. Yes, some rules can be unfair to a few people.

It is because

- Rules might not consider everyone's needs or situations.
- Some people might not have a say in making the rules.
- Rules can be too strict or controlling.
- Rules can be unfair to certain groups, like women or children.
- Rules can be outdated and not relevant anymore.
- Rules can be unclear or confusing.
- Rules can be made with biases or stereotypes.

Q.3 Describe several situations that you have observed where community support makes a difference. You can draw or write about these.

Ans. Some of the situations where I have observed that community support makes a difference are as follows:-

- Distributing free food to poor people during religious ceremonies or through food banks.
- Construction of shelter homes for the homeless during winters.
- Creating a helping unit where people keep their old clothes and other stuffs for needy people.
- Several tribal communities help each other by taking responsibilities during weddings.

REVIEW EXERCISE

Including Competency Based Questions

Part I

Very Short Answer Type Questions

1. Which members are included in a joint family?

Ans. The members such as mother, father, grandparents, uncles, aunts and cousins are included in a joint family.

2. Which Indian language has different terms for elder brother/sister or younger brother/sister?

Ans. Tamil language has different terms for elder brother/sister or younger brother/sister. For example, the elder brother in Tamil language is called 'Anna' and younger brother is called 'Thambi'.

3. What are the key elements that form the basis of relationships among family members?

Ans. Love, care, cooperation and interdependence are the key elements that form the basis of relationships among family members.

4. What is the role of parents in a family?

Ans. The role of parents in a family is to raise their children to become happy individuals and responsible members of society.

5. What values does the family teach children, according to Indian culture?

Ans. Family teaches the values of Ahimsa (non-violence), dana (charity), seva (service) and tyaga (sacrifice) to children according to Indian culture.

6. What type of rules do communities have regarding shared natural resources?

Ans. Communities have unwritten rules regarding the use of shared natural resources like water, grazing lands and forest produce.

7. What is the name of the tradition followed by the Bhil community in Jhabua, Madhya Pradesh?

Ans. Halma tradition is followed by the Bhil community in Jhabua, Madhya Pradesh.

8. Water crisis is a serious issue in many parts of India. Mention some of the activities that can be undertaken to deal with this issue.

Ans. Some of the activities undertaken during the water crisis are planting thousands of trees, digging trenches to conserve rainwater and creating other water harvesting structures.

9. Who received the Padma Shri Award in 2019 for his work with the Bhil community?

Ans. Shri Mahesh Sharma of the Shivganga Movement received the Padma Shri Award in 2019 for his work with the Bhil community.

10. Who provided food to people in need during the Chennai flood in 2015?

Ans. Private spiritual and religious organisations provided food to people in need during the Chennai flood in 2015.

11. What is an example of a new type of community that has emerged in urban areas?

Ans. Residents' Welfare Associations are examples of a new type of community that has emerged in urban areas.

Short Answer Type Questions

1. Describe the two broad types of families in Indian society.

Ans. In Indian society, there are two broad types of families: Joint families and Nuclear families. Joint families consist of multiple generations living together, sharing resources and relying on each other for support.

This type of family structure is deeply rooted in Indian culture and is often seen as a symbol of unity and strength.

Joint families provide a sense of security and belonging to their members, and they play an important role in passing down traditions and values from one generation to the next.

Nuclear families, on the other hand, typically consist of a couple, their children and sometimes one parent and children living together.

This type of family structure is becoming increasingly common in urban areas, where individuals may prioritise their personal goals and aspirations over traditional family values.

2. What is notable about the terms used to describe family relationships in Indian languages compared to English?

Ans. Notably, Indian languages have many specific terms to describe family relationships, whereas English has limited terms. This highlights the importance and complexity of family relationships in Indian culture. Indian languages recognise the nuances of family relationships, acknowledging the unique bonds between relatives.

For example, in Hindi, there are specific terms for different types of cousins, aunts and uncles, which reflects the significance of these relationships in Indian society. This emphasis on family relationships reflects the significance of kinship ties in Indian culture, where family is often seen as a source of support, guidance and identity.

3. "There is no specific term for 'cousin' in most Indian languages." Discuss.

Ans. In most Indian languages, cousins are not referred to by a specific term because they are considered as brothers and sisters, signifying a deep bond among all children in the family. This emphasises the close relationship and shared experiences among cousins in Indian culture.

The absence of a specific term for cousin highlights the inclusive nature of Indian families, where cousins are considered an integral part of the family unit. This lack of distinction between siblings and cousins reflects the importance of family ties and the blurring of boundaries between different family members.

4. What is the importance of assigning duties within a community? Do festivals and events in a community have any significance for the community?

Ans. Assigning specific duties to families and individuals ensures the smooth functioning of the community, promotes a sense of responsibility and maintains social harmony.

By assigning duties, community members can work together towards common goals, share resources and rely on each other for support.

Yes, festivals and events bring community members together, fostering social bonding, collective joy and a sense of belonging. These celebrations strengthen community ties, promote cultural heritage and provide opportunities for socialisation and community engagement. Festivals and events also help to resolve conflicts, promote unity and reinforce community values and traditions.

5. What is the benefit of mutual support in rural communities? How do community rules impact resource management?

Ans. Mutual support in rural communities is crucial for individuals and families to overcome challenges, share knowledge and build stronger relationships. By supporting each other, community members can pool their resources, expertise and labour to achieve common goals, such as farming, irrigation and disaster management. Community rules play a vital role in resource management by ensuring sustainable use and management of shared natural resources. These rules prevent over exploitation, promote equitable access and maintain social harmony.

For instance, community rules may regulate the use of common grazing lands, water sources and forest produce, ensuring that these resources are used in a way that benefits the entire community. Additionally, community rules may also govern the use of shared infrastructure, such as roads, bridges and irrigation canals, to ensure that they are maintained and repaired collectively.

6. What is the significance of community practices in tribal and rural communities?

Ans. Community practices in tribal and rural communities are essential for preserving traditional knowledge, promoting cultural heritage and ensuring the continuation of shared values and customs. These practices, such as festivals, rituals and ceremonies, bring community members together, fostering social bonding, collective joy and a sense of belonging.

Community practices also play a crucial role in passing down traditional skills, knowledge and values from one generation to the next, ensuring the continuation of community traditions and cultural identity.

For example, traditional farming practices, such as crop rotation and organic farming, are passed down through generations, ensuring that the community continues to produce healthy and sustainable food. Similarly, traditional crafts, such as weaving and pottery, are preserved and passed down through community practices, ensuring that the community's cultural heritage is maintained.

7. How did the Bhil community's efforts impact their environment during the water crisis?

Ans. The Bhil community's efforts had a profoundly positive impact on their environment during the water crisis. By planting thousands of trees, conserving rainwater and creating water harvesting structures, they helped mitigate the effects of the water crisis.

These efforts not only ensured a steady supply of water but also helped maintain soil quality, prevent erosion, and support biodiversity. The Bhil community's initiatives demonstrate the importance of community-led conservation efforts in addressing environmental challenges. Additionally, their efforts also helped to reduce the community's reliance on external aid and support, promoting self-sufficiency and resilience.

8. What motivated the Bhil community to undertake their environmental conservation work without payment?

Ans. The Bhil community was motivated by a sense of duty towards their community and the environment, as well as their objective to serve mother earth.

This sense of responsibility and stewardship drove them to undertake their environmental conservation work without payment. Their selfless efforts demonstrate the community's commitment to environmental conservation and their willingness to work together for the greater good.

Additionally, their motivation was also driven by a desire to preserve their traditional way of life and cultural heritage, which is deeply connected to their natural environment.

9. How did private spiritual and religious organisations respond to the Chennai flood?

Ans. Private spiritual and religious organisations played a vital role in responding to the Chennai flood. They proved that community work can help alleviate the suffering of people in need. By cooking and distributing large quantities of food, they helped sustain those affected by the flood.

Their efforts also provided emotional support and comfort to those who had lost their homes and livelihoods. This response demonstrates the importance of community-led initiatives in times of crisis.

Additionally, their response also highlights the role of faith-based organisations in promoting social cohesion and collective action.

Long Answer Type Questions

1. Explain the concept of 'dharma' in Indian culture and its significance in family life. How does it influence individual behaviour and family dynamics?

Ans. In Indian culture, 'dharma' refers to fulfilling one's duty and responsibility, encompassing family, social and personal obligations. In family life, dharma signifies prioritising roles and responsibilities towards family members and society, promoting accountability and commitment.

Embracing dharma encourages selflessness, sacrifice and service, fostering cooperation, interdependence and mutual support within the family. By prioritising duties, family members develop a deeper understanding of each other's needs, leading to a harmonious and supportive environment. Dharma influences individual behaviour by promoting purpose, direction and a long-term perspective.

Individuals make choices aligning with their values and principles, leading to fulfillment, happiness and contentment. Dharma encourages responsibility and stewardship, striving to create a positive legacy for future generations. By embracing dharma, individuals cultivate a sense of trust, loyalty and commitment, forming strong, healthy relationships within the family.

2. Describe the importance of sacrifice and selflessness in family life. How do family members demonstrate these values, and what impact do they have on family relationships?

Ans. Sacrifice and selflessness are essential values in family life, demonstrating love, care and commitment to the family's well-being. Family members often give up their own needs and interests for the benefit of the family, showing selflessness and sacrifice.

This can manifest in various ways, such as parents sacrificing their personal goals for their children's education or family members putting aside their differences for the sake of family harmony. These values strengthen family bonds, promote empathy and understanding and create a supportive and nurturing environment. By demonstrating sacrifice and selflessness, family members build trust, respect, and loyalty, leading to more meaningful and lasting relationships.

3. Describe the role of community duties in promoting social harmony and ensuring the smooth functioning of the community.

Ans. Assigning specific duties to families and individuals within a community promotes a sense of responsibility, encourages cooperation and maintains social harmony, leading to a well-organised and thriving community. By contributing to the community's well-being, members develop a sense of ownership and commitment, fostering a collaborative environment where everyone works together towards a common goal. This system ensures the smooth functioning of the community, as each member plays a vital role in maintaining social balance and collective prosperity. Clear roles and responsibilities also prevent confusion and overlapping efforts, allowing community members to focus on their specific tasks and work efficiently. Ultimately, this approach strengthens community bonds, promotes mutual respect and creates a sense of unity and shared purpose.

4. Discuss the impact of the Bhil community's environmental conservation efforts on their community and the environment and explain how Shri Mahesh Sharma's work contributed to their success.

Ans. The Bhil community's environmental conservation efforts had a profoundly positive impact on their community and the environment. By planting trees, conserving rainwater and creating water harvesting structures, they helped mitigate the effects of the water crisis, ensured a sustainable water supply and promoted eco-friendly practices. Shri Mahesh Sharma's work in the Shivganga Movement played a significant role in supporting and amplifying the Bhil community's efforts. His transformational work helped mobilise the community, facilitated knowledge sharing and encouraged collective action. The Padma Shri Award he received in 2019 recognises his outstanding contributions to the Bhil community's environmental conservation efforts, highlighting the importance of collaborative initiatives in driving positive change.

Part II

Multiple Choice Questions (MCQs)

1. Which of the following is unique about the Tamil language in terms of describing family relationships?

(a) It has only one term for all family members
(b) It has different terms for elder and younger siblings
(c) It has no terms for family relationships
(d) It has only English words for family relationships

2. Which of the following is the significance of not having a specific term for 'cousin' in most Indian languages?

(a) It shows that cousins are not important in Indian culture
(b) It highlights the deep bond among all children in the family
(c) It indicates that cousins are not related by blood
(d) It means that cousins are not part of the family

3. Parents play an important role in the life of the child by teaching them certain values.

What is one of the responsibilities of parents in a family?

(a) Only providing financial support
(b) Only raising children to become happy individuals and responsible members of society
(c) Only teaching children traditions and practices
(d) Only doing household chores

4. Which of the following is an important principle of Indian culture that is taught in a family?

(a) Following one's own desires
(b) Ignoring duties and responsibilities
(c) Following our dharma or doing our duty
(d) Avoiding sacrifices and service

5. Which of the following best describes a community?

(a) A single family living together
(b) A group of people and families connected with each other
(c) A group of individuals with no connection to each other
(d) A group of people living in a city

6. What is the purpose of the 'rules' in a community regarding shared natural wealth?

(a) To restrict access to resources
(b) To ensure secure access to resources for communities
(c) To assign duties only to individuals, not families
(d) To abolish the use of shared natural wealth

7. What is an example of a new type of community that has emerged in urban areas?

(a) Residents' welfare associations
(B) Trading communities
(c) Municipal workers' unions
(d) Religious communities

8. **What is the nature of the concept of community?**
(a) Rigid (b) Flexible (c) Static (d) Dynamic

9. **Which of the following can be the possible reasons behind the interdependence of the communities?**
I. Because they are self-sufficient
II. Because they have no relation with each other
III. Because they depend on each other for different works
IV. Because they are isolated from each other
Which of the above statements is/are incorrect?
(a) I, II and III only (b) III only
(c) I, II and IV only (d) I, II, III and IV

Answers

1. (b) 2. (b) 3. (b) 4. (c) 5. (b)
6. (b) 7. (a) 8. (b) 9. (b)

Fill in the Blanks

1. The Hindi language has specific terms like bua, tau, tai, chacha, mausi, nana, nani and many more to describe .... relationships.
2. In many homes, children learn the .... and practices that their family has been following for generations.
3. In some villages, people help each other in agricultural operations such as preparation of land, ... and harvesting.
4. Resident's welfare associations are dependent on the .... community for the supply of different products.
5. Residents' welfare associations in many .... areas are examples of communities that make their own rules and regulations.
6. Cooperation means .... together.

Ans. 1. family 2. traditions 3. sowing 4. trading 5. urban 6. working

True or False

1. The concept of joint family is unique to Indian society.
2. Hindi language has only a few terms to describe family relationships.
3. Children in a family do not have any responsibilities.
4. The family teaches children to prioritise their own needs over the family's needs.
5. The rules regarding shared natural wealth are rarely written down.
6. Shri Mahesh Sharma received the Padma Shri award for his work with the Bhil Community in 2019.
7. A student is only part of one community in school.

Ans. 1. False 2. False 3. False 4. False 5. True 6. True 7. False

Match the Following

1. Match the value with its description.

	List I		List II
A.	Ahimsa	1.	Non-violence
B.	Dana	2.	Giving
C.	Seva	3.	Sacrifice
D.	Tyaga	4.	Service

Codes

	A	B	C	D		A	B	C	D
(a)	2	1	3	4	(b)	1	2	4	3
(c)	3	2	1	4	(d)	4	1	2	3

Ans. 1. (b)

Assertion-Reason

1. **Assertion** (A) Joint families are common in Indian society.
Reason (R) Joint families allow for a sense of community and shared responsibilities among extended family members.
Codes
(a) Both A and R are true and R is the correct explanation of A
(b) Both A and R are true, but R is not the correct explanation of A
(c) A is false, but R is true
(d) A is true, but R is false

2. **Assertion** (A) Cooperation is an essential aspect of family relationships.
Reason (R) It involves doing work individually to achieve family goals.
Codes
(a) Both A and R are true and R is the correct explanation of A
(b) Both A and R are true, but R is not the correct explanation of A
(c) A is false, but R is true
(d) A is true, but R is false

3. **Assertion** (A) Communities have rules regarding the use of shared natural wealth.
Reason (R) These rules are meant to restrict access to resources for communities.
Codes
(a) Both A and R are true and R is the correct explanation of A

(b) Both A and R are true, but R is not the correct explanation of A
(c) A is false, but R is true
(d) A is true, but R is false

4. Assertion (A) The system of rules in a community assigns specific duties to all families and individuals.
Reason (R) This is done to ensure the smooth functioning of the community.
Codes
(a) Both A and R are true and R is the correct explanation of A
(b) Both A and R are true, but R is not the correct explanation of A
(c) A is false, but R is true
(d) A is true, but R is false

5. Assertion (A) Shri Mahesh Sharma received the Padma Shri Award in 2019.
Reason (R) He received the award for his work in creating water harvesting structures.
Codes
(a) Both A and R are true and R is the correct explanation of A
(b) Both A and R are true, but R is not the correct explanation of A
(c) A is false, but R is true
(d) A is true, but R is false

6. Assertion (A) A student is a part of many communities in a school.
Reason (R) A student can only be part of one community.
Codes
(a) Both A and R are true and R is the correct explanation of A
(b) Both A and R are true, but R is not the correct explanation of A
(c) A is false, but but R is true
(d) A is true, but R is false

Ans. 1. (a) 2. (d) 3. (d) 4. (a) 5. (d) 6. (d)

Case Based Questions

1. Read the source given below and answer the questions that follow.

Shalini lives with her family in a town in Kerala. Her father runs a small business and her mother is a teacher in a nearby school. Shalini has a younger brother.

Her grandmother, Acchamma (father's mother), Chittappa (father's brother or paternal uncle) and her Chitti (aunt or uncle's wife) live with them. They have a daughter, Shalini's cousin, who she calls Chinni. Shalini's uncle has just lost his job and her aunt is a homemaker.

The whole family was preparing for the festival of Onam. Acchamma told Shalini's father that his brother was having financial difficulties, so they were not able to buy new clothes for the festival. When Shalini's parents took her and her brother shopping, they bought new clothes not only for themselves, but also for Chittappa, Chitti and Chinni.

As a result, Shalini did not get the silk dress she had expected; she had to settle for a simple cotton one. Acchamma explained to Shalini that this is how families support each other and share what they have. Shalini did not mind her simpler dress. She was happy that everyone could get some new clothes.

(i) What is the importance of family support in times of financial difficulty?
(a) It provides only emotional support
(b) It provides only financial assistance
(c) It provides both emotional and financial assistance
(d) It has no significance

(ii) How does sharing resources within a family promote unity and cooperation?
(a) By creating competition among family members
(b) By fostering a sense of individualism
(c) By encouraging family members to work together to overcome challenges
(d) By promoting selfishness

(iii) What values can be learned from prioritising the needs of others over personal desires?
(a) Greed and selfishness
(b) Empathy, selflessness and generosity
(c) Anger and frustration
(d) Pride and arrogance

Ans. (i) (c) (ii) (c) (iii) (b)

2. Read the source given below and answer the questions that follow.

My name is Tenzing. I love the mountains we live in, though life is sometimes hard. My father runs a small grocery store. After my mother became busy in a local handicraft cooperative, making our beautiful traditional fabrics, wood carvings and other items for sale to tourists, my father joined in cleaning the house, taking care of our small vegetable garden and other household chores. Often, he helps my grandmother prepare food for us all. Grandmother always has all sorts of interesting stories to tell me, with humour and wisdom; no one seems to understand people better than her! Grandfather helps me with my homework and takes me to the school bus stop. He is also actively involved in social work in our colony and is always offering his help to others.

For example, when there is a power failure in our area, he goes and registers a complaint at the nearby office. When our neighbours' house got damaged in a storm, he collected some money from the whole neighbourhood to help with repairs. We are lucky that my parents can take care of our basic necessities like food and clothing. When any special expenses come up, I have often seen that they discuss them together. Mother says that we should always try to save some money for any unexpected needs that may arise in the future.

(i) What is the importance of shared responsibilities within a family?

(ii) How does involvement in social work benefit individuals and communities?

(iii) What is the value of saving money for unexpected expenses?

Ans. (i) Shared responsibilities within a family promote teamwork, understanding, and mutual respect and help to distribute workload and stress, creating a more harmonious and supportive home environment.

(ii) Involvement in social work benefits individuals by providing a sense of purpose and fulfillment. It also benefits communities by addressing social issues, building connections and fostering a sense of unity and cooperation.

(iii) Saving money for unexpected expenses provides financial security, reduces stress and allows individuals to be better prepared for unforeseen circumstances, such as medical emergencies or natural disasters, ensuring they can respond effectively and maintain stability.

3. Read the source given below and answer the questions that follow.

More than 20 years ago, in an area of Ahmedabad (Gujarat), Kamal Parmar, owner of a small auto-fabrication workshop, noticed a group of underprivileged children on the street. Some had dropped out of school, while others had never been to school.

Kamal started giving them tuition from 5:30 to 9:30 pm every day, after his regular work hours. He also provided the kids with a free dinner. Soon, 150 children were attending those classes regularly and were deeply interested in the lessons! A few teachers from a local school noticed the classes and joined the teaching for a while.

One of them observed, "These children don't get proper benches to sit on, have no 'silence zone' classrooms and the vehicles passing by make lots of noise, yet they pay all their attention to what the teachers tell them. This touched my heart. The love and affection I got from them was unbelievable'. Some older children who were attending regular schools also joined as volunteers to teach in Kamal's classes. One of them remarked, "We went there to teach, instead we learnt a lot from them".

(i) What is the impact of education on underprivileged children?

(ii) How does community involvement in education benefit society?

(iii) What is the value of volunteerism in education?

Ans. (i) Education can have a transformative impact on underprivileged children, providing them with opportunities for personal growth, social mobility, and improved economic prospects, ultimately breaking the cycle of poverty.

(ii) Community involvement in education fosters a sense of social responsibility, promotes intergenerational learning and helps to address educational inequalities ultimately contributing to a more informed and empathetic society.

(iii) Volunteerism in education provides additional support and resources to students, enriches the learning experience and fosters a sense of community and social connection. It also promotes personal growth and development for the volunteers themselves.

Competency Based Questions

1. People in rural areas are knit in a family-like community group who help each other during the time of need. Provide an example of how people help each other in rural communities?

Ans. In some villages, people help each other in agricultural operations like land preparation, sowing and harvesting.

2. Can you give an example of a community based on shared interest or activity?

Ans. A student's sports team, science club or drama club in school are examples of communities based on shared interest or activity.

3. How do family members demonstrate cooperation and interdependence in their relationships? What is the importance of family traditions and practices for children?

Ans. Family members demonstrate cooperation and interdependence in their relationships by doing work together, sharing responsibilities and relying on each other. This cooperation is essential for the smooth functioning of the family and promotes a sense of unity and shared purpose. Learning family traditions and practices is significant for children as it helps them understand their heritage, values and customs, and connect with their roots. Family traditions and practices also foster a sense of belonging and identity among family members, promoting social cohesion and continuity.

By participating in family traditions, children learn important values such as respect, obedience and responsibility, which shape their personalities and guide their actions.

4. Individuals in the family often give up their own needs to take care of the family's needs. Justify the statement.

Ans. Giving up one's own needs for the family's needs means sacrificing personal interests for the benefit of the family. This selflessness is important because a family is based on the foundation of love and support towards each other.

By prioritising family needs, members demonstrate their loyalty and dedication to the family unit, strengthening family bonds and promoting harmony. This willingness to sacrifice personal interests for the family's benefit reflects the importance of family ties in Indian culture, where family is often seen as a source of support, guidance and identity.

By putting family needs first, members can ensure the well-being and prosperity of the family as a whole.

5. "Communities are ultimately interdependent." Comment.

Ans. Communities are interdependent, meaning they rely on each other for various needs and services. For instance, Residents' Welfare Associations depend on the trading community for supplies and municipal workers for waste management. This interdependence illustrates how communities rely on each other for different works.

In another example, farmers may depend on rural artisans for tools and equipment, while artisans may depend on farmers for raw materials. This interdependence promotes cooperation, mutual support, and collective well-being among communities.

Additionally, interdependence also fosters social cohesion, trust and reciprocity among community members, ensuring that communities work together to achieve common goals.

6. Explain the flexibility of the concept of community, describing how it can encompass various groups of people united by shared identity, interest, or activity. Provide examples of different types of communities and explain how they illustrate this flexibility.

Ans. The concept of community is remarkably flexible, encompassing diverse groups of people united by shared identity, interest, or activity. This adaptability enables communities to be defined and organised in various ways, depending on the context and purpose.

For instance, a community can be defined by a shared identity, such as a cultural or ethnic group like Jat or Parsi or by a shared interest, like a sports team, book club or science club.

Additionally, communities can be defined by their location, such as the Indian community in America or by their profession, like a community of doctors, teachers or artists. This flexibility allows the concept of community to be applied and adapted to different contexts, purposes and settings, highlighting its versatility and relevance in various aspects of human life.

Skill Based Questions as per NEP 2020

1. Design a community outreach programme that highlights the importance of family and community in Indian society. Write a detailed proposal outlining the programme's objectives, strategies and activities. Be sure to include examples of community initiatives, cultural practices and social values that promote cooperation and collective responsibility.

Ans. Community Outreach Programme : "United We Thrive"

Objectives

- Promote family and community importance in Indian society
- Foster cooperation and collective responsibility

Strategies

- Organise community events and activities
- Establish community groups and clubs
- Partner with local organisations and businesses

Activities

- Community clean-up drives
- Cultural festivals and celebrations
- Workshops and training programmes

Community Initiatives

- Residents' welfare associations
- Tribal communities preserving traditional practices
- Village communities promoting sustainable agriculture

Social Values

- Ahimsa (non-violence and compassion)
- Dana (generosity and sharing)
- Seva (selfless service)
- Tyaga (sacrifice and selflessness)

This programme aims to build a stronger, more compassionate society by promoting unity, social cohesion and cultural heritage.

2. Imagine you are a member of a joint family living in a rural village. Write a descriptive story about your daily life and experiences.

Ans. I live with my family in a big house in a village. My grandparents, parents, uncles, aunts and cousins all live together. We wake up early in the morning and have tea together.

My grandmother makes breakfast for everyone. My mother helps her. After breakfast, I go to the fields with my uncles and cousins. We work together and help each other. We grow crops like wheat, rice and vegetables. We take a break under a tree and eat lunch together.

In the evening, we all sit together in the courtyard. My grandparents tell us stories about our family. My cousins and I play games and laugh together. My mother and aunts make dinner for everyone.

We all eat together and then go to bed. I like living with my big family. We help each other and make each other happy. We share everything and don't feel alone. On festivals, we all celebrate together. We make traditional food and wear new clothes. We visit our relatives and friends in the village. Everyone is happy and smiling. I like my life in the village. It's simple and happy. I don't want to live anywhere else.

ASSESSMENT EXERCISE

Objective Type Questions

1. What is the fundamental and most ancient unit of any society?

(a) The individual (b) The community

(c) The family (d) The state

2. What is the significance of 'cooperation' in a family?

(a) Doing work individually (b) Doing work together

(c) Avoiding responsibilities (d) Ignoring each other's needs

3. What is one way that members of a community come together?

(a) Only to celebrate festivals

(b) Only to organise weddings

(c) To celebrate festivals and organise other events such as feasts, weddings, etc.

(d) Never, they only live separately

4. What is the main objective of the Halma tradition followed by the Bhil community in Jhabua, Madhya Pradesh?

(a) To serve individual interests

(b) To serve mother earth

(c) To receive awards and recognition

(d) To get paid for their work

5. Assertion (A) Indian languages have a limited number of terms to describe family relationships.

Reason (R) Indian languages have a simple family structure.

Codes

(a) Both A and R are true and R is the correct explanation of A

(b) Both A and R are true, but R is not the correct explanation of A

(c) A is false, but R is true

(d) A is true, but R is false

6. In a joint family, individuals from .... generations live together.

7. Relationships among family members are based on ...., care, cooperation and interdependence.

8. The nuclear family consists of only one parent and their children. (True/False)

9. The system of rules in a community only assigns duties to families, not individuals. (True/False)

Subjective Questions (VSA, SA & LA)

1. What are the different types of families present in Indian society today?

2. What do children learn from their family traditions and practices?

3. What was the objective of the Halma tradition?

4. What natural disaster hit Chennai in 2015?

5. Explain the flexibility of the concept of community, providing examples of different types of communities.

6. Do you think there is any role of residents in a resident's welfare association? Comment.

7. How does the concept of 'dharma' influence family dynamics and individual behaviour?

8. What is unique about Indian languages when it comes to describing family relationships?

9. Describe the characteristics of joint and nuclear families in Indian society. How do they differ from each other?

10. Explain the significance of community rules regarding shared natural resources and their impact on resource management.

Governance

CHAPTER 10

In a community, rules are essential to maintain order and harmony. Whether at home, school, on the road,or in the country ,rules guide our actions and interactions. Governance is the process of creating and enforcing these rules, while the government is the system that manages this process. Laws can be updated based on public input, ensuring that rules evolve with society's needs.

Human beings have been a part of community life for a very long time. Disagreements and disorders are common when many people live together. Therefore, rules become necessary to maintain order and harmony in society.

Rules are followed by people in several spheres of life such as

- Simple rules at home for family members
- Rules at school for students and teachers
- Traffic rules for drivers on road
- Rules set by the employers for employees
- Rules committed to the employees by the employers

A society would not be able to function if nobody follows these rules.

10.1 Governance and Making of Rules

- Governance is the process of taking decisions, organisation of social life with different sets of rules and ensuring that these rules are followed.
- **Government** is a group of people or the system responsible for making rules and ensuring that these rules are followed. Some of the more important rules are called **laws.**
- The rules and laws can be changed or updated as needed. People or citizens have a role in making or changing the rules and laws of their society.

10.2 Three Organs of Government

There are three branches or 'organs' of the government as follows

(i) **The Legislature** It is the organ that legislates or makes new laws. In the legislature, an assembly of representatives of people makes new laws and sometimes it also updates or removes existing laws.

(ii) **The Executive** It is the organ that executes or implements the laws. It includes the authorities that are responsible for enforcing 'law and order' such as

- The head of state (President, a Prime Minister or a Chief Minister).
- The ministers
- Any other agency that maintains law and order e.g. Police.

(iii) **The Judiciary** It is the system of courts responsible for the following

- Deciding whether a law has been broken by someone.
- Deciding the course of action or punishment for breaking the law.
- Examine whether the decision taken by the executive is right or not.
- Examine the fairness of the laws passed by the legislature.

These three organs of the government work together. This can be understood with the example of **cybercrime. Cybercrime** is a new form of criminal activity. Government passes new laws to overcome these criminal activities **(Work of Legislature)**. Cyber police then take action against these criminals and arrest them **(Work of Executive)**. Criminals are then convicted in courts and jailed for some years **(Work of Judiciary)**.

Separation of Power

- The three organs of the government work and interact with each other. However, in any good system of governance, these organs must be kept separate. This separation is called 'separation of powers'. It helps to maintain the system of **checks and balances**.

- Under this system, each organ of the government can check the work of other organs and restore balance if any organ is acting beyond its expected role.

Functions of Three Organs at National and State Level

	National/All India Level	State Level
Judiciary	Supreme Court of India function of the national level	High Court functions at the state level
Legislature	It has two houses –Lok Sabha and Rajya Sabha. These houses formulate national laws.	There is one state assembly or Vidhan Sabha. Few states have two assemblies.
Executive	**Central Government** It is led by the President of India. He is the **nominal head** and the Supreme Commander of the Indian armed forces. Prime Minister is the executive head.	**State Government** It is led by the Governor. Chief Minister is the executive head.
	The functions and responsibilities of the national level executive are as follows • Defence • Foreign affairs • Atomic energy • Communications • Currency • Interstate commerce • Education • Formulation of national policies	The functions and responsibilities of the state level executive are as follows • Police, law and order • Adaptation and implementation of laws made by the Central government at the State level. • Public health • Education • Agriculture • Irrigation • Local government

10.3 Three Levels of Government

- Governments usually operate at two levels-local and national. In some countries, including India, government also functions at 3 levels–National, State and Local level. Each of these levels deals with different matters.
- In India, there is local government at the town or village level, state government at the state level and central government at the national level.
- The scope of the functions of the different levels of the government are
  - Local authorities handle local issues.
  - State government addresses regional issues affecting multiple towns and villages.
  - Central government deals with national issues affecting vast areas.

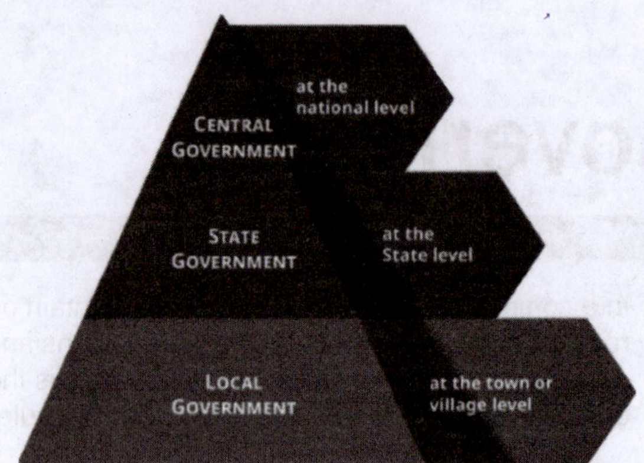

Level of Government

Indian Mottos and their Meanings

Many of our institutions have mottos inspired by the wisdom of our ancient texts.
For example,

- ***Satyameva Jayate*** It is the motto of the government of India. It means 'Truth alone triumphs'.
- ***Yato Dharmastato Jayah*** It is the motto of the supreme Court. It means 'Where there is dharma, there is victory'.

10.4 Democracy

- The word 'democracy' comes from two Greek words. ***'demos'*** meaning 'people', and ***'kratos'*** meaning 'rule' or power. Hence, democracy means the **rule of the people**.
- It is not possible for all people to rule and hence people vote for their representatives through elections. The representatives rule on behalf of all the people. The representatives are elected members of their respective assemblies.
- The system of election of representatives is present both at the state and national levels.
  They are called **Members of Legislative Assembly (MLAs)** at the state level and **Members of Parliament (MPs)** at the national level.
- These members hold discussions in the assembly related to laws, problems and solutions and try to convince each other when there is a difference of opinions.

Representative Democracy

- India, like any modern democracy, is a representative democracy. India is also the **world's largest democracy**. It has around 970 million voters as of 2024.
- All the Indian citizens above the age of 18 years have the right to participate in the elections.

- Voting is a method for making decisions where everyone has a chance to contribute their opinion. It is done in the following ways
  - Options are presented
  - Each person chooses their preferred option by voting
  - The option with the most votes wins

Direct Democracy and Grassroots Democracy

- When every person's opinion is heard and counted to make a decision, it is called **direct democracy**. For example, to choose a picnic spot for a school picnic, each student gives their vote between two options. The option with the most votes is chosen.
- Grassroots democracy is a system that empowers ordinary citizens to participate in decision-making processes. It gives ordinary people a voice in the decisions that affect their lives.

Dr APJ Abdul Kalam

Dr APJ Abdul Kalam , nicknamed as the **Missile Man of India**, was a famous scientist known for his crucial role in the development of India's space programme, missile programme and nuclear capabilities.

- He was born in Rameswaram , Tamil Nadu in 1931. He served as the 11th President of India from 2002 to 2007. Despite this high position, he remained deeply connected with people and youths through his passion for education and innovation.
- He was dedicated to social causes and committed to the nation. He inspired so many young Indians to dream big and work hard.
- He proved that despite his nominal position as the President, he could play an important role by impacting so many lives.

Try These

1. **Government is present at how many levels in India?**
2. **Rahul, a concerned citizen, notices that the local government is not following the rules and regulations. He wants to take action. Which organ of the government Rahul should he approach ?**
3. **What is meant by a system of checks and balances?**
4. **A group of students are divided on the matter of selection of class monitors. Which process should they adopt for a fair selection of the monitor with the agreement of whole class?**

Glossary

Governance The process of decision-making, organisation and rule-following to maintain social order.

Government A group of people or system responsible for making and enforcing rules .

Laws Important rules that can be changed or updated as needed.

Nominal In name only, having a title or position without actual authority or power.

Separation of Powers The division of government into three organs to maintain checks and balances.

Checks and Balances A system that ensures each organ of government has some power to limit or check the actions of the other two, preventing any one organ from becoming too powerful.

Democracy A system of government where people vote for representatives to rule on their behalf.

Elections The process of voting for representatives to make decisions on behalf of the people.

GOVERNANCE

Rules and Governance
- Simple rules at home, school, traffic and employers
- Governance: decision-making, organisation, and rule-following

Separation of Powers
- Each organ keeps a check on the other two organs
- Maintains checks and balances

Three Levels of Government
- Local, State/Regional, National
- Each level deals with different matters

Three Organs of Government
- Legislature: makes new laws
- Executive: implements laws
- Judiciary: interprets laws and ensures justice

Community Life
- Disagreements disorder
- Need for rules

Government
- Group of people/system responsible for making and enforcing rules
- Three organs: Legislature, Executive and Judiciary

Democracy
- Rule of the people
- Derived from Greek words 'Demos' (people) and 'Kratos' (rule/power).

Types of Democracy
- Representative democracy
- People vote for representatives
- Representatives rule on behalf of the people

Voting Process
- Options are presented
- Each person chooses their preferred option by voting
- Option with the most votes wins

Representative Democracy in India
- India is a representative democracy
- Citizens above 18 years can participate in elections
- Elected representatives: MLAs (state level) and MPs (national level)

Direct Democracy
- Every person's opinion is heard and counted
- Example: volting for school picnic

Grassroots Democracy
- Ordinary citizens participate in decision-making
- Gives people a voice in decisions affecting their lives

NCERT FOLDER

Detailed Answers of All NCERT Questions

Let's Explore (Page 150)

Q.1 Describe the two pictures given below. What difference does you see between them?

Ans. The two pictures are described below.

Picture 1

This is a well managed picture of a crossroad. We can see people moving systematically in the picture. There are two traffic lights on the opposite side of the road to guide the traffic.

No parking area has been highlighted through a cross sign. No vehicle is parked on the road. Zebra lines on the road are clear. People are walking on the footpath safely. A man riding a bike on the road can be seen wearing a helmet.

Picture 2

This is the sight of a chaotic road. There are no rules for people moving on the road. People can be seen walking in the middle of the road, while vehicles are moving on the footpath. People are not following any safety measures. They can be seen sitting on the top of the vehicle, on the window of the car and also on the bonnet of the vehicles. No person riding a two wheeler is wearing a helmet. There are no traffic lights, nor any Zebra crossing.

Difference between the two pictures

We can clearly see that the people in the first picture are obeying the traffic rules while the people in the second picture are not following any rules. This has led to a chaotic situation on the road in the second picture. This shows that following proper rules can prevent such chaotic situations in our day to day lives.

Q. 2 How do you connect the images given in question 1 with our discussion on rules?

Ans. Rules are made to maintain order and harmony in the society. We can clearly see the contrasting situations in both the pictures. The road in picture 1 is functioning so well just because people are seriously obeying the rules. If no one follows these rules, the situation can become just like shown in picture 2. Hence , society would not be able to function without rules.

Q. 3 What are some of the rules in your school? Who made them?

Ans. Some of the rules in my school are as follows

- Come school on time
- Follow a timetable everyday for classes
- Eat lunch only during the lunch time
- Make a decent hairstyle in school
- Wear only school uniform during school time

Most of these rules are decided by the school administration while some of them are also made by the principal or the class teacher.

Let's Explore (Page 153)

Q.4 Can you identify the categories of public service or other activities that are represented in the images below?

Ans. Yes, the following public service and other activities are represented in these ten pictures .

1. Road construction
2. Rail transport
3. Soldiers on duty
4. A doctor checking on a patient
5. Firefighters rescuing an injured man
6. Traffic police administering the traffic
7. The Supreme Court of India
8. A teacher teaching in a classroom
9. A postman
10. A bank with questions of people

Q.5 What role do you think the government plays in each of these activities?

Ans. The government plays an important role in these activities by ensuring that everyone gets access to these services in a cost effective manner. The government runs hospitals, schools, post offices and banks , trains, soldiers and police officers, builds and repairs roads and also runs trains for the citizens.

Q.6 Can you think of other aspects of your daily life where the government plays an important role?

Ans. The other aspects of our daily life where the government plays an important role are as follows

- By collecting garbage daily from our home
- By installing streetlights
- By running public buses
- By constructing public toilets
- By constructing and maintaining public parks, etc.

Let's Explore (Page 154)

Q.7 Explain how the three government organs are at work in the case of the cyber criminals.

Ans. The three government organs work in the following ways to prevent and control such criminals

- **Legislature** Government or legislature passed a new law to deal with cybercrimes.
- **Executive** The executive organ or the cyber police implemented the law against cyber criminals by arresting them.
- **Judiciary** The judiciary or the court examined the case, convicted the criminals and passed a hail sentence for them.

Let's Explore (Page 155)

Q.8 As a class activity, can you imagine the sort of disorder we might witness if all three organs were under the control of the same group of people? Can you describe any such real-life situation you may have heard of?

Ans. Let's imagine a scenario where one person or group is in charge of making laws, enforcing laws and judging laws. It would be like having one person as the teacher, principal and parent all at once!

If this happened, the following could happen

- Unfair rules that benefit only the person incharge
- No one to stop the person incharge from doing something wrong
- People being treated unfairly or bullied

Hence, if all three organs were under the control of the same group of people a sort of disorder might be created. A real-life example is a country called North Korea. Their leader, Kim Jong-un, has complete control over the government, military and courts. This means he can make laws, enforce them and judge people all by himself. Here, a single person has all the authority, making it difficult for people to speak up or disagree. The people in the country can do nothing against his will and they have no freedom and rights. Separate branches of government helps keep everyone in check and ensures fair treatment for all.

Let's Explore (Page 156)

Q.9 Observe the table given below. Highlight the functions and responsibilities that affect your life the most.

	All India	State Level
Judiciary	Supreme Court of India	High Court
	National Level	**State Level**
Legislature	Two houses–Lok Sabha and Rajya Sabha–formulate national laws	One State Assembly or Vidhan Sabha (Note that most States have a single assembly, a few State have two)
	Central Government	**State Government**
Executive	Led by the President of India (nominal head and Supreme Commander of the Indian Armed Forces), Prime Minister as the executive head	Led by the Governnor (nominal head), Chief Minister as the executive head
Functions and Responsibilities of the Executive (the list is not exhaustive)	• Defence • Foreign Affairs • Atomic Energy • Communications • Currency • Interstate Commerce • Education • Formulation of National Policies	• Police, law and order • Adaptation and Implementation of laws made by the Central Government at the State Level • Public Health • Education • Agriculture • Irrigation • Local Government

Ans. The functions and responsibilities that affects our life are

- **Defence** The defence forces of our country provides security to us so that we can live a peaceful life.
- **Communications** We are connected to the distant world through various communication means such as television, telephone, internet, etc.
- **Currency** It facilitates our day to day transaction in the market.
- **Education** This is very important aspect of our life, as without education our life would be so difficult and directionless.
- **Police, Law and Order** It helps to maintain a peaceful society by preventing any sort of disorder.
- **Public Health** Cheap and affordable public health facilities are very beneficial in the life of a common man.

Q.10 Ask two or three adults about their connection or interaction with the government at what levels does it take place and for what purpose?

Ans. I asked three adults in India about how they interact with the government as follows

(i) Ramesh, who runs a shop, talks to local officials to pay taxes and get permissions.

(ii) Smita, a teacher works with the state government for school things and pays taxes to the Central government.

(iii) Raj, a farmer, meets with local leaders for village development, state officials for farming help and Central government for insurance.

They interact with the government to

- Get help with local things like roads and water.
- Get services like education and healthcare.
- Follow national rules and get benefits like insurance.

Questions, Activities and Projects

Q.1 Test yourself-What is the meaning of democracy? What is the difference between direct democracy and representative democracy?

Ans. Democracy means 'rule of the people'. It's a system where people choose their representatives to make decisions on their behalf.

Difference between direct democracy and representative democracy are as follows

Direct democracy	Representative democracy
Every person's opinion is heard and counted to make a decision.	People vote for representatives who make decisions on their behalf.
Example Voting for a picnic spot in school.	**Example** Voting for MLAs or MPs in India.

Q.2 Recall the three organs of government. What are their different roles?

Ans. The three organs of government are the Legislature, the Executive and the Judiciary. Their roles are as follows

(i) The Legislature (Law making)
- Makes new laws
- Updates or removes existing laws
- Composed of representatives elected by the people.

(ii) The Executive(Law enforcement)
- Implements laws
- Enforces law and order
- Includes authorities like the head of state, ministers, police and other agencies.

(iii) The Judiciary (Law interpretation)
- Decides if laws have been broken
- Determines punishment for breaking laws
- Examines the correctness of executive decisions and fairness of laws.

Q.3 Why do we need three tiers of government?

Ans. A government is like a team that solve problems and makes decisions for our country, state and local area. We need three tiers of government because each tier deals with different matters helping in better administration. These are as follows

- **Local Government** They take care of small problems in our village or town, like fixing streetlights or keeping our local parks clean.
- **State Government** They help with bigger problems that affect many villages or towns, like building roads or supporting schools in the state.
- **National Government** They make big decisions and help with huge problems that affect the whole country, like natural disasters or national security.

Q.4 Project: Many of you will remember the lockdown that took place during the COVID-19 pandemic. Make a list of all the actions that were taken at that time? Which tiers of government were involved in managing the situation? What was the role of each of the organs of government?

Ans. The actions that were taken during the COVID-19 pandemic lockdown were as follows

- Everyone had to stay at home.
- Schools and colleges were closed.
- No buses, trains or autos were allowed.
- No parties or gatherings were allowed.
- Only essential shops like grocery stores were open.
- Doctors and nurses worked hard to help sick people.
- We had to wear masks and use sanitisers.
- Vaccines were given to protect us.
- The tiers of government involved in managing the situation were Central government (like the Prime Minister and his team) State governments (like the Chief Minister and his team) Local governments (like the Mayor and his team).

The role played by each organ of the government during the lockdown were as follows

Legislature

Lawmakers made new rules to keep us safe. It gave money to help people who lost their jobs.

Executive

Central government told everyone to stay at home. It helped states and local governments and made sure hospitals had what they needed.

State governments made sure people followed the rules. It helped local governments and made sure hospitals had what they needed.

Local governments made sure people followed the rules and helped hospitals and doctors.

Judiciary

Courts made sure the government was being fair. It helped solve problems related to the lockdown.

REVIEW EXERCISE

Including Competency Based Questions

Part-I

Very Short Answer Type Questions

1. Mention the significant role of the executive organ of the government?

Ans. The executive branch of government has a crucial role in enforcing laws and keeping the country safe by maintaining law and order. It carries out government policies, protects citizens and oversees government programme.

2. What significant role does the local government play?

Ans. Local governments address local issues, providing essential services and making decisions that impact the community. They are closest to the people, understanding their needs and ensuring effective governance.

3. What is the scope of power of the Central government?

Ans. The Central government deals with matters affecting vast areas, setting policies, laws and regulations that have far-reaching impacts. It addresses larger issues like national security, foreign policy and economic development, ensuring national interests and unity.

4. What is the motto of the government of India?

Ans. The motto of the government of India is "Satyameva Jayate" (Truth alone triumphs). It emphasises truth, honesty and integrity in governance. It guides the government to ensure transparency, accountability and fairness in actions and decisions.

5. How do people participate in democracy?

Ans. Citizens participate in democracy by voting for representatives, exercising their right to choose leaders who represent their interests. Participation goes beyond voting, including public debates, expressing opinions and holding elected representatives accountable.

6. What is the core principle of representative democracy?

Ans. Representative democracy is a system where citizens elect representatives to make decisions on their behalf.

7. How does grassroots democracy differ from traditional democracy?

Ans. Grassroots democracy empowers ordinary citizens to participate directly in decision-making, unlike traditional democracy where citizens elect representatives to make decisions for them. This approach leads to inclusivity, transparency and accountability, enabling citizens to contribute to policy-making and drive change.

8. What are the key responsibilities of the Prime Minister?

Ans. The Prime Minister is the executive head of the Central government. He is responsible for executing decisions, leading the Council of Ministers and representing the nation internationally. They provide strategic direction, advise the President and ensure accountability.

9. How are representatives elected in India?

Ans. In India, representatives are elected through a democratic process where citizens vote at both state and national levels to choose their leaders.

Short Answer Type Questions

1. What is the difference between government and governance?

Ans.

Government	Governance
The group or system that makes and enforces rules and laws.	The process of making decisions, organising society, and ensuring rules are followed.
Involves officials and institutions.	It involves government, civil society and private sectors.

2. What are the key functions of the judiciary?

Ans. The judiciary plays a vital role in upholding the rule of law, ensuring justice and protecting citizens' rights.

The key functions of judiciary are

- Interpretation of laws.
- Taking decision on cases.
- Determining guilt or innocence.
- Reviewing executive decisions.
- Examining legislative actions.

The judiciary provides a platform for resolving disputes, addressing grievances and promoting fairness. It ensures that the legal system serves the greater good, maintains social order and holds the government accountable.

3. What is the significance of the Supreme Court's motto?

Ans. The Supreme Court's motto is *"Yato Dharmastato Jayah"* where there is dharma, there is victory. This motto is significant as

- It emphasises the importance of justice, fairness, morality, ethics and constitutional values.
- It reflects the court's commitment to upholding the principles of justice, ensuring that the legal system serves the greater good and promoting social justice.
- It reminds the judiciary to remain impartial, independent and accountable.

4. How do citizens participate in the democratic process and what role do representatives play in this system? How representative democracy is implemented in India?

Ans. Citizens participate in democracy by voting, engaging in public debates, contacting representatives, joining political parties or organisations and exercising their right to free speech.

Representatives play a crucial role by representing citizens' interests, making informed decisions, holding the government accountable and facilitating communication between citizens and government.

In India, representative democracy is implemented through periodic elections, Universal Adult Franchise, reservation of seats for marginalised groups and decentralisation of power to local governments. This ensures that citizens' voices are heard and their interests are represented.

5. Direct democracy embodies the principle of "by the people, for the people". Explain with an example of direct democracy in action.

Ans. Direct democracy is a system where every individual's opinion is heard and counted to make a decision, ensuring direct participation and equal influence. This contrasts with representative democracy, where elected representatives make decisions on behalf of the people.

In direct democracy, citizens engage actively, voting on policies, laws or decisions, fostering inclusivity and accountability.

A simple example of direct democracy is choosing a picnic spot for a school picnic, where each student votes between two options, and the majority choice prevails.

This approach ensures collective ownership and empowers citizens, promoting transparency and legitimacy. Direct democracy thus embodies the principle of "by the people, for the people".

6. Why is voting important in a democratic system and what impact does it have on the country's future?

Ans. Voting is crucial in a democratic system as it allows citizens to have a direct say in decisions, ensuring their voices are heard and counted. Voting enables people to choose representatives, shape policy directions and influence the country's trajectory. It holds leaders accountable, ensures representation of diverse perspectives and promotes democratic legitimacy. By exercising their right to vote, citizens contribute to a healthy democracy, shaping their collective future.

Voting impacts the country's future by determining policy directions, resource allocation and protection of rights, ultimately shaping the nation's destiny.

Long Answer Type Questions

1. Why is it essential for individuals to follow rules and what would happen if no one followed these rules in a society?

Ans. Following rules is crucial for maintaining social order, harmony and stability. Rules provide a framework for behaviour, ensuring safety, promoting cooperation and enabling individuals to coexist peacefully. Rules impact daily life in various spheres, guiding actions and decisions. By following rules, individuals contribute to the greater good, fostering responsibility, respect and trust within the community. This promotes a sense of belonging, social cohesion and collective well-being. Moreover, rules protect individual rights, prevent exploitation and ensure fair treatment.

If no one followed rules, society would descend into chaos, disorder and harmful situations.

Confusion, conflicts and unpredictability would prevail, making it challenging for individuals to live and work together. Without rules, society would struggle to function and progress would be hindered.

2. Governance, government and laws relate to each other. Examine the statement.

Ans. Governance, government and laws are interconnected and relate to each other. Governance is the overall process of decision-making and implementation of laws within a society. It includes the methods in which power is exercised by the government in power, resources are allocated and how various institutions interact to maintain order and promote the common good.

Government is the authority to make and enforce laws within a society. It consists of different branches (executive, legislative, and judicial) and is responsible for creating policies, administering public services and ensuring security and justice. It is also accountable to the people and the legislature.

Laws are the rules and regulations established by the government that guide behaviour and maintain order within society. Laws are created through the legislative process, enforced by the executive branch and interpreted by the judiciary.

Thus, governance provides the framework within which the government operates. The government creates and enforces laws which are the instruments through which governance objectives are achieved.

3. How do the three organs of government work together, and what is the significance of separation of powers in maintaining a good system of governance?

Ans. The legislature, executive and judiciary work together to maintain social order and harmony. The legislature passes laws, the executive enforces them and the judiciary interprets and adjudicates.

Separation of powers prevents any one organ from becoming too powerful, ensuring checks and balances. This division promotes accountability, transparency and good governance, safeguarding individual rights and preventing abuse of authority. Separation of powers leads to collaboration, coordination and healthy competition among organs, ensuring effective governance and protecting democratic values. Additionally, it prevents tyranny, ensures due process and promotes judicial independence. This balance of power enables each organ to perform its functions efficiently, maintaining the rule of law and upholding the Constitution.

4. What are the three levels of government in India, and how do they deal with different matters?

Ans. India's governance structure comprises local, state/regional and national levels, each addressing distinct matters. Local authorities manage local issues like municipal services, community development and public health.

State governments handle matters involving several towns and villages, including law and order, education, healthcare and agriculture. The Central government addresses matters affecting vast areas, such as defense, foreign affairs, national policies and interstate commerce. This division ensures effective governance, enabling each level to focus on specific needs and priorities, promoting decentralised decision-making and regional development. Moreover, it facilitates coordination and cooperation among levels, ensuring a unified approach to national development.

5. The functions and responsibilities of the executive at the national and state levels in India contribute to governance. Explain.

Ans. The national executive oversees critical areas like defense, foreign affairs, atomic energy, communications, currency, interstate commerce, education and national policy formulation. The state executive manages police, law and order, adaptation and implementation of central laws, public health, education, agriculture, irrigation and local government.

These functions enable the executive to contribute to governance by ensuring effective policy implementation, promoting citizen welfare and maintaining social order. The executive's responsibilities foster economic development, social justice and human well-being, contributing to India's growth and prosperity. Additionally, the executive ensures coordination among various departments, implements development programme and responds to emergencies, making it a crucial component of governance.

Part-II

Multiple Choice Questions (MCQs)

1. What is the consequence of not following rules in a society?

(a) Harmony and order (b) Disorder and chaos
(c) No impact (d) Benefits for all

2. Which organ of the government has the power to update or remove existing laws?

(a) The Executive (b) The Legislature
(c) The Judiciary (d) The Head of State

3. What is the purpose of the judiciary in examining the decisions taken by the executive?

(a) To support the executive
(b) To oppose the executive
(c) To ensure the correctness of the decisions
(d) To ignore the decisions

4. How do the three organs of government address a new form of criminal activity like cybercrime?

(a) They ignore it (b) They work independently
(c) They work together (d) They blame each other

5. What is the significance of the motto "Satyameva Jayate"?

(a) It emphasises the importance of victory
(b) It highlights the power of truth
(c) It promotes the idea of Dharma
(d) It encourages the pursuit of wealth

6. Who is the executive head of the State government in India?

(a) Chief Minister (b) Governor
(c) Prime Minister (d) President

7. Which of the following is a function of the Central government?

(a) Police, law and order (b) Education
(c) Defence and foreign affairs (d) Local government

8. What was Dr APJ Abdul Kalam's contribution to India's development?

(a) He was a renowned economist
(b) He was a celebrated artist
(c) He played a crucial role in India's space and missile programme
(d) He was a prominent politician

9. What is the process of voting in a democracy?

(a) Options are presented and the majority decides.
(b) Options are presented and each person chooses their preferred option.
(c) Options are presented and the government decides
(d) Options are presented and only the elected representatives decide

10. What is a key feature of India's democratic system?

(a) Only the majority gets to decide
(b) Only the government gets to decide
(c) All citizens above 18 have the right to participate in elections
(d) Only elected representatives get to decide

Answers

1. (b)	2. (b)	3. (c)	4. (c)	5. (b)
6. (a)	7. (c)	8. (c)	9. (b)	10. (c)

Fill in the Blanks

1. Governance is the process of taking .... and organising social life with different sets of rules.
2. .... are some of the more important rules that can be changed or updated as needed.
3. The State government is responsible for matters such as education, agriculture and ....
4. The .... is responsible for the administration of the state government.
5. The word 'democracy' is derived from two Greek words, 'demos' meaning .... and 'kratos' meaning 'rule' or 'power'.
6. ...... are elected representatives at the national level.

Ans. 1. decisions 2. Laws
3. irrigation 4. Chief Minister
5. people 6. Members of Parliament (MPs)

True or False

1. The government is responsible for making rules but not ensuring that they are followed.
2. The three organs of government work independently of each other.
3. The executive branch includes the head of state, ministers and agencies responsible for maintaining law and order.
4. The Central government is responsible for public health and agriculture.
5. The President is the Supreme Commander of the Indian Armed Forces.
6. Democracy means the rule of a king or queen.
7. Voting is a way to make decisions where only a few people get a say.
8. Grassroots democracy empowers only the educated citizens to participate in decision-making processes.

Ans. 1. False 2. False 3. True 4. False 5. True 6. False 7. False 8. False

Match the Following

1.

List I (Executive)	List II (Function)
A. Chief Minister	1. The nominal head of the Central Government
B. Governor	2. The executive head of the Central Government
C. Prime Minister	3. The head of the State Government
D. President of India	4. The executive head of the State Government.

Codes

	A	B	C	D		A	B	C	D
(a)	2	3	4	1	(b)	4	3	2	1
(c)	3	2	1	4	(d)	4	1	2	3

2.

List I (Terms)	List II (Meaning)
A. Direct Democracy	1. The process used by representatives to convince each other in case of different opinions.
B. Election	2. A way to make decisions where everyone gets a say.
C. Dialogue and Debate	3. A system where every person's opinion is heard and counted.
D. Voting	4. The process through which representatives are chosen.

Codes

	A	B	C	D		A	B	C	D
(a)	2	3	1	4	(b)	4	3	2	1
(c)	3	4	1	2	(d)	4	1	2	3

Ans. 1. (b) 2. (a)

Assertion-Reason

1. **Assertion** (A) The Lok Sabha and Rajya Sabha are the two houses of the national legislature.
   Reason (R) The Lok Sabha is the upper house of the national legislature.
   Codes
   (a) Both A and R are true and R is the correct explanation of A
   (b) Both A and R are true, but R is not the correct explanation of A
   (c) A is true, but R is false
   (d) A is false, but R is true
2. **Assertion** (A) The executive head of the Central government is the President.
   Reason (R) The President has the power to make laws.
   Codes
   (a) Both A and R are true and R is the correct explanation of A
   (b) Both A and R are true, but R is not the correct explanation of A
   (c) A is true, but R is false
   (d) A is false, but R is true
3. **Assertion** (A) In a democracy, all people rule directly.
   Reason (R) Democracy means the 'rule of the people'.
   Codes
   (a) Both A and R are true and R is the correct explanation of A
   (b) Both A and R are true, but R is not the correct explanation of A.
   (c) A is true, but R is false
   (d) A is false, but R is true
4. **Assertion** (A) Grassroots democracy empowers ordinary citizens to participate in decision-making processes.
   Reason (R) It gives only influential people a voice and a say in decisions.
   Codes
   (a) Both A and R are true and R is the correct explanation of A
   (b) Both A and R are true, but R is not the correct explanation of A
   (c) A is true, but R is false
   (d) A is false, but R is true

Ans. 1. (c) 2. (d) 3. (d) 4. (c)

Case Based Questions

1. Read the source given below and answer the questions that follow.

Born in a humble family in Rameswaram, Tamil Nadu, in 1931, Dr. A P J Abdul Kalam was a renowned scientist, nicknamed the 'Missile Man of India' for his crucial role in the development of India's space programme, missile programme and nuclear capabilities. Dr. Abdul Kalam served as the 11th President of India from 2002 to 2007. Despite his high status, he remained deeply connected to the people, and the youth in particular, through his passion for good education and innovation. He inspired millions with his humility, dedication to social causes and commitment to the nation. He tirelessly encouraged young Indians to dream big and work hard to achieve their goals. Dr. Kalam showed that even though his position as the President of India was nominal, he could play an important role, impacting countless lives.

(i) What value did Dr. Abdul Kalam demonstrate through his connection with the people, especially the youth?

(a) A strong desire for personal recognition and accolades.

(b) Humility and a willingness to serve others despite holding a high position.

(c) A focus on accumulating wealth and material possessions

(d) A tendency to prioritise his own interests over the needs of others.

(ii) What quality enabled Dr. Kalam to inspire millions and make a significant impact on countless lives?

(a) His ability to prioritise his own ambitions and interests above all else.

(b) His unwavering dedication to social causes and commitment to the betterment of society.

(c) His tendency to seek power and control over others.

(d) His focus on personal gain and self-promotion.

(iii) What message did Dr. Kalam convey to the youth through his life and work?

(a) Success comes easily with wealth and status.

(b) Hard work and determination are essential for achieving goals.

(c) Only some people in society can make a difference.

(d) Education is not important for success.

(iv) What was Dr. Kalam's approach towards the youth of India?

(a) He encouraged them to avoid risks.

(b) He motivated them to dream big and work hard.

(c) He focused solely on technical education.

(d) He remained indifferent to their aspirations.

(v) How did Dr. Kalam's humility influence his role as President?

(a) It led to him avoiding public appearances.

(b) It made him more relatable and accessible to the people.

(c) It diminished his influence in political decisions.

(d) It caused him to focus solely on scientific research.

Ans. (i) (b), (ii) (b), (iii) (b), (iv) (b), (v) (b)

2. Read the source given below and answer the questions that follow.

You may have noticed that we earlier mentioned 'representatives of the people'. This is one of the foundation stones of the system of governance adopted by most countries of the world-democracy. The word 'democracy' comes from two Greek words . demos meaning 'people', and kratos meaning 'rule' or 'power'; so 'democracy' literally means the 'rule of the people'. But can all people actually rule? It is clearly not possible. Imagine there is a problem that your class wants to bring to the attention of your school's principal– maybe there is something wrong with the classroom, or with the school's infrastructure, or perhaps you would like to propose a certain date for a field trip. Will the entire class go to the principal? It would clearly not be practical. In many schools, classes have a 'class monitor' or 'class representative', whom the whole class elected; even if there is none, one representative can be selected for this specific purpose. It will be enough to send the representative to the principal.

(i) Why is it impractical for all people to directly participate in decision-making in a democracy?

(ii) How do democratic systems address the challenge of direct participation by all people?

(iii) What is the role of representatives in a democratic system, and how do they facilitate decision-making?

Ans. (i) It is impractical for all people to directly participate in decision-making in a democracy because it would be difficult to manage and make decisions with a large group of people. For instance, in the example of a class wanting to bring a concern to the principal's attention, having the entire class go to the principal would be chaotic and inefficient. It would be hard to ensure everyone's voice is heard, and it would take a lot of time and resources.

(ii) Democratic systems address this challenge by electing representatives who can make decisions or convey concerns on behalf of the larger group. This allows for more efficient decision-making and ensures that everyone's voice is represented. In the class example, electing a class monitor or selecting a representative to go to the principal ensures that the class's concerns are heard without the need for everyone to be present.

(iii) Representatives act as intermediaries between the people and decision-makers. Thus, conveying concerns and ideas and facilitate decision-making. This allows for more effective and efficient decision-making.

Competency Based Questions

1. "India follows the policy of separation of power". What is meant by separation of power?

Ans. Separation of powers means non interference of the three organs of the government in each other's sphere of work. Separation of powers is important between the three organs of the government because it helps to maintain checks and balances among the three organs.

2. Separation of powers is important. Comment.

Ans. Separation of powers is important because

- It prevents abuse of power
- It promotes accountability and ensures effective governance.
- Each organ checks and balances the others, preventing concentration of power.
- It encourages collaboration, safeguards individual rights and freedoms and ensures a smooth functioning of government.
- It also promotes transparency, accountability and responsiveness to citizens' needs.

3. MLAs and MPs play crucial roles in the democratic process. Analyse.

Ans. MLAs (Members of Legislative Assembly) are elected representatives at the state level, responsible for addressing regional issues and concerns. MPs (Members of Parliament) are elected representatives at the national level, responsible for addressing national issues and concerns.

Both MLAs and MPs play crucial roles in the democratic process. They represent citizens' interests, participate in legislative debates and discussions, vote on laws and policies, hold the government accountable and address constituents' concerns. They serve as bridges between citizens and the government, ensuring that voices are heard and represented.

4. Grassroots democracy plays an important role in empowering citizens. Justify the statement.

Ans. Grassroots democracy is a system that empowers ordinary citizens to participate directly in decision-making processes, giving them a voice in decisions affecting their lives.

This approach fosters community engagement, inclusivity and transparency, ensuring diverse perspectives are represented. By empowering citizens, grassroots democracy promotes active citizenship, builds trust in institutions and strengthens democratic foundations. It enables citizens to contribute to policy-making, hold leaders accountable, and drive change from the bottom up, ultimately enhancing democratic governance.

Skill Based Questions as per NEP 2020

1. A student, Rohan, is curious about how laws are made in India. He wants to know who is responsible for making laws and how they are enforced. Explain to Rohan the role of the Legislature and the Executive in lawmaking.

Ans. The Legislature, which consists of elected representatives (MPs and MLAs), is responsible for making laws in India. They discuss, debate and vote on bills in the Parliament or State Assemblies. Once a bill is passed, it becomes a law. The Executive, which includes the President, Prime Minister and other officials, is responsible for enforcing these laws.

The Executive ensures that the laws are implemented and followed by the citizens. In other words, the Legislature makes the laws and the Executive enforces them.

2. Research and given an example of grassroots democracy in action, where ordinary citizens participate in decision-making.

Ans. In Rajasthan, India, Swaraj Abhiyan, an NGO, helped villagers participate in decision-making through Gram Sabhas (village assemblies).

They worked in the following manner

- Villagers met to discuss their needs and priorities.
- They elected representatives to present their ideas.
- The representatives worked with local officials to create a plan.
- Villagers voted on the final plan.

This process helped villagers decide how to spend funds on projects like

- Building roads
- Providing clean water
- Creating schools

This is an example of grassroots democracy in India, where ordinary citizens participated in decision-making and improved their community.

ASSESSMENT EXERCISE

Objective Type Questions

1. Which of the following is true with respect to the relationship between governance and rules?
   (a) Governance is the absence of rules
   (b) Governance is the process of making rules
   (c) Governance is the process of taking decisions and organising social life with different sets of rules
   (d) Governance is the enforcement of rules
2. Separation of powers in governance ensures which of the following ?
   (a) Concentration of power (b) Conflict between organs
   (c) Checks and balances (d) Inefficiency
3. Who are the elected representatives at the state level in India?
   (a) Members of Parliament (MPs)
   (b) Members of Legislative Assembly (MLAs)
   (c) Members of the State Council
   (d) Members of the Local Government
4. What is the result of citizens participating in grassroots democracy?
   (a) They have no participation in decision-making
   (b) They have a limited participation in decision-making
   (c) They have a huge say in decision-making
   (d) They have complete control over decision-making
5. People or citizens have a say in making or changing the .... of their society.
6. In a representative democracy, people vote for their .... through elections.
7. The judiciary is responsible for making new laws. (True/False)
8. The minimum age to participate in elections in India is 21 years. (True/False)

Subjective Questions (VSA, SA & LA)

1. Democracy is the essence of our nation. What is direct democracy?
2. Who is the head of the executive at the national level?
3. What is the minimum age to participate in elections in India?
4. How do local governments address local issues?
5. What is the importance of voting in a democratic system and how does it impact decision-making?
6. Who has the right to participate in Indian democracy and what is the minimum age requirement?
7. What is the role of representatives in the democratic process and what are their responsibilities?
8. Explain the significance of rules in maintaining social order, and how they impact our daily lives in various spheres.
9. What are the roles and responsibilities of the judiciary, legislature and executive at the national and state levels in India?
10. Highlight the importance of the judiciary in the governance process and how does it contribute to upholding the rule of law?
11. Discuss the three organs of government and their respective roles in the governance process.

Local Government in Rural Areas

India is a diverse and vast country. There are around 600,000 villages, 8,000 towns and over 4,000 cities in the country. The population in India is more than 1.4 billion. Around 2/3rd of India's total population lives in rural areas or villages. So there is a need of system for governing such population in the rural areas.

- There are many governance related issues that arise in villages. These are as follows
  - Requirement of water for irrigation
  - Maintenance of damaged roads
  - Maintenance of village primary school
  - Land disputes and theft of crops
  - Many other issues related to day-to-day lives of the villagers.
- All the above issues cannot be taken to the state or national level for its resolution. Hence, governance at the local level is important.

11.1 Panchayati Raj System

- Panchayat' refers to a village council. It is a system of **local government** which brings governance closer to people.
- The system of Panchayat makes it possible for the people to actively participate in the decision-making processes. Thus, the Panchayat system, also known as **Panchayati Raj**, is a form of **self government**.
- Panchayats play an important role in taking care of local issues and promoting development. It ensures that the benefit of the government schemes reach to the people at grassroots level (community level).

Three-tier System of Panchayati Raj

The Panchayati Raj system operates on three levels, the village level at the bottom, the block level and the district level. This system is known as the three-tier system. The three levels are as follows

(i) **Village level** It consists of Gram Panchayat or Village Parishad.

(ii) **Block level** It consists of Block Panchayat/Panchayat Samiti / Mandal Parishad.

(iii) **District level** It consists of District Panchayat / Zila Parishad.

- These institutions together are responsible for almost all aspects of life in the district. This includes agriculture, housing, maintenance of roads, management of water resources, education, healthcare, social welfare and cultural activities.
- Special rules have been framed for each of the three levels of local government so that disadvantaged sections of the population can present their needs and problems. These institutions also reserve one-third of the seats for women.
- The structure and functions of the Panchayati Raj institutions differ across the states because states have authority over these institutions.

  However, they have the same objective of enabling villagers to take an active part in the management and development of their villages and local areas.

Gram Panchayat

- This is the **lowest level** of the three-tier system. This is closest to the people in rural areas. The members of the Gram Panchayat are elected directly by the **Gram Sabha**.
- The Gram Sabha is a group of adults from a village or a group of neighbouring villages who are enrolled as voters. In the Gram Sabha, people discuss all matters related to their area and make decisions.
- Each Gram sabha has an **elected head** or President called the **Sarpanch** or **Pradhan**. In recent years more women have become Sarpanchs.
- The Gram Panchayat is assisted by two officers which are as follows

  (i) **Panchayat Secretary** He performs administrative **functions** like calling meetings and maintaining records.

(ii) **Patwari** He maintains land records of the villagers. In some cases, he also keeps years old maps for future use.

Some Remarkable Sarpanchs

- **Dnyaneshwar Kamble** Kamble is a trans-gender person who became sarpanch of the Tarangfal village in the Solapur district of Maharashtra in 2017. Kamble defeated six other candidates to become Sarpanch. Kamble's motto is 'lok seva, gram seva' which means 'service to the village is service to the public'.
- **Vandana Bahadur Maida** She is a member of the Bhil community from Khankhandvi village in Madhya Pradesh. She challenged patriarchal norms to become the first female sarpanch of her village. She earned recognition by addressing important issues like education, sanitation and motivated women in the village to participate in sabha meetings. Her journey reflects how women can participate in the transformation of rural India.
- **Popatrao Baguji Pawar** Popatrao was a Sarpanch of Hiware bazar village in Ahmednagar district of Maharashtra which used to be affected by frequent droughts and poor agricultural yield. The Sarpanch applied Anna Hazare's model of rainwater harvesting, watershed conservation and massive tree plantation. His efforts along with the support of villagers led to the recharge of groundwater. Soon, this village became green and prosperous . Shri Popatrao Pawar was awarded with Padma Shri in 2020.

Child-friendly Panchayat Initiative

- Panchayats are meant to address the concerns of everyone including children. Child-friendly Panchayat initiative enables the children to express their ideas and opinions on matters that affect their well-being.
- Several states have taken initiative to encourage the participation of children in **Bal Sabhas** and **Bal Panchayats** on a regular basis. Village elders on the other hand try to resolve their issues in these sabhas.
- An example of **Bal Panchayat** is in **Maharashtra** which have worked to
  - eliminate child labour and child marriage.
  - bring many children back to school.
  - stop marriages of girls who are in their educational age.
- Several Gram Panchayats have won awards for taking child friendly initiatives, e.g., the **Sangkhu Radhu Khandu Gram Panchayat** in West Sikkim. It has taken following steps to address the child's needs and rights due to which it has been declared a child friendly Gram Panchayat
  - It has built compound walls for schools to make them safer for children.
  - It has constructed kitchens in the schools to ensure hygienically cooked mid-day meals for students.

Children's Parliament Initiative in Rajasthan

- This initiative is an result of Bunkers Roy' **Barefoot College initiative'**. In this initiative, underprivileged children in the rural areas of Rajasthan were empowered through education and democratic participation.
- Night schools and Parliament-like elections were conducted for children aged 8-14, to involve them in the governance process, learn about democracy and social responsibility.
- Formal procedures like voter-ID cards, campaigning, etc were followed in these parliaments.
- A cabinet formed by the elected representatives was then given the responsibility of overseeing school management and advocating for community needs.
- This initiative enabled the children to develop leadership skills and become socially aware.
- This initiative can enable them to challenge norms of society and demand for change. Children learned to address issues such as education, sanitation, social equality and contributing to community development.
- This initiative received many awards including the **World's Children's Honorary Award** in 2001.

Panchayat Samiti and Zila Parishad

- The institutions at the **block level** is known as Panchayati Samiti, and at the **district level** is known as Zila Parishad.
- The members of both these institutions are elected by local people but they may also have other members like Sarpanchs of the villages in the area and local members of the State Legislative Assembly.

Role of Panchayat Samiti

- Panchayat Samiti forms a link between the Gram Panchayats and Zila Parishad. Its composition differs from state to state but its basic role in strengthening the participation of local people remains the same.
- Panchayat Samiti co-ordinates between Gram Panchayats. For example, it collects development plans from all the Gram Panchayats and then puts them together to present them at the district or state levels.

- The task of co-ordination of Panchayat Samiti facilitates the allotment of funds for development projects and government schemes. One such scheme is **Pradhan Mantri Gram Sadak Yojana** which promotes the construction of all-weather roads in rural areas.

Administrative Structure in Kautilya's Arthshastra

Arthshastra is an ancient text of governance written by Kautilya around 2300 years ago. It describes the following

- the structure of the state
- how the economy can be made prosperous.
- duties of the ruler
- how to conduct of war

Kautilya was an expert in statecraft . He has explained the whole administrative structure from the village to the regional capital. He mentioned the establishment of 4 headquarters by the king as follows

(i) **Sangrahana** A sub-district headquarters for every 10 villages.

(ii) **Karvatika** District headquarters for every 100 villages

(iii) **Dronamukha** A headquarters for every 400 villages

(iv) **Sthaniya** Provincial headquarters for every 800 villages.

Try These

1. What proportion of India's population lives in rural areas?

2. Priya went with her grandmother to the Gram Panchayat in her village. She noticed that the Sarpanch was the head of the meeting. How is a Sarpanch chosen?

3. Name the institution that forms a link between Gram Panchayats and Zila Parishad.

4. Recent years have seen the success stories of several women Sarpanchs. What proportion of seats is reserved for women in Panchayati Raj institutions?

Glossary

Panchayat A village council or local government body.

Panchayati Raj A system of local self-government in India.

Gram Panchayat The bottommost level of the Panchayati Raj system, responsible for village-level governance.

Gram Sabha A group of adults from a village or neighbouring villages who are enrolled as voters.

Sarpanch/Pradhan The elected head of the Gram Panchayat.

Panchayat Secretary An officer who performs administrative functions for the Gram Panchayat.

Patwari An officer responsible for maintaining land records in the village.

Child-Friendly Panchayat Initiative An initiative to involve children in the decision-making process at the local level.

Bal Sabhas and Bal Panchayats Forums for children to express their ideas and opinions on matters affecting them.

Panchayat Samiti The block-level institution responsible for co-ordinating between Gram Panchayats and Zila Parishad.

Zila Parishad The district-level institution responsible for overseeing development projects and government schemes.

Kautilya's Arthshastra An ancient text on governance that describes the structure of the state, economy and administrative structure.

Resolution It is the process of solving a problem.

Gram Panchayat Assistance
- Panchayat Secretary (Administrative functions)
- Patwari (maintains land records and old maps)

Gram Sabha
- Groups of adult voters from village or neighbouring villages
- Discusses and decides on local matters
- Elected head: Sarpanch or Pradhan

Exemplary Sarpanchs
- Dnyaneshwar Kamble (transgender)
- Vandana Bahadur Maida (first female Sarpanch)
- Popatrao Baguji Pawar (applied Anna Hazare's model)

Gram Panchayat
- Bottom-most level of three-tier system
- Members elected by Gram Sabha

Three-Tier System
- Village Level Gram Panchayat/ Village Parishad
- Block Level-Block Panchayat/ Panchayat Samiti/Mandal Parishad
- District Level-District Panchayat/ Zila Parishad

Governance Issues in Villages
- Water requirement for irrigation
- Damaged road maintenance
- Village primary school maintenance
- Land disputes
- Crop theft
- Day-to-day life issues

Panchayati Raj System
- Local Government System
- Brings governance closer to people
- Self-government
- Active participation in decision-making

LOCAL GOVERNMENT IN RURAL AREAS

Children's Parliament Initiative (Rajasthan)
- Empowers underprivileged children through education and democratic participation
- Addresses issues: education, sanitation, social equality, community development
- Won World's Children's Honorary Award in 2001

Panchayat Samiti and Zila Parishad
- Institutions above village level
- Block level: Panchayat Samiti
- District level: Zila Parishad
- Members:
  - Elected by local people
  - Sarpanchs of villages
  - Local members of State Legislative Assembly

Administrative Structure in Kautilya's Arthshastra
- Establishes 4 headquarters
  - (i) Sangrahana (sub-district)
  - (ii) Karvatika (district)
  - (iii) Dronamukha (regional)
  - (iv) Sthaniya (provincial)

Role of Panchayat Samiti
- Links Gram Panchayats and Zila Parishad
- Coordinates between Gram Panchayats
- Collects development plans
- Presents plans to district/state levels

Child Friendly Panchayat Initiative
- Addresses concerns of children
- Enables children to express ideas and opinions
- Bal Sabhas and Bal Panchayats for children's participation

NCERT FOLDER

Detailed Answers of All NCERT Questions

Think About It (Page 150)

Q.1 How do you think can the old maps used by Patwari be helpful for us? Can they tell us something about the past and the present?

Ans. Old maps kept by the village Patwari can be helpful in the following ways

- showing land use changes over time
- revealing village expansion or shrinkage
- locating traditional water sources
- resolving boundary disputes
- tracking infrastructure development
- identifying environmental changes
- preserving cultural heritage
- understanding demographic changes

These maps provide insights into the village's past, helping us understand the present and make informed decisions for the future.

Let's Explore (Page 169)

Q.2 As a class activity, let four or five students form a Bal Panchayat and the rest of the class imagine they are the villagers. What issues will the Gram Sabha discuss? What challenges could it encounter? What solutions will it propose?

Ans. Gram Sabha can discuss following issues

- Lack of clean drinking water
- Poor condition of village roads
- Insufficient electricity supply
- Need for a new school building
- Waste management issues

Challenges that may be encountered by the panchayat are as follows

- Limited funds
- Resistance from some villagers to change
- Lack of co-operation from local authorities
- Limited resources and expertise
- Balancing individual interests with collective needs

Some of the solutions proposed at the panchayat were as follows

- **Clean drinking water** Install new water pumps and pipes and implement rainwater harvesting systems.
- **Village roads** Repair and maintain existing roads and build new roads to connect remote areas.
- **Electricity supply** Install solar panels or wind turbines and upgrade existing power infrastructure.
- **New school building** Raise funds through donations and grants and collaborate with local authorities for support.
- **Waste management** Implement recycling programs and build a community composting facility.

Bal Panchayat's role is as follows

- Facilitate discussion and decision-making
- Allocate tasks and responsibilities
- Manage funds and resources
- Co-ordinate with local authorities and experts
- Ensure transparency and accountability

Think About It (Page 170)

Q.3 Why do you think it is important for the government to pay more attention to the needs and problems of the disadvantaged sections of society?

Ans. The government should pay more attention to the needs of disadvantaged groups because

- they are often left out and ignored.
- they face big obstacles that prevent them from getting basic rights and opportunities.
- they are more likely to be poor and treated unfairly.
- helping them can break cycles of poverty and inequality.
- it's a matter of fairness and human rights.
- it can benefit everyone and help the economy grow.
- disadvantaged groups have unique experiences that can help improve decision-making.

By focusing on their needs, the government can create a fairer and more just society.

Let's Explore (Page 170)

Q.4 What similarities and differences do you notice between the governance system at the Central level and at the Panchayat level? (Hint: refer back to Chapter 10 if required.)

Ans. The similarities between the governance system at the Central and Panchayat levels are as follows

- Both have leaders who are chosen by people. (For Ex- MPs in central level and Panchayat members at Panchayat levels).
- Both have a system to make sure everyone works together and follows rules.

- Both want to help people and make their lives better.
- Both levels hold meetings for discussions of the issues.

The differences between the governance system at the Central and Panchayat levels are as follows

- The Central government governs a vast area while the local government governs only the local area.
- The Central government has more power and money than the Panchayat government.
- The Central government makes decisions for the whole country, while Panchayat government makes decisions for a small area.
- The Central government is answerable to the whole country, while Panchayat government is answerable to the people in their small area.
- There are two heads at Central level (President and Prime Minister) while only one head (Sarpanch) at local level.

Q.5 If you get an opportunity to meet a few Panchayat members, what questions would you like to ask them? Discuss in small groups to create a questionnaire. Meet some Gram Panchayat members or invite them to your school. Ask them the questions in your questionnaire and write a short report.

Ans. If I get an opportunity to meet a few Panchayat members, I would ask the following questions

- What inspired you to become a Panchayat member?
- What are the biggest challenges you face in your role?
- How do you ensure everyone's voice is heard in decision-making?
- What initiatives have you taken to improve Our village/town?
- How do you balance individual interests with the greater good?
- What role do you think youth can play in community development?
- How can we, as students, contribute to the Panchayat's efforts?
- What message would you like to share with our school community?

Short Report

We met with three Gram Panchayat members, Mr. Kumar, Ms. Devi and Mr. Patel and asked them the questions from our questionnaire. Here's what we learned

- They became Panchayat members to serve their community and make a positive impact.
- Challenges they face include limited resources, conflicting opinions and ensuring everyone's participation.
- They ensure everyone's voice is heard by conducting regular meetings and encouraging open discussion.
- Initiatives they've taken include building new roads, improving healthcare facilities and promoting education.
- They balance individual interests with the greater good by prioritising community needs and seeking expert advice.
- They believe youth can play a vital role in community development by bringing new ideas and enthusiasm.
- We, as students, can contribute by participating in Panchayat meetings, volunteering for community projects and spreading awareness about important issues.
- Their message to our school community is to become active citizens, work together and strive for the betterment of our community.

Questions, Activities and Projects

Q.1 Test yourself–without looking at the text above, can you name the three–tiers of the Panchayati Raj System? What are the key functions of each of the three–tiers?

Ans. The three-tiers of the Panchayati Raj system are Gram Panchayat, Panchayat Samiti and Zila Parishad. The key functions of these three tiers are as follows

(i) **Gram Panchayat (Village Level)** The Gram Panchayat develops the village and provides basic needs like water, roads and sanitation. It also supports agriculture, health and education in the village.

(ii) **Panchayat Samiti (Block Level)** The Panchayat Samiti co-ordinates the activities of the Gram Panchayats in its block. It implements development programs and monitors their progress.

(iii) **Zilla Parishad (District Level)** The Zila Parishad oversees the activities of the Panchayat samitis in its district. It plans and manages resources and funds for the development of the district.

Q.2 Write a letter to the Sarpanch regarding the issue of plastic bags lying on the roadside in the village.

Ans. Do it yourself.

Q.3 In your view, what type of person should be a Gram Panchayat member?

Ans. In my view a Gram Panchayat member should possess the necessary following qualities

- A good friend to the community who cares about the people and their problems.
- A truthful and fair person who always speaks the truth and is fair to everyone.
- A leader who helps and shows others the way and works together.
- A good listener and speaker who hears what others say and explains things clearly.
- A kind and caring person who thinks about how others feel and helps those in need.

- A dreamer who thinks about what the community needs in the future.
- A team player who works together with others for the community's good.
- Someone who takes responsibility for their actions and decisions.
- Someone who loves to help and wants to make the community a better place.
- Someone who understands local rules and ways to help the community.

Q.4 Let us suppose that you study in a village school. The school is located next to a highway and students find it difficult to cross the road when they come to school or leave at the end of the day. What are the options to solve this issue? Which institutions in the Panchayati Raj can help you? What can the students do?

Ans. If our village school is located next to a highway, making it difficult for students to cross the road safely, some of the options that can be taken to solve the issue are as follows

- **Pedestrian crossing or Zebra crossing** Paint a zebra crossing or install a pedestrian crossing signal to alert drivers to slow down.
- **Speed bump or speed breaker** Install speed bumps or speed breakers to reduce vehicle speed near the school.
- **School crossing guard** Appoint a school crossing guard or a traffic volunteer to help students cross the road safely.
- **Footbridge or Overpass** Construct a footbridge or overpass for students to cross the highway safely.
- **Alternate route** Identify an alternate route for students to reach school, avoiding the highway.

Institutions in Panchayati Raj that can help are

- **Gram Panchayat** The local village council can take up the issue and work with other authorities to implement a solution.
- **Panchayat Samiti** The block-level council can provide guidance and support to the Gram Panchayat.
- **Zila Parishad** The district-level council can allocate funds and resources for infrastructure development, such as footbridges or speed breakers.

The students can do the following

- **Raise awareness** Organise awareness campaigns to educate drivers about the importance of slowing down near schools.
- **Petition** Create a petition signed by students, parents, and teachers to submit to the Gram Panchayat or other authorities.
- **Meet with authorities** Meet with Gram Panchayat members, Panchayat Samiti officials, or Zila Parishad representatives to discuss the issue and potential solutions.
- **Participate in safety initiatives** Participate in safety initiatives, such as painting zebra crossings or installing speed breakers, under the guidance of authorities.

By working together, students, schools and Panchayati Raj institutions can find a solution to ensure safe crossing for students.

REVIEW EXERCISE

Including Competency Based Questions

Part-I

Very Short Answer Type Questions

1. Panchayat forms the base of governance in India. What is the role of Panchayats in India?

Ans. The vital role of Panchayats in India is in addressing local issues, promoting development and ensuring government schemes reach the grassroots level. They empower rural communities, decentralise power and foster participatory governance, making them the foundation of India's democratic framework.

2. Three levels of the Panchayat together look after development of the whole district. What are the three levels of the Panchayati Raj system?

Ans. The three levels of the Panchayati Raj System are Village (Gram Panchayat), Block (Panchayat Samiti) and District (Zila Parishad). These levels work collaboratively to ensure holistic development, effective governance and citizen participation.

3. What aspects of life are looked after by the three tiers of the Panchayati Raj system?

Ans. The aspects of life looked after by the three tiers of the Panchayati Raj system are agriculture, housing, road maintenance, water management, education, healthcare, social welfare and cultural activities.

4. Who elects the members of the Gram Panchayat?

Ans. The Gram Panchayat members are elected directly by the Gram Sabha which comprises of enrolled voters from a village or neighbouring villages. This democratic process ensures representative governance and citizen participation.

5. What is the role of the Sarpanch or Pradhan in a Gram Sabha?

Ans. The elected Sarpanch or Pradhan play a role in leading the village council, ensuring smooth Gram Panchayat functioning, representing the village's interests and facilitating development initiatives. They serve as a bridge between the community and government, fostering collaboration and progress.

6. Who is Dnyaneshwar Kamble?

Ans. Dnyaneshwar Kamble is a pioneer transgender individual who became Tarangfal village's Sarpanch in 2017 by defeating six candidates. He advocated for "lok seva and gram seva."

7. Which officer is responsible for assisting the Gram Panchayat?

Ans. The Gram Panchayat receives crucial support from two key officers: the Panchayat Secretary and the Patwari. The Panchayat Secretary handles administrative tasks like convening meetings, maintaining records and ensuring smooth functioning.

The Patwari, on the other hand, is responsible for maintaining accurate land records, vital for village development and dispute resolution.

8. What is the significance of the Child Friendly Panchayat initiative?

Ans. The Child Friendly Panchayat initiative is a pioneering programme and holds significance for empowering children to express their thoughts and opinions on matters affecting them. By promoting child participation, this initiative ensures their needs and rights are addressed, fostering a supportive environment for their growth and development.

9. Which award did the Children's Parliament initiative win in 2001?

Ans. The Children's Parliament initiative received the prestigious World's Children's Honorary Award in 2001, recognising its innovative approach to child empowerment and community development.

10. What is the main role performed by the Panchayat Samiti?

Ans. Panchayat Samiti performs a multifaceted role, coordinating between Gram Panchayats, collecting development plans and presenting them to district or state levels for fund allocation and government schemes. This ensures effective planning, resource mobilisation, and implementation of development initiatives.

11. What is the special feature of Panchayati Raj institutions?

Ans. Panchayati Raj institutions have a special or distinctive feature - reserving one-third of the seats for women and implementing special rules to facilitate participation from disadvantaged sections of the population. This ensures inclusive representation, addressing the needs and concerns of marginalised communities.

12. Mention the four headquarters mentioned in Kautilya's Arthshastra.

Ans. Kautilya's Arthshastra mentions four headquarters that are Sangrahana (sub-district), Karvatika (district), Dronamukha (regional) and Sthaniya (provincial). These administrative divisions formed a structured framework from village to regional capital, showcasing ancient India's governance sophistication.

Short Answer Type Questions

1. Why is local governance important in India? What are some examples of governance-related issues that arise in villages?

Ans. Local governance is important in India as numerous governance-related issues emerge in villages, and every such issue cannot be taken to the state or national level for its resolution.

Examples of governance-related issues that arise in villages are as follows

- Water scarcity for irrigation
- Damaged road maintenance
- Village primary school management
- Land disputes
- Crop theft
- Electricity supply
- Healthcare access
- Sanitation and waste management

These issues significantly impact villagers' daily lives, making local governance essential for effective problem-solving and decision-making. By addressing these concerns locally, villages can ensure timely solutions, promoting overall development and improving quality of life.

2. How Bal Panchayats in Maharashtra proved significant? Mention its outcomes and achievements.

Ans. The Bal Panchayats in Maharashtra have achieved significant success. The outcomes of Bal Panchayats in Maharashtra are as follows

- Elimination of child labour and child marriage
- Convincing parents to send their wards back to school

The achievements of Bal Panchayats in Maharashtra are as follows

- Reduction in social evils
- Increase in educational enrollment
- Safer and more inclusive environment
- Promotion of holistic development

3. What is the relationship between Panchayat Samiti, Gram Panchayats and Zila Parishad?

Ans. Panchayat Samiti forms a crucial link between Gram Panchayats and Zila Parishad. It serves as a co-ordinating body that collects development plans from Gram Panchayats. It then presents them to district or state levels for fund allocation and government schemes. This facilitates effective implementation of development projects and ensures that local needs are addressed.

By bridging the gap between Gram Panchayats and Zila Parishad, Panchayat Samiti plays a vital role in promoting decentralised governance and local participation.

4. Explain the structure and composition of Panchayat Samitis and discuss how these structures vary across different states in India.

Ans. Panchayat Samitis are part of the Panchayati Raj system. They are present at the block level and is the link between the Gram Panchayat and Zila Parishad. They play a crucial role in local governance in India.

The structure and composition of Panchayat Samitis can vary from state to state based on regional requirements and administrative decisions.

Typically, a Panchayat Samiti is composed of elected members from the Gram Panchayats within a specific block, with representation including the elected members of the Gram Panchayats, and sometimes nominated members based on specific criteria.

5. Describe the administrative structure proposed by Kautilya in the Arthashastra.

Ans. Kautilya's administrative structure, as described in The Arthashastra, is a hierarchical system designed to efficiently manage and govern the state. This structure includes several levels of administration

- Sangrahana manages local administration, overseeing basic governance tasks and ensuring the implementation of state policies at the village level.
- Karvatika is responsible for coordinating between multiple sangrahanas, managing resources and addressing issues that affect a larger area.
- Droanamukha is tasked with higher-level coordination, resource management and ensuring the smooth functioning of the karvatika and sangrahana units.
- Sthanaya is the highest level in the local administration is responsible for overall regional governance, strategic planning, and implementation of policies across the entire province.

6. How do Panchayati Raj institutions promote women's participation in local governance?

Ans. Panchayati Raj institutions promote women's participation in local governance by reserving one-third of seats for women enabling them to participate in the development process, present their needs and problems and take an active part in local governance.

This empowerment of women leads to more inclusive decision-making and ensures that their perspectives are considered in development initiatives. By increasing women's participation, Panchayati Raj institutions foster a more equitable and representative local governance system.

Long Answer Type Questions

1. What is the relationship between the Panchayati Raj system and the concept of self-government?

Ans. The Panchayati Raj system is a form of self-government where the villagers govern themselves through their elected representatives. This system empowers villagers to participate in decision-making processes by bringing governance closer to the people. Through the three-tier system, villagers can actively participate in planning and implementing development initiatives. This system also enables villagers to hold their elected representatives accountable, fostering transparency and accountability in governance. Villagers can address their local issues, promote development, and ensure that the benefits of government schemes reach the grassroots level, all while maintaining autonomy and self-governance.

2. What are the key characteristics of a successful Gram Panchayat and how do they contribute to rural development?

Ans. A successful Gram Panchayat possesses key characteristics such as

- active community participation
- effective leadership
- transparency
- inclusive decision-making

These characteristics contribute to rural development in the following ways

- ensuring local needs are addressed
- promoting grassroots governance
- facilitating effective implementation of government schemes
- fostering community engagement
- encouraging sustainable development

By addressing local issues and promoting development, successful Gram Panchayats contribute significantly to rural development, leading to improved livelihoods, social cohesion, and economic growth. Moreover, they serve as a model for other Gram Panchayats, promoting best practices and innovative approaches to rural development.

3. Discuss the achievements of exemplary Sarpanchs like Dnyaneshwar Kamble, Vandana Bahadur Maida and Popatrao Baguji Pawar.

Ans. Exemplary Sarpanchs like Dnyaneshwar Kamble, Vandana Bahadur Maida, and Popatrao Baguji Pawar have revolutionised rural development through innovative leadership and community engagement. Their achievements are as follows

- They addressed critical issues like education, sanitation and healthcare by implementing initiatives like rainwater harvesting and tree plantation.
- They empowered marginalised communities and promoted social inclusion and gender equality.
- They established self-help groups and encouraged entrepreneurship among marginalised communities.
- Their leadership demonstrates the impact of grassroots initiatives, inspiring others to replicate their models and redefining the Sarpanch role.

4. Describe the structure and functions of Panchayati Raj institutions and their differences across states. Comment on the importance of Panchayat secretary and Patwari in Panchayati Raj system.

Ans. Panchayati Raj institutions have a three-tier structure– Gram Panchayats at the village level, Panchayat Samiti at the block level and Zila Parishad at the district level.

Their functions include facilitating development projects, government schemes and promoting participation of local people in governance. However, Panchayati Raj institutions differ across states in their structure and functions as they are under the authority of states. Despite these differences, they have a similar objective of enabling villagers to take an active part in the development of their villages and local areas.

The Panchayat Secretary and Patwari are essential support systems for the Gram Panchayat. The secretary performs administrative functions, while the Patwari maintains land records and assists in administrative tasks. These support systems ensure smooth implementation of government schemes, address land-related issues efficiently and enable the Gram Panchayat to function effectively. Additionally, they provide critical support in areas like financial management, record-keeping and communication, enabling the Gram Panchayat to focus on development initiatives and community engagement.

Part-II

Multiple Choice Questions (MCQs)

1. What is the main objective of the Panchayati Raj system?

(a) To provide employment opportunities
(b) To promote industrialisation
(c) To enable villagers to take an active part in the development of their villages and local areas
(d) To increase the power of the Central Government

2. The head of the Gram Panchayat is known by which of the following names?

(a) Sarpanch (b) Pradhan
(c) Panchayat Secretary (d) Patwari

3. Which of the following is not a level of the Panchayati Raj system?

(a) Village level
(b) Block level
(c) District level
(d) State level

4. The officer who maintains land records in a Gram Panchayat is known as

(a) Panchayat Secretary (b) Patwari
(c) Sarpanch (d) Pradhan

5. What is the name of the initiative that enables children to express their ideas and opinions on matters that affect them?

(a) Child Friendly Panchayat initiative
(b) Bal Sabha
(c) Bal Panchayat
(d) Children's Parliament

6. Which initiative is an offshoot of Bunkers Roy' 'Barefoot College initiative'?

(a) Child Friendly Panchayat initiative
(b) Children's Parliament
(c) Bal Sabha
(d) Bal Panchayat

7. Which scheme aids in the construction of all-weather roads in rural areas?
(a) Pradhan Mantri Gram Sadak Yojana
(b) Panchayati Raj Yojana
(c) Gram Panchayat Yojana
(d) Zila Parishad Yojana

8. Which ancient text of governance was written by Kautilya?
(a) Arthshastra (b) Panchayati Raj
(c) Gram Panchayat (d) Zila Parishad

9. Arthshastra mentions the establishment of four headquarters for administrative purposes. In which year was the book written?
(a) 2000 years ago (b) 2300 years ago
(c) 2500 years ago (d) 2800 years ago

10. Arrange the following events in chronological order.
(i) Kautilya wrote Arthshastra
(ii) Panchayati Raj system was established
(iii) Child Friendly Panchayat Initiative was launched
(iv) Pradhan Mantri Gram Sadak Yojana was launched

Options
(a) (i), (ii), (iii), (iv) (b) (i), (iii), (ii), (iv)
(c) (ii), (i), (iii), (iv) (d) (iii), (ii), (i), (iv)

11. Which of the following statements is/are correct?
I. Panchayat Samiti forms a link between Gram Panchayats and Zila Parishad.
II. Panchayat Samiti collects development plans from all Gram Panchayats.
III. Panchayat Samiti presents the development plans to the Central Government.
IV. Panchayat Samiti co-ordinates between Gram Panchayats.

Codes
(a) I and II (b) I, II and IV
(c) I, II, III and IV (d) II and IV

12. Which among the following statements is/are correct?
I. Gram Panchayat is the highest level of the Panchayati Raj system.
II. Panchayat Samiti is the block level institution.
III. Zila Parishad is the district level institution.
IV. Panchayati Raj institutions are same across all states.

Codes
(a) I and II (b) I, II and III
(c) II and III (d) III and IV

Answers

1. (c)	2. (a)	3. (d)	4. (b)	5. (a)
6. (b)	7. (a)	8. (a)	9. (b)	10. (a)
11. (b)	12. (c)			

Fill in the Blanks

1. The Zila Panchayat is the .... level of the Panchayati Raj system.
2. Kautilya's .... describes the administrative structure from the village to the regional capital around 2300 years ago.
3. The .... Gram Panchayat in West Sikkim has been declared a Child Friendly Gram Panchayat due to its Child Friendly initiatives.
4. The Panchayati Raj system works at three levels–the village, the .... and the district.
5. The Panchayat Samiti collects development plans from all the Gram Panchayats and then puts them together to present it before the .... levels for funding and implementation.

Ans. 1. highest 2. Arthshastra
3. Sangkhu Radhu Khandu 4. block 5. district or state

True or False

1. The Panchayati Raj system is a form of national government.
2. The Gram Panchayat is responsible for collecting development plans from Gram Sabhas and presenting them to the Panchayat Samiti.
3. Kautilya's Arthshastra describes the structure of the state and how the economy could be made prosperous around 1000 years ago.
4. The Dronamukha is a provincial headquarters for every 400 villages according to Kautilya.
5. One-third of the seats in Panchayati Raj institutions are reserved for men.

Ans. 1. False 2. False 3. False 4. True 5. False

Match the Following

1.

List I (Personalities)	List II (Achievements)
A. Dnyaneshwar Kamble	1. First transgender sarpanch in Maharashtra
B. Vandana Bahadur Maida	2. First female Sarpanch from Bhil community in Madhya Pradesh
C. Popatrao Baguji Pawar	3. Implemented rainwater harvesting and watershed conservation in Hiware Bazar village
D. Kautilya	4. Authored Arthshastra, an ancient text on governance

Codes

	A	B	C	D		A	B	C	D
(a)	3	4	2	1	(b)	4	2	3	1
(c)	1	2	3	4	(d)	2	3	1	4

2.

List I (Terms)	List II (Description)
A. Sangrahana	1. Provincial headquarters for every 800 villages
B. Karvatika	2. Sub-district headquarters for every 10 villages
C. Dronamukha	3. District headquarters for every 100 villages
D. Sthaniya	4. Headquarters for every 400 villages

Codes

	A	B	C	D		A	B	C	D
(a)	4	2	3	1	(b)	2	3	4	1
(c)	1	4	3	2	(d)	3	2	1	4

Ans. 1. (c) 2. (b)

Assertion-Reason

1. Assertion (A) The Panchayat Secretary performs administrative functions.

Reason (R) He is responsible for maintaining land records.

Codes

(a) Both A and R are true and R is the correct explanation of A

(b) Both A and R are true, but R is not the correct explanation of A

(c) A Is false, but R is true

(d) A is true, but R is false

2. Assertion (A) Panchayat Samiti plays a crucial role in co-ordinating between Gram Panchayats.

Reason (R) It collects development plans from all the Gram Panchayats and presents them to the district or state levels.

Codes

(a) Both A and R are true and R is the correct explanation of A

(b) Both A and R are true, but R is not the correct explanation of A

(c) A is false, but R is true

(d) A is true, but R is false

3. Assertion (A) The Children Parliament initiative has empowered underprivileged children in Rajasthan.

Reason (R) It has enabled them to develop leadership skills and become socially aware.

Codes

(a) Both A and R are true and R is the correct explanation of A

(b) Both A and R are true, but R is not the correct explanation of A

(c) A is false, but R is true

(d) A is true, but R is false

4. Assertion (A) Kautilya's Arthshastra mentions the establishment of headquarters by the king.

Reason (R) It describes the structure of the state and how the economy can be made prosperous.

Codes

(a) Both A and R are true and R is the correct explanation of A

(b) Both A and R are true, but R is not the correct explanation of A

(c) A is false, but R is true

(d) A is true, but R is false

5. Assertion (A) The Sangkhu Radhu Khandu Gram Panchayat has been declared a Child Friendly Gram Panchayat.

Reason (R) It has taken steps to cater to the needs and rights of children.

Codes

(a) Both A and R are true and R is the correct explanation of A

(b) Both A and R are true, but R is not the correct explanation of A

(c) A is false, but R is true

(d) A is true, but R is false

Ans. 1. (a) 2. (a) 3. (d) 4. (b) 5. (a)

Case Based Questions

1. Read the case given below and answer the questions that follows.

Vandana Bahadur Maida, a member of the Bhil community from the village of Khankhandvi in Madhya Pradesh, defied patriarchal norms to become the first female Sarpanch of her village. She convinced women in the village to attend the Sabha meetings and addressed critical issues like education and sanitation, earning recognition far and wide. Vandana's journey shows how women can play a leading role in transforming rural India.

Hiware Bazar, a village in Ahmednagar district of Maharashtra, used to be affected by frequent droughts and poor agricultural yield. After Popatrao Baguji Pawar became its Sarpanch, he started applying Anna Hazare's model of rainwater harvesting, watershed conservation and massive tree planting of lakhs of trees, all of which contributed to the recharge of groundwater. With the collaboration of the villagers, Hiware Bazar became a green and prosperous village in a few years. Shri Popatrao Pawar was awarded the Padma Shri in 2020.

(i) What is the significance of Vandana Bahadur Maida's achievement as the first female Sarpanch of Khankhandvi village in terms of promoting gender equality?

(a) It highlights the need for reservation of seats for women in local governance.

(b) It demonstrates the impact of education on women's empowerment.

(c) It shows that women can lead and bring about positive change in rural communities.

(d) It emphasises the importance of patriarchal norms in maintaining social order.

(ii) What is the underlying value that drove Popatrao Baguji Pawar's initiatives in Hiware Bazar village, leading to its transformation from a drought-prone area to a prosperous one?

(a) Individualism and personal gain

(b) Community development and collective well-being

(c) Environmental conservation for its own sake

(d) Technological innovation for economic growth

(iii) What does the recognition of Popatrao Baguji Pawar's efforts with the Padma Shri award signify in terms of valuing citizen-led initiatives?

(a) That only government-led initiatives are effective in bringing about change.

(b) That citizen-led initiatives are not recognised or valued.

(c) That community-led efforts can lead to significant positive impact and deserve recognition.

(d) That awards and recognition are not important for social change.

(iv) What was the major problem faced by Hiware Bazar before the initiatives taken by Popatrao Pawar?

(a) Lack of education

(b) Frequent droughts and poor agricultural yield

(c) Lack of medical facilities

(d) Overpopulation

Ans. (i) (c) (ii) (b) (iii) (c) (iv) (b)

2. Read the case given below and answer the questions that follows.

The 'Children's Parliament', an offshoot of Bunker Roy's 'Barefoot College' initiative a few decades ago, empowered underprivileged children in Rajasthan's rural areas through education and democratic participation. Children aged 8 to 14 are engaged in governance processes, learning about democracy and social responsibility through night schools and Parliament-like elections. The 'Parliament' followed formal procedures, including voter ID cards and campaigning. Elected representatives formed a 'Cabinet', overseeing school management and advocating for community needs. The initiative fostered leadership skills and social awareness, enabling children to challenge societal norms and advocate for change. Children actively addressed issues such as access to education, sanitation and social equality, contributing to community development. The Children's Parliament initiative received many accolades, including the World's Children's Honorary Award in 2001.

(i) What does the Children's Parliament initiative reveal about the potential for children to drive social change in rural communities?

(ii) In what ways can the Children's Parliament model be seen as an innovative approach to leadership development and community engagement?

(iii) What does the success of the Children's Parliament initiative suggest about the importance of inclusive and participatory approaches to community development?

Ans. (i) The Children's Parliament initiative reveals that children can be powerful agents of social change in rural communities, as they bring fresh perspectives, creativity, and energy to addressing complex social issues.

(ii) The Children's Parliament model can be seen as an innovative approach to leadership development and community engagement because it empowers children to take ownership of governance processes, builds their confidence and skills and fosters a sense of social responsibility and citizenship.

(iii) The success of the Children's Parliament initiative suggests that inclusive and participatory approaches to community development, which involve marginalised groups like children, can lead to more sustainable and equitable outcomes, as they tap into the collective wisdom and creativity of the community.

Competency Based Questions

1. An institution similar to Gram Panchayat exists at the block level. Mention its name.

Ans. Panchayat Samiti is the institution similar to Gram Panchayat at the block level, serving as a vital link between Gram Panchayats and Zila Parishad.

2. Panchayati Raj institutions were established in India through a constitutional amendment. What is the objective of Panchayati Raj institutions?

Ans. The primary objective of Panchayati Raj institutions is to empower villagers to actively participate in developing their villages and local areas. Although structures and functions vary across states, the core aim remains decentralisation, democratisation and inclusive development.

ASSESSMENT EXERCISE

Objective Type Questions

1. With which name does the system of local government in India known as?
   (a) Panchayati Raj (b) Gram Panchayat
   (c) Zila Parishad (d) Panchayat Samiti
2. Which of the following is the name of the bottom most level of the Panchayati Raj system?
   (a) Gram Panchayat
   (b) Panchayat Samiti
   (c) Zila Parishad
   (d) Block Panchayat
3. Which of the following awards was received by the Children's Parliament initiative in 2001?
   (a) World Children's Honorary Award
   (b) Panchayati Raj Award
   (c) Gram Panchayat Award
   (d) Zila Parishad Award
4. How many headquarters did Kautilya mention in his book Arthshastra?
   (a) 2 (b) 3
   (c) 4 (d) 5
5. **Assertion** (A) Panchayati Raj system is a form of self-government.
   Reason (R) It brings governance closer to the people.
   Codes
   (a) Both A and R are true and R is the correct explanation of A.
   (b) Both A and R are true, but R is not the correct explanation of A
   (c) A is false, but R is true
   (d) A is true, but R is false
6. The Panchayati Raj system is a form of government .... that brings governance closer to the people.
7. The Panchayat Samiti is responsible for co-ordinating between .... and presenting development plans to the district or state levels.
8. The Panchayati Raj system has been successful in empowering rural communities and promoting local self-governance. (True/False)
9. The Pradhan Mantri Gram Sadak Yojana is a scheme that aids in the construction of rural healthcare facilities. (True/False)

Subjective Questions (VSA, SA & LA)

1. Panchayati Raj system is a three -tier system. Name the bottommost level of the three-tier system in rural areas.
2. What is the motto of Dnyaneshwar Kamble?
3. What is the Children's Parliament initiative in Rajasthan?
4. Who wrote the ancient text of governance, Arthshastra?
5. Describe the role of Panchayati Raj system in promoting development.
6. Panchayat Samiti forms the middle tier of the three-level Panchayati Raj system. What is the scope of work of the Panchayat Samiti?
7. Describe the role and function of the Patwari in a Gram Panchayat.
8. Comment on the contribution of Vandana Bahadur Maida in her village. What is her achievement?
9. Explain how the Panchayati Raj system empowers villagers to participate in decision-making processes.
10. The Panchayati Raj system functions through a system in which many persons are involved. What are the essential support systems that enable the Gram Panchayat to function effectively? Comment.

Local Government in Urban Areas

CHAPTER 12

Urban local bodies are essential decentralised governance structures in cities and towns, overseeing local services and infrastructure. Depending on the city's size, these include Municipal Corporations, Municipal Councils, or Nagar Panchayats. They manage crucial functions like waste management, infrastructure upkeep, and local taxation. Effective urban governance depends on both the administrative effectiveness of these bodies and active citizen involvement, reflecting the core principles of participatory democracy.

- Like in rural areas, urban areas also have the system of local government. This government caters to the day-to-day needs of the citizens living in urban areas.
- It also aims to empower the citizens so they may actively participate in their country functioning at the urban level. Local government is important in shaping the quality of urban life within urban areas.

12.1 Governance in Urban Areas

- In a democracy, good governance empowers the citizens so that they can actively participate in the functioning of the country.
- This participation can be at the rural, regional, urban, state or national level. This is the concept of **participatory democracy**.
- Urban areas are more complex and diverse than the rural areas. Hence, the governance system in urban areas needs to be more complex.
- The Indian system of governance works at three levels. These levels are local government, state government and Union government.
- The local government is further sub-divided into local government in rural areas (Panchayati raj institutions) and local government in urban areas (urban local bodies).

Urban Local Bodies

- Local government structures in urban areas are called 'urban local bodies'. They are decentralised, which means the local communities have a direct say in the management of their areas and the issues they face. They don't operate under a central authority at the top.
- In this mechanism, the citizens living in an area come together and take decisions which are best for them.
- In the system of local government in urban areas, cities and towns are divided into smaller units known as **'wards'**.
- The ward committees help in organising activities such as health camps and campaigns like anti plastic drives, etc.
- The committees also identify and report issues to authorities such as water leaks, blocked drains and damaged roads, etc.
- The functioning of wards dependent upon the rules made by the state. Hence, it differs from state to state.

Responsibilities of the Urban Local Bodies

Urban local bodies are responsible for a variety of functions such as

- Maintaining infrastructure
- Managing burial grounds
- Collection and disposal of garbage
- Monitoring the implementation of government schemes
- Collecting local taxes and fines
- Contribute to planning for the area's economic and social development

Responsibilities of the Citizens

In a participatory democracy, the people living in the area must also perform their duties. This helps urban local bodies to perform their functions efficiently.

Citizens can participate by performing the following duties

- Participating in waste segregation
- Report issues promptly (e.g. water leakage)
- Show care and concern for their area

Indore has been named the cleanest city in India for seven consecutive years under the Swachh Survekshan scheme. This success is largely due to the active participation of its residents, who follow cleanliness guidelines, report issues like garbage problems, and support waste management efforts. Their commitment to keeping their city clean plays a crucial role in achieving this award.

Different Kinds of Urban Local Bodies

The highest urban local body differ from cities to cities according to their population as follows

- **Municipal Corporation** (*Mahanagar Nigam*) It is the highest urban body in cities having a population above 10 lakhs. In 1865, Municipal Corporation of Greater Mumbai was created. It was originally known as Bombay Municipal Corporation.
- **Municipal Council** (*Nagar Palika*) It is the highest body in cities with a population between 1 and 10 lakhs.
- **Nagar Panchayat** It is an urban body in the cities and towns with smaller populations.

Madras Municipal Corporation

- The Madras Corporation which is now known as the Greater Chennai Corporation was established on 29th September, 1688. It is India's oldest municipal institution.
- In 1687, the East India Company issued a charter constituting the town of Fort St. George and its surrounding 16-kilometer radius into a corporation.
- The Madras Corporation began its municipal administration after it gained the power to collect municipal taxes in 1792 through a Parliamentary Act.

Glossary

Participatory Democracy A system of governance where citizens actively participate in decision-making processes at various levels (rural, regional, urban, state or national).

Urban Local Bodies Decentralised local government structures in urban areas, responsible for managing local issues and providing services.

Wards Smaller units of cities and towns, divided for administrative purposes.

Decentralised A system where power is distributed among local communities, rather than being controlled by a central authority.

Participatory Governance A system where citizens are involved in decision-making processes, ensuring that their needs and concerns are addressed.

LOCAL GOVERNMENT IN URBAN AREAS

Wards

- Smaller units of cities and towns – Ward committees:
- Organise activities (health camps, anti-plastic drives)
- Identify and report issues (water leaks, blocked drains, damaged roads)
- State-specific rules govern functioning of wards

Functions

- Maintain infrastructure
- Manage burial grounds
- Collect and dispose of garbage
- Monitor government schemes
- Collect local taxes and fines
- Contribute to economic and social development planning

Types of Urban Local Bodies

- Municipal Corporation (population above 10 lakhs)
- Municipal Council (population between 1 and 10 lakhs)
- Nagar Panchayat (smaller populations)

Urban Local Bodies

- Decentralised local government structures
- Citizens have direct say in management of their areas

Participatory Democracy

- Citizens participate in country's functioning
- Urban areas are more complex and diverse than rural areas
- Decentralised governance in urban areas

Responsibilities of Citizens

- Participate in waste segregation
- Report issues promptly
- Show care and concern for their area

Madras Corporation

- India's oldest municipal institution (established 1688)
- Began municipal administration in 1792

NCERT FOLDER

Detailed Answers of All NCERT Questions

Let's Explore (Page 174)

Q.1 Why is a city like Kolkata, Chennai or Mumbai more complex and diverse than a village or a town?

Ans. A city like Kolkata, Chennai or Mumbai is more complex and diverse than a village or a town because of the following reasons

- Larger population with varied socio-economic backgrounds, cultures and lifestyles.
- Diverse range of industries, businesses and economic activities.
- Complex infrastructure, including transportation systems, utilities and public services.
- Higher density of population, leading to unique urban challenges and issues.
- Greater need for specialised services, such as healthcare, education and waste management.
- More complex governance and administrative structures to manage the city's affairs.

Overall, the larger size, density and economic activity of a city create a more complex and diverse environment compared to a smaller village or town.

Q.2 With your classmates, make a list of diverse communities residing in any city that you are familiar with. How many were you able to list? What else do you observe in the list?

Ans. The list of diverse communities in a city is as follows

- Religious groups (Hindus, Muslims, Christians, etc.)
- Ethnic groups (North Indians, South Indians, etc.)
- Language groups (Bengali, Tamil, Hindi, etc.)
- Socio-economic groups (Rich, Middle class, Poor)
- Cultural groups (Artists, Writers, Food vendors)
- Other groups (Seniors, People with disabilities, Migrant workers)

Key observations in the list are

- Many communities exist in a city
- Individuals can belong to multiple communities
- Communities can overlap
- Diversity makes a city rich and complex
- Understanding and appreciating diversity is important for a harmonious city

Let's Explore (Page 175)

Q.3 In the figure given below, what similarities and differences do you notice between the Panchayati Raj system and the urban local government?

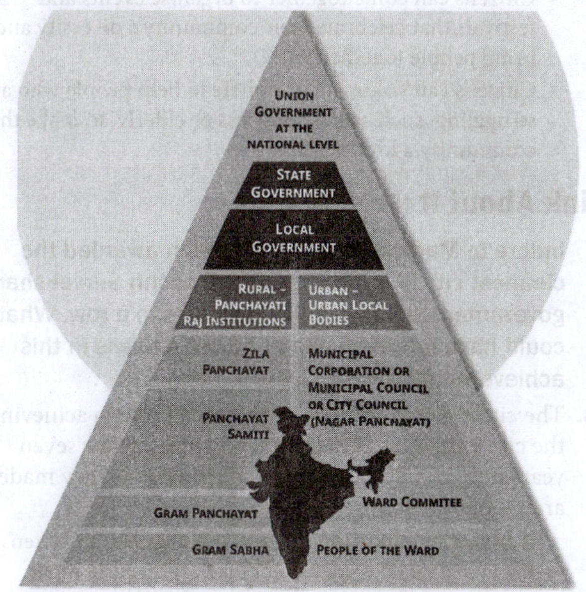

Ans. The similarities between the Panchayati Raj system and the urban local government area as follows

- Both occupy the bottom position in the pyramid of government working in the country.
- Both the governments are closer to the common people.
- Both work for smaller and local areas.
- Both include the participation of people living in the area.
- Both have elected representatives.

The differences between the Panchayati Raj system and the urban local government area as follows

- Panchayati Raj system is for rural areas while urban local government is for urban areas.
- Panchayati Raj system is sub-divided into three bodies at the village, block and district level while urban local government is of different types depending upon the population of the city.

Let's Explore (Page 177)

Q.4 Can you think of four or five more actions that responsible citizens might take to help their area of the city?

Ans. The actions that responsible citizens might take to help their area of the city are as follows

- Citizens can plant trees and help keep the area clean to make it a nicer place to live.
- Citizens can share their skills and experience with young people to help them learn and grow.
- Citizens can help reduce waste, recycle and conserve resources to make their area cleaner and healthier.
- Citizens can come together to organise events and festivals that celebrate their community's diversity and bring people together.
- Citizens can volunteer or donate to help people who are struggling, such as the homeless or elderly, to make their community a kinder place.

Think About It (Page 179)

Q.1 Indore in Madhya Pradesh has been awarded the cleanest city in India under the Swachh Survekshan government scheme for seven years in a row. What could have been the role of Indore citizens in this achievement?

Ans. The citizens of Indore played a crucial role in achieving the city's status as the cleanest city in India for seven years in a row. Some possible contributions they made are as follows

- **Active Participation in Waste Management** Citizens may have taken responsibility for segregating waste, recycling and properly disposing of trash.
- **Community Initiatives** Residents might have organised cleanliness drives, awareness campaigns and rallies to promote cleanliness and hygiene.
- **Cooperation with Municipal Authorities** Citizens may have worked closely with the municipal corporation, providing feedback and supporting their efforts to improve sanitation and waste management.
- **Adoption of Sustainable Practices** Indore citizens might have adopted eco-friendly habits, such as reducing plastic use, conserving water and using public transport.
- **Social Pressure and Accountability** Citizens may have held their neighbours, local businesses and authorities accountable for maintaining cleanliness, creating a sense of collective responsibility.
- **Education and Awareness** Residents might have educated themselves and others about the importance of cleanliness, hygiene and sanitation, leading to a cultural shift towards cleanliness.

The collective efforts of Indore's citizens, combined with effective governance and municipal initiatives, likely contributed to the city's remarkable achievement.

Let's Explore (Page 174)

Q.1 Select a few cities, from your state and from a few neighbouring states. These may include the city you live in or the city nearest to your town or village. How will you find out if they have a Nagar Panchayat, Municipal Council or Municipal Corporation? Draw a table with the names of the cities and the type of urban local body each of them has.

Ans. The following is a table with a few cities from different states and their corresponding urban local bodies

City	State	Urban local body
Indore	Madhya Pradesh	Municipal Corporation
Bhopal	Madhya Pradesh	Municipal Corporation
Mumbai	Maharashtra	Municipal Corporation
Pune	Maharashtra	Municipal Corporation
Nagpur	Maharashtra	Municipal Corporation
Jaipur	Rajasthan	Municipal Corporation
Udaipur	Rajasthan	Municipal Council

To find out the type of urban local body for each city, I would take the following steps

- Check the official website of the city's municipal body or local government.
- Look for information on the city's wikipedia page or other reliable online sources.
- Contact the city's municipal office or local government department directly to ask about their urban local body.

Q.2 How do urban local bodies fund their activities? (Hint: Look carefully at the pictures of the functions performed by Indore Municipal Corporation in Figure 12.4 on page 178.) Are some of them paid services?

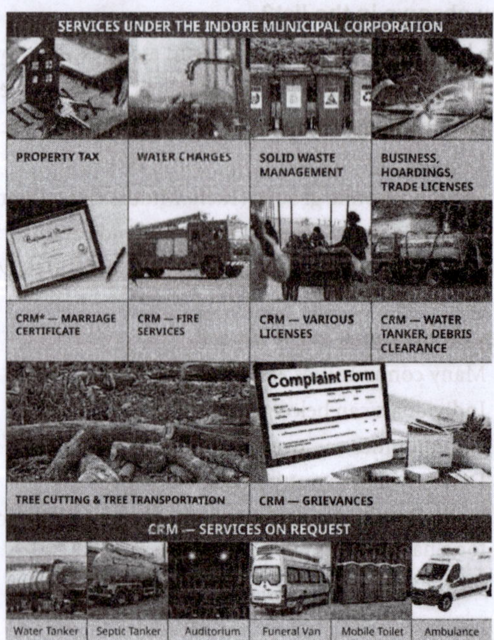

Ans. Urban local bodies fund their activities through a combination of sources, including

- Property taxes which are collected from property owners within the city limits.
- Water and sewerage charges which are collected from residents and businesses for water supply and sewerage services.
- Garbage collection fees which are collected from residents and businesses for waste management services.
- Parking fees which are collected from vehicle owners for parking in public spaces.
- Licenses and permits which are issued to businesses, vendors and other entities for various activities.
- Grants and aid received from state and central governments for specific projects and initiatives.
- User charges which are collected for services like public toilets, streetlights and other amenities.

Yes, some of the services provided by Indore municipal corporation are paid services, such as water supply, sewerage services, garbage collection, property, licenses and permits.

Questions, Activities and Projects

Q.1 On your way to school, you and your friends notice that a water pipe is leaking. A lot of water is being wasted on account of the leak. What would you and your friends do in such a situation?

Ans. If my friends and I noticed a leaking water pipe on our way to school, we would

- Take a photo or video of the leak as evidence.
- Note the location of the leak, including the nearest landmark or address.
- Report the leak to the local municipal authority or water department immediately, either by
  - Calling their helpline number
  - Sending an email or message through their website or social media
  - Informing a nearby authority figure, such as a school teacher or local shopkeeper
- If possible, try to temporarily stop the leak by turning off the valve (if accessible) or using a makeshift plug (like a cloth or stick) to reduce water waste.
- Follow up with the authorities to ensure the leak is fixed promptly.

By taking these steps, we can help conserve water, prevent wastage, and contribute to a more responsible and sustainable community.

Q.2 Invite a member of an urban local body near you to your class. Discuss with them their role and responsibilities. Prepare a set of questions to ask them so that the meeting is fruitful.

Ans. The following is a set of questions that can be asked to a member of an urban local body

- Can you introduce yourself and explain your role in the urban local body?
- What are your key responsibilities and areas of focus?
- How do you interact with citizens and address their concerns?
- What initiatives has the urban local body taken to improve infrastructure, sanitation and public services?
- How do you prioritise projects and allocate resources?
- How does the urban local body handle emergencies like natural disasters or public health crises?
- What measures are taken to ensure transparency and accountability in decision-making and fund allocation?
- How can citizens like us get involved and contribute to the urban local body's efforts?
- What challenges do you face in your role and how do you overcome them?
- What message would you like to share with our class about the importance of urban governance and civic engagement?

Q.3 Discuss with adult members of your family and neighbourhood, and make a list of their expectations from the urban local bodies.

Ans. From the discussions with adult members of my family and neighbourhood, I made the following list of their expectations from the urban local bodies

- Keep our streets and public spaces clean and free of waste.
- Maintain good roads and provide adequate streetlights for safety.
- Ensure we have access to clean water and proper sewage management.
- Keep our community safe with effective law enforcement and emergency services.
- Protect the environment by planting trees, controlling pollution and managing waste.
- Support vulnerable populations like seniors and the disabled by organising social programmes and providing affordable healthcare.
- Be transparent and accountable by sharing information on projects, budgets and expenditures.
- Encourage citizen participation by listening to feedback, involving us in decision-making and supporting community-led initiatives.

These expectations highlight what urban local bodies can do to improve our daily lives and create a better community.

Q.4 Make a list of characteristics of a good urban local body.

Ans. The list of characteristics of a good urban local body is as follows

- A good urban local body is responsive to citizens' concerns and addresses them promptly.
- It is transparent in its decisions, budgets and projects.
- It is accountable for its actions and decisions.
- It is inclusive and represents all communities.
- It delivers quality services efficiently and effectively.
- It prioritises sustainability and environmental conservation.
- It communicates regularly with citizens and is adaptive to changing circumstances.

These characteristics help urban local bodies serve their citizens well and build trust.

Q.5 What are the similarities and differences between the Panchayati Raj system in rural areas and the urban local bodies?

Ans. The similarities between the Panchayati Raj system in rural areas and the urban local bodies are as follows

- Both are local self-governance systems, empowering citizens to manage their own affairs.
- Both have elected representatives (Gram Panchayat/ Municipal Councilors) accountable to the people.
- Both focus on providing basic services like water, sanitation, roads and healthcare.
- Both encourage citizen participation and involvement in decision-making.

The differences between the Panchayati Raj system in rural areas and the urban local bodies are as follows

- **Location** Panchayati Raj system operates in rural areas, while urban local bodies operate in cities and towns.
- **Structure** Panchayati Raj has a three-tier system (Gram Panchayat, Block Panchayat and District Panchayat), while urban local bodies have a single-tier system (Municipal Corporation or Council).
- **Powers and functions** Urban local bodies have more powers and responsibilities, such as urban planning, transportation and taxation, whereas Panchayati Raj focuses on rural development and basic services.
- **Funding** Urban local bodies receive more funding and have greater financial autonomy compared to Panchayati Raj institutions.
- **Election process** Urban local body elections are more formalised, while Panchayati Raj elections may have more informal or traditional processes.

In summary, while both systems aim to decentralise power and empower local communities, they differ in structure, powers and focus due to the unique needs and contexts of rural and urban areas.

REVIEW EXERCISE

Including Competency Based Questions

Part-I

Very Short Answer Type Questions

1. Why are urban governance systems more complex?

Ans. Urban governance systems are more complex due to the diversity and complexity of urban areas, which have a higher population density, varied socio-economic profiles and intricate infrastructure needs. This complexity requires more nuanced and multi-faceted governance structures to address the unique challenges of urbanisation.

2. What is the role of ward committees?

Ans. Ward committees play a crucial role in organising activities, identifying and reporting local issues and facilitating citizen participation in governance. They serve as a bridge between citizens and urban local bodies, ensuring that local concerns are addressed and community needs are met.

3. Why does the functioning of wards differ from state to state?

Ans. The functioning of wards differs from state to state because it is determined by state-specific rules, regulations and governance structures. Each state has its own laws and guidelines governing urban local bodies, leading to variations in ward administration, powers and responsibilities.

4. What is the purpose of participatory democracy?

Ans. The purpose of participatory democracy is to empower citizens to participate in the functioning of the country, ensuring that their voices are heard and their needs are addressed.

5. **What is the primary responsibility of urban local bodies regarding infrastructure?**

Ans. The primary responsibility of urban local bodies regarding infrastructure is maintaining and upgrading existing infrastructure, as well as planning and developing new infrastructure to meet the growing needs of urban populations. This includes roads, public transportation, water supply, sanitation and other essential services.

6. **What is the role of citizens in a participatory democracy?**

Ans. Citizens play a vital role in participatory democracy by participating in waste segregation, reporting issues promptly, showing care for their area and engaging in community decision-making processes.

7. **What is the significance of the East India Company charter in 1687?**

Ans. The East India Company's charter in 1687 was significant because it constituted the town of Fort St. George and its surrounding area into a corporation, marking one of the earliest forms of urban governance in India. This charter laid the foundation for modern municipal governance in India.

8. **What is the primary focus of urban local bodies in cities?**

Ans. The primary focus of urban local bodies includes taking care of the infrastructure and providing range of service.

9. **How do urban local bodies found their activities?**

Ans. Urban local bodies found their activities through taxes and fees.

Short Answer Type Questions

1. **How do urban local bodies differ from central authorities?**

Ans. Urban local bodies differ from central authorities in the following ways

Urban Local Bodies	Central Authorities
They are decentralised and operate independently without a central authority.	They are operated with a central authority controlling them from the top.
They are responsible for administration only in urban areas.	They are responsible for framing rules and laws for the entire country.
Their functions include local governance, urban planning, sanitation, etc.	Their functions include national policy making, defence, foreign relations, etc.
They are directly accountable to local residents of an area.	They are accountable to Parliament and the citizens of the country.

2. **Highlight the functions of ward committees.**

Ans. Ward committees organise various activities, such as health camps, anti-plastic drives, and other local initiatives, aimed at improving the quality of life for citizens and addressing specific community needs.

These activities foster community engagement, promote social cohesion, and help build a sense of ownership among residents, ultimately contributing to a better living environment.

By organising such activities, ward committees demonstrate their commitment to community development and well-being. Additionally, these initiatives provide opportunities for citizens to come together, share ideas, and work collaboratively towards common goals.

3. **What are the impacts of state-specific rules on ward functioning?**

Ans. The impact of state-specific rules on ward functioning is that it allows for flexibility and adaptability in addressing local needs, but also means that the functioning of wards can differ significantly from state to state.

This variation can lead to innovative solutions and best practices, but also requires careful consideration to ensure consistency and equity in service delivery across different regions.

State-specific rules can also influence the allocation of resources, with some states prioritising certain services over others. Therefore, it is essential to strike a balance

between flexibility and standardisation, ensuring that ward committees can respond to local needs while maintaining consistency and equity in governance.

4. **How do citizens contribute to the efficient functioning of urban local bodies?**

Ans. Citizens can significantly contribute to the efficient functioning of urban local bodies in the following ways

- Citizens can contribute by taking ownership of their responsibilities, such as participating in waste segregation, reporting issues promptly, and showing care and concern for their area. This collaborative approach enables urban local bodies to serve citizens better, fosters community engagement, promotes social cohesion and builds trust between citizens and government institutions.
- By working together, citizens and urban local bodies can create a better quality of life, address complex urban challenges and ensure sustainable development.
- Citizen participation also helps identify local needs, prioritise services and evaluate the effectiveness of urban local body initiatives.

5. How does the Municipal Corporation differ from a Nagar Panchayat in terms of functions and responsibilities?

Ans. Municipal Corporation differs from a Nagar Panchayat in terms of functions and responsibilities. Due to its large population, the Municipal corporation handles complex and extensive functions including large-scale infrastructure development, comprehensive waste management, and significant revenue collection. It is responsible for more sophisticated urban planning and public services. In contrast, a Nagar Panchayat serves smaller towns. It deals with fewer and less complex functions, focusing on basic services and local infrastructure suited to a smaller population.

6. Most of the government schemes aim to provide basic services to the people in general. What role do urban local bodies play in implementing government schemes?

Ans. Urban local bodies act as a bridge between citizens and government schemes, monitoring their implementation and ensuring that benefits reach the intended beneficiaries. This critical role requires effective coordination and communication between urban local bodies and government agencies.

Urban local bodies must also identify gaps in service delivery, advocate for citizen's needs and ensure that government schemes align with local priorities. By doing so, urban local bodies can enhance the impact of government schemes, improve the overall quality of life for citizens and promote inclusive development.

Urban local bodies must also build capacity, leverage resources, and foster partnerships to ensure successful implementation.

Long Answer Type Questions

1. Participatory democracy is essential in a democratic setup because it empowers citizens to contribute to the functioning of the country. Explain this statement, highlighting the key features and benefits of participatory democracy.

Ans. Participatory democracy is indeed essential in a democratic setup, as it empowers citizens to take an active role in decision-making processes, thereby contributing to the functioning of the country. This system ensures that citizens' voices are heard and their concerns are addressed, leading to more inclusive and responsive governance.

Key features of participatory democracy include citizen engagement, transparency and accountability, which foster trust and cooperation among community members.

The benefits of participatory democracy are numerous, including improved service delivery, better resource allocation and more effective solutions to community problems. By empowering citizens, participatory democracy promotes social capital, community ownership, and a sense of responsibility, leading to a more prosperous and stable society.

2. Urban local bodies should prioritise citizen participation in decision-making processes to ensure that their needs and concerns are addressed. Discuss.

Ans. Prioritising citizen participation in decision-making processes is essential for effective urban governance. By engaging citizens, urban local bodies can tap into local knowledge, expertise and resources, leading to more effective and sustainable solutions. Citizen participation ensures that decisions reflect community needs and priorities, builds trust, promotes accountability and builds a sense of community ownership.

Urban local bodies must create opportunities for citizen engagement through various channels, such as public meetings, surveys and digital platforms, to ensure inclusive decision-making processes.

This can be achieved by establishing citizen committees, conducting regular town hall meetings and using social media to gain feedback. By doing so, urban local bodies can ensure that citizens are empowered to contribute to the development of their city.

3. Describe the different types of urban local bodies and their characteristics.

Ans. Urban local bodies in India are categorised based on population size, each with distinct responsibilities and functions.

The different types of urban local bodies are

- **Municipal corporations** serve cities with a population above 10 lakhs, providing advanced civic amenities and implementing development projects. They have a larger budget, more powers, and a wider range of responsibilities compared to other urban local bodies.
- **Municipal councils** cater to cities with a population between 1-10 lakhs, focusing on basic services like water supply, sanitation and waste management.
- **Nagar panchayats** serve smaller towns and cities, addressing local needs and promoting community development. Each type of urban local body plays a vital role in delivering essential services, promoting economic growth and enhancing the quality of life for citizens. Understanding the characteristics of each type of urban local body is crucial for effective urban governance.

Part-II

Multiple Choice Questions (MCQs)

1. Which of the following is not typically a function of urban local bodies?
(a) Collecting local taxes
(b) Planning national economic policies
(c) Maintaining local infrastructure
(d) Implementing government schemes at the local level

2. What is a primary function of a ward committee in an urban area?
(a) National policy making
(b) Enforcing state laws
(c) Setting international tariffs
(d) Conducting health camps and reporting local issues

3. What is the characteristic of urban local bodies that allows them to function independently?
(a) Centralised authority (b) Decentralised governance
(c) State-level control (d) National-level oversight

4. What is the outcome of citizens participation in waste segregation and reporting issues promptly?
(a) Inefficient waste management
(b) Effective service delivery
(c) Increased tax burden
(d) Decreased civic engagement

5. Which of the following is correct with respect to the concept of participatory democracy?
(a) Citizens' participation in national-level decisions
(b) Citizens' participation in local-level decisions
(c) Citizens' participation in state-level decisions
(d) Citizens' participation in regional-level decisions

6. Urban local bodies are involved in checking the implementation of
(a) National policies (b) Government schemes
(c) International regulations (d) Corporate strategies

7. Which of the following is not a responsibility of urban local bodies?
(a) Maintaining infrastructure
(b) Managing burial grounds
(c) Collecting local taxes and fines
(d) Implementing national-level schemes

8. What is the highest urban local body in cities with a population above 10 lakhs?
(a) Municipal Council (b) Municipal Corporation
(c) Nagar Panchayat (d) Nagar Palika

9. Chennai and Indore have which type of urban body as their highest authority?
(a) Nagar Panchayat
(b) Municipal Council
(c) Municipal Corporation
(d) Gram Panchayat

10. Consider the following statements
I. Urban local bodies are responsible for maintaining infrastructure.
II. Urban local bodies are responsible for collecting local taxes and fines.
III Urban local bodies are responsible for implementing national-level schemes.
Which of the above statements is/are correct?
(a) I and II only (b) II and III only
(c) I and III only (d) All of these

11. Consider the following statements
I. Urban local bodies are decentralised.
II. Urban local bodies operate under a central authority.
Which of the above statements is/are correct?
(a) I only (b) II only
(c) Both I and II (d) Neither I nor II

Answers

1. (b)	**2.** (d)	**3.** (b)	**4.** (b)	**5.** (b)
6. (b)	**7.** (d)	**8.** (b)	**9.** (c)	**10.** (a)
11. (a)				

Fill in the Blanks

1. The concept of citizens actively participating in the functioning of the country is known as .... democracy.

2. Urban local bodies are ...., meaning that local communities have a direct say in the management of their areas.

3. Cities and towns are divided into smaller units known as ....

4. The Madras Corporation gained the power to collect municipal taxes in .... through a Parliamentary Act.

5. .... are the highest urban local bodies in cities with a population between 1 to 10 lakhs.

6. Urban local bodies have .... members who represent the local citizens.

Ans. 1. participatory 2. decentralised
3. wards 4. 1792
5. Municipal councils 6. elected

True or False

1. Citizens cannot report about a damaged road in their area to local authorities.

2. Urban local bodies have the power to collect local taxes and fines.

3. The functioning of wards is the same across all states.
4. Citizens can contribute to the functioning of urban local bodies by participating in waste segregation.
5. The Greater Chennai Corporation is India's oldest municipal institution.

Ans. 1. False 2. True 3. False 4. True 5. True

Match the Following

1.

List I (Terms Related To Urban Governance)	List II (Description)
A. Urban local bodies	1. Citizen active participation in country's functioning
B. Wards	2. Decentralised local government structures in urban areas
C. Participatory democracy	3. Groups that organise activities and report local issues
D. Ward committees	4. Smaller units of cities and towns

Codes

	A	B	C	D
(a)	1	3	4	2
(b)	2	4	1	3
(c)	3	4	2	1
(d)	2	3	1	4

2.

List I (Terms)	List II (Meaning)
A. Madras Corporation	1. Established in 1688
B. Nagar Panchayat	2. Population between 1-10 lakhs
C. Municipal Council	3. Smaller towns and cities
D. Bombay Municipal Corporation	4. Established in 1865

Codes

	A	B	C	D		A	B	C	D
(a)	4	2	3	1	(b)	2	4	1	3
(c)	1	4	3	2	(d)	1	3	2	4

Ans. 1. (b) 2. (d)

Assertion-Reason

1. **Assertion** (A) Urban local bodies perform tasks like garbage collection and maintaining burial grounds.
Reason (R) They are responsible for handling local administrative functions and collecting taxes.
Codes
(a) Both A and R are true and R is the correct explanation of A
(b) Both A and R are true, but R is not the correct explanation of A
(c) A is true, but R is false
(d) A is false, but R is true

2. **Assertion** (A) Citizens should show care and concern for their area.
Reason (R) It helps urban local bodies to perform their functions inefficiently.
Codes
(a) Both A and R are true and R is the correct explanation of A
(b) Both A and R are true, but R is not the correct explanation of A
(c) A is true, but R is false
(d) A is false, but R is true

3. **Assertion** (A) Nagar Panchayats are found only in cities like Delhi and Kolkata.
Reason (R) They are responsible for contributing to planning for the area's economic development.
Codes
(a) Both A and R are true and R is the correct explanation of A
(b) Both A and R are true, but R is not the correct explanation of A
(c) A is true, but R is false
(d) A is false, but R is true

4. **Assertion** (A) Indore has been awarded the cleanest city in India for ten consecutive years.
Reason (R) The achievement is largely due to the active participation of Indore citizens in maintaining cleanliness.
Codes
(a) Both A and R are true and R is the correct explanation of A
(b) Both A and R are true, but R is not the correct explanation of A
(c) A is true, but R is false
(d) A is false, but R is true

Ans. 1. (a) 2. (c) 3. (d) 4. (d)

Case Based Questions

1. Read the paragraph given below and answer the questions that follow.

Altogether, urban local bodies are responsible for a range of functions helping take care of the infrastructure, maintaining the burial ground, garbage collection and disposal, checking the implementation of government schemes, collecting local taxes and fines and so on. They also have some role in planning for the area's economic and social development. However, for these bodies to be able to perform their functions efficiently, people living in the city must also perform their duties, which means that they must show care and concern for their area (remember, this is a participatory democracy). For instance, if people carefully follow instructions regarding waste segregation, garbage collection becomes easier; or if they notice a water leakage in a street, reporting it promptly will prevent further wastage of precious water.

(i) What is the underlying value that enables urban local bodies to perform their functions efficiently?

(a) Individualism and personal gain
(b) Community involvement and collective responsibility
(c) Government control and authority
(d) Technological advancements and infrastructure

(ii) What is the value that urban local bodies should prioritise in their planning and decision-making processes?

(a) Economic growth and development
(b) Social welfare and citizen engagement
(c) Environmental sustainability and conservation
(d) Political power and control

(iii) What is the outcome of citizens' active participation in reporting issues like water leakage?

(a) Increased bureaucracy and red tape
(b) Decreased accountability and transparency
(c) Improved resource management and conservation
(d) Enhanced government control and surveillance

(iv) How can citizens contribute to making garbage collection easier?

(a) By ignoring waste segregation instructions
(b) By carefully following instructions regarding waste segregation
(c) By leaving waste unsegregated at the curbside
(d) By not reporting garbage collection issues

Ans. (i) (b), (ii) (d), (iii) (c) (iv) (b)

2. Read the paragraph given below and answer the questions that follow.

Anita Hello! Yes, I'm visiting my grandparents who live nearby. I am from the city. It's quite different from here!

Sameer Oh, really? What's it like in the city?

Anita Well, it's busy and crowded, with tall buildings everywhere. There are so many people rushing around all the time, and it's noisy compared to the quietness here. Also, people are more independent and often don't even know their neighbours.

Sameer Wow! Here, everyone knows everyone else and pitches in to help each other out we work together in the fields, celebrate festivals together, and even make decisions as a community.

Sameer Doesn't the local government help in such cases?

Anita Yes, it does. In fact, we have local bodies and elected representatives who represent us and our interests.

Here are the three indirect questions with longer answers written in simpler language

(i) What does Anita's description of city life reveal about her values and preferences?

(ii) How does Sameer's community differ from Anita city life in terms of social relationships and collective action?

(iii) What does Anita's mention of local bodies and elected representatives suggest about the role of governance in her city?

Ans. (i) Anita's description of city life shows that she likes being independent and living in a busy place. She is used to people rushing around and not knowing their neighbours. But she also appreciates the quiet and friendly atmosphere of the village, where people know and help each other. This means she values both independence and community, and maybe feels like something is missing in her city life.

(ii) Sameer's community is very different from Anita's city life. In the village, people work together, help each other and celebrate together. They have a strong sense of community and look out for one another. In contrast, Anita's city life is more individualistic, with people focusing on their own goals and not knowing their neighbours as well.

This difference highlights the importance of community and social relationships in Sameer's village.

(iii) Anita's mention of local bodies and elected representatives shows that the government plays a role in representing citizens' interests and addressing their needs.

This means that there are people and organisations in place to help make decisions and provide services for the community..

Competency Based Questions

1. In some cities the main urban local body is known as Municipal Corporation while in some, it is known as Municipal Council. What is the difference between a Municipal Corporation and a Municipal Council?

Ans. The primary difference between a Municipal Corporation and a Municipal Council is the population threshold, with Municipal Corporations serving areas with a population above 10 lakhs and Municipal Councils serving areas with a population between 1-10 lakhs. This distinction affects the powers, responsibilities and governance structures of these urban local bodies.

2. Local bodies are created to solve the local issues that exist at the grassroot level. How can urban local bodies promote economic development in their areas?

Ans. Urban local bodies can promote economic development in the following ways

- By creating a conducive business environment, investing in infrastructure, supporting local entrepreneurship and facilitating public-private partnerships.
- They can also encourage innovation, develop skills training programmes and promote local industries. By doing so, urban local bodies can stimulate economic growth, create job opportunities and improve the overall quality of life for citizens.
- Urban local bodies must also foster a culture of innovation, support start-ups and attract investments to drive economic development.

3. Effective waste management is crucial for maintaining public health and hygiene in urban areas. How can urban local bodies play a vital role in ensuring this? Discuss.

Ans. Effective waste management is indeed critical for maintaining public health and hygiene in urban areas. Urban local bodies are responsible for collecting, disposing and managing waste, which has a direct impact on the health and well-being of citizens.

Proper waste management prevents the spread of diseases, maintains a clean environment and promotes overall well-being.

Urban local bodies must prioritise waste management by investing in adequate infrastructure, implementing efficient collection systems and promoting recycling and composting practices. Additionally, they must engage citizens in waste management efforts through education and awareness programmes, encouraging responsible waste disposal practices. This can be achieved through door-to-door collection, waste segregation and proper disposal methods.

Furthermore, urban local bodies can adopt innovative technologies like waste-to-energy conversion, reducing the environmental impact of waste disposal.

Skill Based Questions as per NEP 2020

1. Activity: Organise a campaign to promote waste segregation in your neighbourhood.

Ans. Campaign theme - Let's Keep Our Neighbourhood Clean!

Waste segregation is separating trash into different bins like plastic, paper and glass.

This helps keep our environment clean and healthy.

Steps to organise a campaign are as follows

- **Form a Team** Gather 5-7 friends and classmates to help with the campaign. Assign roles like team leader, poster maker and bin distributor.
- **Make Posters and Banners** Create eye-catching signs to spread the message. Use colorful paper, markers, and glue to make posters that say 'Segregate Waste' or 'Keep Our Neighbourhood Clean'.
- **Distribute Bins** Provide separate bins for different types of waste. Label each bin clearly so people know what to put in them.
- **Educate Neighbours** Explain the importance of waste segregation. Tell them how it helps keep our environment clean and healthy.
- **Monitor Progress** Check if people are segregating waste correctly. Encourage them to keep up the good work!

2. Project Work : Design a community garden in an urban area.

Ans. Project theme - Let's Grow a Garden!

A community garden is a shared space where people grow fruits, vegetables and flowers.

Steps to design a community garden

- **Choose a Location** Find a sunny spot with good soil. Make sure it's close to a water source.
- **Plan the Garden** Decide what to grow and how to arrange the plants. Consider a mix of fruits, vegetables and flowers.
- **Prepare the Soil** Add nutrients like compost or manure to make the soil fertile. Remove weeds and rocks that can harm plants.
- **Build Garden Beds** Create separate areas for different plants. Use wooden planks or bricks to make raised beds.
- **Water and Maintain** Ensure everyone helps with upkeep. Create a schedule for watering, pruning and harvesting.

Benefits

- Fresh produce for the community
- Beautiful green space for relaxation
- Opportunity to learn about gardening and sustainability

ASSESSMENT EXERCISE

Objective Type Questions

1. In a democratic setup, what enables citizens to take an active part in the country functioning at various levels?

(a) Representative democracy (b) Participatory democracy
(c) Direct democracy (d) Indirect democracy

2. The primary function of urban local bodies is

(a) to collect taxes and fines
(b) to maintain infrastructure and provide services
(c) to implement government schemes
(d) to plan for economic development

3. What is the name of India oldest municipal institution?

(a) Greater Chennai Corporation
(b) Madras Corporation
(c) Municipal Corporation of Delhi
(d) Municipal Corporation of Mumbai

4. Which urban local body works in cities and towns with smaller populations?

(a) Municipal Corporation (b) Municipal Council
(c) Nagar Panchayat (d) Nagar Palika

5. Assertion (A) Ward committees are responsible for organising activities like health camps.

Reason (R) They are responsible for maintaining infrastructure.

Codes

(a) Both A and R are true and R is the correct explanation of A
(b) Both A and R are true, but R is not the correct explanation of A
(c) A is true, but R is false
(d) A is false, but R is true

6. Assertion (A) Cities and towns are divided into wards for water management by urban local bodies.

Reason (R) Ward committees are established to facilitate local administration and community activities.

Codes

(a) Both A and R are true and R is the correct explanation of A
(b) Both A and R are true, but R is not the correct explanation of A
(c) A is true, but R is false
(d) A is false, but R is true

7. Good governance in a democracy empowers citizens to participate in the functioning of the country at various levels, including the .... level.

8. Citizens can help urban local bodies by segregating .... at source.

9. Urban local bodies are responsible for maintaining infrastructure. (True/False)

10. The citizens also have duties to ensure that the local bodies are able to perform their functions efficiently. (True/False)

Subjective Questions (VSA, SA & LA)

1. What is participatory democracy?

2. What are urban local bodies?

3. What are wards?

4. Urban local bodies works on the principle of participatory democracy. Who makes decisions in urban local bodies?

5. How are the local issues identified? Who identifies and reports local issues to authorities?

6. What is the benefit of citizens coming together to make decisions?

7. What are the key functions of urban local bodies in maintaining public health and hygiene?

8. Urban local bodies play a major role in delivering variety of services to the citizens. What are the challenges faced by urban local bodies in providing effective services to citizens?

The Value of Work

CHAPTER 13

"This chapter explores the significance of different activities people engage in, dividing them into economic and non-economic categories. Economic activities involve earning money or creating wealth, such as a baker selling bread or a pilot flying a plane. Non-economic activities, like volunteering or family care, enrich our lives without monetary gain. This chapter highlights how both types of work contribute to personal well-being and societal development.

13.1 Economic and Non-Economic Activities

- Everyone around us performs various types of activities. These activities can be classified as **economic** or **non-economic activities**.
- Economic activities are performed in exchange of money or money's worth. For example, a vendor selling fruits in the **market**, or a lawyer arguing a case to get **fees**.
- The people involved in economic activities generally receive a **salary/payment** for their services.
- Non-economic activities do not generate income or wealth. They are performed out of feelings like gratitude, love, care and respect. For example, parents cooking food for their family or youth taking care of their grandparents.

Types of Economics Activities

We can classify the types of economic activities based on their form of payments as follows

- **Salaried Employment** The activities for which one receives monthly payment as salary are considered as salaried employment. Examples of such activities can be engineer, technician, government employees, etc.
- **Waged Employment** The activities for which a daily wage or payment is given are considered as waged employment. Wages simply means that the labour is paid on a periodic basis for their services. Examples of such services are farm labours, masons, etc.
- **Payment in Kind Employment** The economic activities that are not paid through money rather some goods are given in return are 'payment in kind' type of employment. For example, a mango farm labour receiving mangoes in return for his services.

Value Addition

Value addition if the process of increasing the value of a product at each stage of production by transforming it into another form.

For example, Rajesh is a carpenter who buys wood from a nearby market to make furniture. He uses special tools and other materials to make chairs.

Rajesh sells a chair for ₹ 1,000 each in the market. The wood for the chair costs him ₹ 600. So, profit for Rajesh is the remaining ₹ 400 (₹ 1,000 – ₹ 600). It is the **monetary value** of Rajesh's skill, time and effort, in making that chair. In this process, Rajesh has added value to the wood by turning it into furniture.

Importance of Non-Economic Activities

- The non-economic activities might not involve money but the values they generate are important for our lives.

An example of non-economic activities is **Seva: Selfless Service.**

- The act of seva can be seen at many places such as temples, gurudwaras, mosques and churches. For example, langars or community kitchens at gurudwaras serve free food to every visitor.
- These practices develop a sense of satisfaction and gratitude. They are also a way of contributing to society without expecting anything in return.

13.2 Community Participation

- Community participation is the collective efforts of a community to achieve something collectively. Some examples of community participation include **Swachh Bharat Abhiyan** and **Van Mahotsav**.
- The Swachh Bharat Abhiyan is based on the collective efforts of all Indian citizens to keep their surroundings clean. Individually, we keep our homes and surroundings clean. However, in this programme, people also come together to clean up streets, roads, parks and other public places or community areas. Together, these efforts lead to a clean home, neighbourhood, society and nation.
- Van Mahotsav (the festival of forests) in India is celebrated to promote awareness about the value of trees and the conservation of forests. This initiative brings together members of the community and encourages them to plant trees in their surroundings.

Glossary

Money's Worth The monetary value that a person gives to an object, based on the benefits they take from it.

Market A place where people engage in the exchange of goods and services. People may exchange goods and services for other goods but in most markets these are exchanged for money.

Fee A payment made to a person or organisation in exchange for professional advice or services.

Salary A fixed regular payment generally paid monthly by an employer to an employee.

Wage A payment made by the employer to the worker for a specific period of time.

Payment in kind A non-cash payment that is received for the work performed.

Manufacturing It is the process of converting raw materials into finished products through the use of tools, machinery and labour.

THE VALUE OF WORK

Economic Activities

Includes activities that are done in exchange for money

Different forms of payments

- **Salary** A fixed regular payment generally paid monthly by an employer to an employee.
- **Fees** A payment made to a person or organisation in exchange for professional advices or services.
- **Wages** A payment made by the employer to the worker for a specific period of time.
- **Payment in Kind** A non-cash payment that is received for work done.

Value Addition

- Economic activity adds value at each stage of the process of transforming something into a another form.

Non-Economic Activities

- Such activities do not generate income or wealth.
- They are performed as a feeling of gratitude, love, care and respect.

Selfless Service

- Such activities develop a sense of satisfaction and gratitude, for what we have.
- One contributes to the society without expecting any returns.

Community Participation

- Collective efforts
- Initiatives like Van Mahotsav and Swachh Bharat Mission brings people together for good deeds.

NCERT FOLDER

Detailed Answers of All NCERT Questions

Let's Explore (Page 185)

Q.1 What activities did the people in Anu's and Kabir's story engage in? Mention them in the table given below

Character in the story	Activities they are engaged in

Ans.

Character in the story	Activities they are engaged in
Geeta	Pilot
Kabir's grandfather	Retired officer, teaches geography, gardening, helping in household tasks
Anu's parents	Shopkeepers
Anu's brother, Rohan	Software engineer

Let's Explore (Page 187)

Q2. In the table given below, did you notice the third empty column? Label this column 'economic / non-economic activity'. Now classify them according to the nature of activity.

Character in the story	Activities they are engaged in

Ans.

Character in the story	Activities they are engaged in	Type of activity
Geeta	Pilot	Economic activity
Kabir's grandfather	Retired officer, teaches geography, gardening, house errands	Non- economic activity
Anu's parents	Shopkeepers	Economic activity
Anu's brother, Rohan	Software engineer	Economic activity

Think About It (Page 187)

Q3. When Kabir's grandfather voluntarily teaches the neighbourhood kids for free, is that an economic activity or a non-economic activity?

How is it different from your teachers teaching you at school? Discuss with your classmates.

Ans. Kabir's grandfather teaches the neighbourhood kids for free voluntarily. He is not getting fees for his services hence, it is a non-economic activity. When a teacher teaches at school they receive a salary for their teaching services. The school teachers are involved in economic activities. Therefore, it is different from what Kabir's grandfather does voluntarily.

Q4. What are some non-economic activities that are important to you and your family? Why are they valuable?

Ans. Some of the non- economic activities that are valuable to us and our family are

- Cooking food for family
- Taking care of grandparents
- Watering plants
- Helping our parents in cleaning house

They are valuable to us because it develops a sense of care, love and responsibility.

Think About It (Page 189)

Q5. On your way from home to school today, can you recall the various economic activities that people are engaged in? In what ways do you think those people are paid?

Ans. The various economic activities that people are engaged in are given below

Economic activity	How people are paid
Fruit selling vendor	Money
Taxi driver	Salary
Shopkeeper	Money
Construction labourer	Wages

Let's Explore (Page 191)

Q6. Put a (✓) against those activities/professions that you think create monetary value. Can you add two activities and examples of money related value creation to the empty rows at the end?

Activity/ Profession	Example of money related value creation
Baker	
Tailor	
Farmers repairing their tractor	
Doctor	
Parents cooking dinner for the family	
Scientist	
Person taking care of a sick grandparent	

Ans.

Activity/Profession	Example of money related value creation
Lawyer	✓
Teacher	✓
Tailor	✓
Scientist	✓
Doctor	✓
Baker	✓

Think About It (Page 193)

Q7. Many communities in India have similar practices that involve community participation. Can you identify a few from your area?

Ans. Some examples of community practices are Swachh Bharat Abhiyan, Van Mahotsav, Polio Immunisation campaign, Blood Donation camps, etc.

Q8. We celebrate many festivals in India. During these festivals, people gather to organise all the various activities. They decorate the place together and share the food that they cook. Are these non-economic activities? Why do you think they still hold value?

Ans. During festivals, decoration of places and sharing of cooked food are non-economic activities.

Yes, these activities hold values. These activities develop the value of satisfaction, respect and appreciation for what we have.

Q9. Can you identify community programmes that have been undertaken by your school or in your locality? What did you observe during these programmes?

Ans. A community programme that has been undertaken by my school was organising an educational support programme.

During the programme, students can donate their books, notebooks and stationeries to the NGO. The school also asked teachers voluntarily to teach students from slums.

Questions, Activities and Projects

Q1. How are economic activities different from non-economic activities?

Ans. The differences between economic and non- economic activities are as follows

Economic activities	Non-economic activities
These activities are performed in exchange for money or money's worth.	These activities are performed out of love, care, gratitude, or social service and do not generate monetary value.
For example, a businessperson selling school bags in the market, a farmer selling produce in the market, a lawyer arguing a case and earning a fee.	For example, parents cooking food for the family, family members helping with household chores, youth taking care of grandparents.

Q2. What kind of economic activities do people engage in? Illustrate with examples.

Ans. People get engaged in various types of economic activities. Some of them are as follows

- A person working as a labour at farm for wages.
- A person teaching at school for a salary.
- A technician working at a construction site for salary.
- A driver transporting goods from one place to another for wages.
- A farm labourer receiving a portion of the harvested crops, instead of money for his work.

Q3. There is a great value attached to people who are engaged in community service activities. Comment on this statement.

Ans. There is a great value attached to people who are engaged in community service activities. The community services provides a sense of satisfaction for the people. Involving in community services showcase the individual's responsibility towards humanity and the environment.

Q4. What are the various ways in which people are compensated for various economic activities? Give some examples.

Ans. There are various ways in which people are compensated for economic activities.

Some of them are as follows

- **Salary** Salary is a fixed regular payment generally paid monthly by an employer to an employee. For example, an employee at the post office receives a salary every month.
- **Fees** It is a payment made to a person or organisation in exchange for professional advice or services. For example, a fee paid to a doctor and a lawyer.
- **Wages** Wages are payment made by the employer to the worker for a specific period of time. For example, a mason is paid weekly at construction sites.
- **Payment in kind** It is a non-cash payment that is received for the work performed. Generally, such types of payments are given to farm labourers. For example, a labourer is getting paid by a share of wheat from the total cultivation.

REVIEW EXERCISE

Including Competency Based Questions

Part I

Very Short Answer Type Questions

1. Which type of activities are considered as economic activities?

Ans. The activities that involve money or are performed in exchange for money or its equivalent are considered as economic activities.

2. Which form of activities do not generate income but are done out of feelings like love, care or respect?

Ans. Non-economic activities are the ones that do not generate income but are done out of feelings like love, care or respect.

3. What does a lawyer earn by arguing a case for the client?

Ans. A lawyer earns a fee for arguing a case for the client.

Short Answer Type Questions

1. How does the concept of value addition apply to economic activities? Explain with an example.

Ans. The concept of value addition applies to economic activities by adding value at each stage of the process of transforming something into another form. For example, in the process of making a chair, initially, the value is added when raw timber is cut and processed into planks. These planks are then shaped and assembled into a chair. Finally, the chair is painted or finished. Thus, each stage of this process increases the overall value of the chair, transforming it from a simple piece of wood into a finished product that is more valuable and useful.

2. "Software engineer can be involved in both economic and non-economic activities." Explain how.

Ans. A person may be involved in both economic and non-economic activities. While an economic activity is meant for earning money or wealth, non-economic activities are done for a sense of self satisfaction, love and care.

A software engineer works for a company and earns a salary for that. In this way, he is engaged in economic activity. If a software engineer is spending his weekends teaching computer to kids at an NGO for free, then he/she is involved in a non-economic activity.

Long Answer Type Question

1. How do economic activities contribute to our everyday lives? Provideexamples.

Ans. Economic activities greatly impact our daily lives by supplying essential goods and services. For example, a baker's work provides us with fresh bread, while a teacher's role equips students with critical knowledge and skills for their future. These activities not only fulfill our basic needs but also support trade, create job opportunities, and generate income. By facilitating the exchange of products and services, economic activities help improve our standard of living and promote overall economic growth. This process enhances our quality of life and contributes to community development, showcasing the integral role of economic activities in both personal and societal well-being.

Part II

Multiple Choice Questions (MCQs)

1. Anu's brother teaches computer skills to young people on weekends. What type of economic activity is it?

(a) Economic activity (b) Non-economic activity
(c) Social activity (d) Recreational activity

2. Which of the following is an example of payment in kind?

(a) Salary given to the employee
(b) Fee paid to a lawyer
(c) Daily wage given to plumber
(d) Mangoes given to a farm labourer

3. What does the term "money's worth" refer to?

(a) The physical appearance of money
(b) The monetary value placed on an object
(c) The total amount of money a person has
(d) The exchange rate of money

4. Geeta is a pilot in the Indian Air Force and brings honour to the country. How will she be paid for her services as a pilot?

(a) Salary (b) Fees
(c) Wages (d) Payment in kind

5. Consider the following statements.

(i) A farmer selling fruits or vegetables in the market is performing a non-economic activity.
(ii) Non-economic activities are done out of feelings like gratitude, love, care and respect.
(iii) Taking care of your grandparents is a non-economic activity.
(iv) A pilot in the Indian Air Force is performing an economic activity.

Which of the above statements are correct?

(a) (i) and (ii) (b) (iii) and (iv)
(c) (ii), (iii) and (iv) (d) None of these

Ans. 1. (b) 2. (d) 3. (b) 4. (a) 5. (c)

Fill in the Blanks

1. Economic activities are those that involve money or are performed in exchange for ....
2. .... activities do not generate income but are done out of feelings like love, care and respect.
3. A .... is a payment made to a person or organisation in exchange for professional advice or services.
4. Value addition involves enhancing the value of a product at each stage of ....
5. Community participation, such as the celebration of ...., promotes awareness about forest conservation.

Ans. 1. money 2. Non-economic 3. fees 4. transformation 5. Van Mahotsav

True or False

1. Parents cooking dinner for their family is an example of an economic activity.
2. Mamta, a school teacher, performs an economic activity by receiving a salary for her work.
3. The value generated by non-economic activities is important for social welfare and personal well-being.

Ans. 1. False 2. True 3. True

Match the Following

List I (Economic Activity)	List II (Form of Payment)
A. Engineer	1. Weekly fee
B. Farm labourer	2. Monthly salary
C. Carpenter	3. Daily wage
D. Online class instructor	4. Payment in kind

Codes

	A	B	C	D		A	B	C	D
(a)	2	4	3	1	(b)	3	4	2	1
(c)	4	3	2	1	(d)	1	2	3	4

Ans. (a)

Assertion-Reason

1. **Assertion** (A) Teaching children for free is a non-economic activity.
   Reason (R) Non-economic activities do not generate income and are driven by feelings like love and care.
   Codes
   (a) Both A and R are true and R is the correct explanation of A
   (b) Both A and R are true, but R is not the correct explanation of A
   (c) A is true, but R is false
   (d) A is false, but R is true
2. **Assertion** (A) Economic activities add value at each stage of transforming something into another form.
   Reason (R) Economic activities involve monetary transactions that reflect the value addition process.
   Codes
   (a) Both A and R are true and R is the correct explanation of A
   (b) Both A and R are true, but R is not the correct explanation of A
   (c) A is true, but R is false
   (d) A is false, but R is true

3. Assertion (A) Economic activities are always performed out of love and care.

Reason (R) Economic activities are performed in exchange for money.

Codes

(a) Both A and R are true and R is the correct explanation of A

(b) Both A and R are true, but R is not the correct explanation of A

(c) A is true, but R is false

(d) A is false, but R is true

4. Assertion (A) The Swachh Bharat Abhiyan aims to keep public places clean through collective efforts.

Reason (R) Swachh Bharat Abhiyan is an individual effort to clean personal homes.

Codes

(a) Both A and R are true and R is the correct explanation of A

(b) Both A and R are true, but R is not the correct explanation of A

(c) A is true, but R is false

(d) A is false, but R is true

Ans. 1. (a) 2. (a) 3. (d) 4. (c)

Case Based Questions

1. Read the source given below and answer the questions that follows.

The Swachh Bharat Abhiyan is based on the collective efforts of all Indian citizens to keep our surroundings clean. Individually, we keep our homes and surroundings clean. People have also come together to clean up streets, roads, parks and other public places or community areas. Together, these efforts lead to a clean home, neighbourhood, society and nation. Another example of collective community participation is the celebration of Van Mahotsav (the festival of forests) in India to promote awareness about the value of trees and the conservation of forests. The initiative brings together members of the community for tree plantation drives.

(i) **What is the main objective of the Swachh Bharat Abhiyan?**

(a) To celebrate traditional Indian festivals

(b) To keep homes and surroundings clean through collective efforts

(c) To promote urbanisation in rural areas

(d) To conserve water resources

(ii) **A community celebration like Van Mahotsav is celebrated with the purpose such as ....**

(a) to organise cultural festivals

(b) to promote awareness about the value of trees and forest conservation

(c) to increase industrial activities

(d) to support technological innovations

(iii) **How do community members participate in Van Mahotsav?**

(a) By organising sports events

(b) By participating in tree plantation drives

(c) By attending educational workshops

(d) By donating to charitable organisations

(iv) **Which of the following activities is not associated with the Swachh Bharat Abhiyan?**

(a) Cleaning streets (b) Planting trees

(c) Cleaning parks (d) Cleaning roads

Ans. (i) (b), (ii) (b), (iii) (b), (iv) (b)

2. Read the source given below and answer the following questions.

Kavya was excited to go to her aunt's house in the village of Kamlapur. On the way, she saw that a highway was being built near the village and the construction site was abuzz with activity.

Large machines, such as excavators and bulldozers, were being operated by dedicated technicians. This new highway promised to reduce the travel time to the nearest town from five hours to just two hours. Kavya thought that she would be able to visit her aunt more often once the highway was ready, since it would take less time to travel there. Happy with this thought, Kavya ran to greet her aunt and to eat the delicious jalebis that she had made. They were joined by Kavya's uncle, who had just returned home from work. He is a technician in a construction company and operates a bulldozer. He receives a monthly salary for his services.

The next day, Kavya's aunt woke up early to finish her share of the household chores and left for work. She is employed at the village post office and is paid a monthly salary. In the evening, after her office work, she also conducts online classes to help students prepare for school exams. She charges a weekly fee for these classes. On the weekend, Kavya visited a local mango orchard with her aunt to have some delicious mangoes. There she saw Sahil, a farm labourer who was using a tractor to till a farmer's land nearby. He earns a daily wage for his efforts. He gets some payment for his work in cash, and the remaining part of the payment in the form of mangoes of equal value. The mangoes that he receives as a part of his work are called payment in kind.

(i) **What roles do Kavya's uncle and aunt play in their professional lives and how are they paid for their work?**

(ii) **In what ways does Kavya's aunt contribute to the community besides her primary job and how does she earn additional income?**

(iii) **How does the presence of modern machinery, such as excavators and bulldozers, at the construction site reflect the nature of the highway project Kavya observed?**

Ans. (i) Kavya's uncle is a technician in a construction company who operates a bulldozer and receives a monthly salary for his services.

Kavya's aunt works at the village post office, also earning a monthly salary. Additionally, she conducts online classes to help students prepare for school exams, for which she charges a weekly fee.

(ii) The primary job of Kavya's aunt is an employee at the post office. She contributes to the community by conducting online classes to help students prepare for school exams. She earns additional income by charging a weekly fee for these educational services.

(iii) The presence of modern machinery like excavators and bulldozers at the construction site indicates that the highway project near Kamlapur is a large-scale and technologically advanced project. This reflects the significant effort and resources being invested to improve infrastructure and reduce travel time in the area.

Competency Based Questions

1. If Aisha volunteers to clean up the local park without receiving any payment, what kind of activity is she performing?

Ans. If Aisha volunteers to clean up the local park without receiving any payment, then she is performing a non-economic activity.

2. Economic activities also add value at each stage of transformations. Explain with an example.

Ans. Economic activities add value at each stage of transformation by transforming something to another form. For example, a carpenter makes a chair from wood. In this way he is adding value to wood by transforming it into a chair.

3. "Non-economic activities may not involve money, but the value they generate is important in our lives". Explain with an example.

Ans. Non-economic activities may not involve money, but the value they generate is important in our lives. For example,

- Langars or community kitchens at gurudwaras serve food to every visitor for free. These practices foster a sense of satisfaction and gratitude for what we have and they are also a way of contributing to society without expecting anything in return.
- Community participation helps in keeping the environment clean. People have also come together to clean up streets, roads, parks and other public places or community areas just to contribute towards development of the country. Together, these efforts lead to a clean home, neighbourhood, society and nation.

4. "Kavya's uncle and aunt receive a monthly salary for their services." Define salary. In what other ways can a person involved in economic activities be paid?

Ans. A person generally receives a salary for their services. Salary is a fixed regular payment generally paid monthly by employer to an employee.

The other ways in which a person can be paid for their services are as follows

- **Fees** It is a payment made to a person or organisation in exchange for professional advice or services. For example, a fee paid to a doctor or a tutor.
- **Wages** Wages are the payment made by the employer to the worker for a specific period of time. For example, a mason being paid on a weekly basis.
- **Payment in kind** It is a non-cash payment that is received for the work or services provided. For example, a farm labour being paid through mangoes for his services.

Skill Based Questions as per NEP 2020

1. Discuss how the balance between economic and non-economic activities can contribute to personal and societal well-being.

Ans. Balancing economic and non-economic activities is essential for both personal and societal well-being. Economic activities provide financial resources necessary for sustaining livelihoods. However, non-economic activities, such as Kabir's grandfather teaching kids and community participation in cleanliness drives, develop social connections and emotional fulfillment. Together, they ensure not only material prosperity but also emotional and social well-being. This balance promotes a more fulfilling and harmonious life, demonstrating the need for both types of activities in a well-rounded community.

2. In every family, each member is doing some activities. Based on your understanding, list down both economic and non-economic activities performed by different members.

Ans. In a family there are parents, grandparents and children. All of them do some economic and non-economic activities. Some of them are given below

Member	Economic activity	Non-economic activity
Grandparents	Most of them are retired and don't do economic activities.	Activities such as gardening, helping children in studies.
Parents	Do different jobs like vendors, business, government employee, doctor, lawyer, etc.	• Making food for the family. • Washing the clothes • Taking care of children.
Children	Children are not involved in any economic activity.	• Taking care of pets • Helping their parents in house chores.

3. Illustrate how volunteer activities can complement formal education and contribute to overall development.

Ans. Volunteer activities complement formal education by providing practical experiences and fostering community spirit. Some of these can be explained through following examples

- Kabir's grandfather's voluntary teaching geography classes helps the children's learning beyond the classroom, enhancing their knowledge and curiosity.
- Rohan's weekend computer classes for young adults provide them with essential skills that may not be covered in their formal education, preparing them for future job opportunities.
- These volunteer activities not only fill educational gaps but also instill values of service and social responsibility. Such contributions are integral to overall development, developing individuals equipped with both academic knowledge and practical skills.

ASSESSMENT EXERCISE

Objective Type Questions

1. Which of the following activities can be considered non-economic activity?

(a) Operating a bulldozer
(b) Teaching kids for free
(c) Earning a salary as a technician
(d) Selling goods in a market

2. What could be the major objective of conducting any non-economic activity?

(a) Financial gain
(b) Professional advancement
(c) Feelings of love and care
(d) Monetary transactions

3. Assertion (A) Kabir's grandfather's gardening is an economic activity.

Reason (R) Economic activities involve activities done in exchange for money.

Codes

(a) Both A and R are true and R is the correct explanation of A
(b) Both A and R are true, but R is not the correct explanation of A
(c) A is true, but R is false
(d) A is false, but R is true

4. Rohan volunteers to teach .... skills to young adults on weekends.

5. Sahil, a farm labourer, receives .... and payment in kind for his work.

6. A technician earning a monthly salary is engaged in a non-economic activity. (True/False)

7. Teaching children for free is considered an economic activity. (True/False)

Subjective Questions (VSA, SA & LA)

1. What is the primary objective of non-economic activities?

2. How does Rohan contribute to the community on weekends?

3. What do technicians operating machines during highway construction earn?

4. Describe the role of Geeta Aunty in the community.

5. What does Kabir's grandfather do for the neighbourhood children and why is it significant?

6. Sahil is a farm labour who receives mangoes in return for his services. Discuss which type of activity is this?

7. Explain the importance of both economic and non-economic activities in the lives of individuals, using examples.

8. Discuss the significance of volunteer work in enhancing community relationships and personal growth, with examples.

Economic Activities Around Us

CHAPTER 14

Activities that create **monetary value** are called economic activities. Various economic activities have developed over decades. For example, most people were involved in agriculture, livestock rearing, the production of tools, pottery and cloth weaving earlier. But today, there are diverse economic activities such as manufacturing computers, mobile phones and drones, working in banks, schools and hotels, etc.

14.1 Classification of Economic Activities

- The economic activities with similar characteristics can be grouped or classified into broader groups called **economic sectors**.
- We can classify economic activities based on their functions as **primary**, **secondary** or **tertiary**. All these activities are interdependent to each other.

Primary Sector

- Under primary sector economic activities, people are directly dependent on nature to produce goods.
- The group of activities that extract raw materials **directly from nature** such as farming, fishing, forestry, etc. are included in the primary sector.
- For example, the cultivation of grains and vegetables from agricultural farms, collection of wood from the forests, extraction of coal from mines, fish from fisheries, eggs from poultry farms, etc. are all primary sector economic activities.

Secondary Sector

- Secondary sector activities are a group of activities that process outputs **derived from the primary sector** into products for sale or consumption.
- The secondary sector activities include the construction of buildings, roads, etc. and providing utilities like water, electricity, gas and other such necessities.
- It also includes the manufacturing of products in factories and production units to process raw materials from the primary sector into some other form that can be further sold or consumed.
- For example, the processing of grains to make flour in mills, processing of tea leaves and manufacturing of furniture from wood.

Tertiary Sector

- Tertiary sector economic activities are a group of activities that include the services that **support both primary and secondary sectors**, such as transportation, banking and management of business.
- This sector is also called the **service sector**. Some examples of tertiary sector activities include fruit or vegetable vendors selling the farm produce to household consumers.
- Doctors, nurses, teachers, lawyers and pilots who provide their services to those who need them are also included in the tertiary sector.

Interdependence among Sectors

- The three types of economic activities or economic sectors play an important role in the process of conversion of natural raw materials into finished products for final consumption.
- These three sectors are interdependent. For example, extracting pulp from trees to make paper and finally producing a book, requires all the three sectors to work together.

- Another example to understand the interdependence of three sectors is the co-operative, named **Anand Milk Union Limited** (AMUL). It was set up in 1946 under the leadership of **Tribhuvandas Patel** and **Dr. Varghese Kurien**. The activities of this co-operative are interconnected in the following ways
  (i) **Primary Activities** The milk used at AMUL is sold in the market at a later time. This process is a primary activity as the product (milk) is obtained directly from the natural resource (cows).
  (ii) **Secondary Activities** The milk is processed to make milk products like butter, cheese or ghee.
  (iii) **Tertiary Activities** AMUL uses trucks, trains, planes and ships to distribute its products to retail stores and other shops across Gujarat, as well as other states of India to transport and sell its products. Here, transportation, trading and retail are tertiary activities.

Must Know !

There are many other milk co-operative brands like AMUL. Some of them are Nandini from Karnataka, Mother Dairy from Delhi- NCR, Aavin from Tamil Nadu, Sudha from Bihar, etc. There is a co-operative named **SEWA** that supports women to become self-reliant.

Glossary

Monetary Value When the value of something is measured in terms of money.

Economic Sectors The groups in which various economic activities are classified.

Primary Sector The groups of activities that include extraction of raw materials directly from nature.

Secondary Sector The group of activities that include the processing of raw materials taken from the primary sector.

Tertiary Sector The group of activities that provide services to different sectors.

Extraction The process of taking out resources from their natural source.

Retail The sale of goods to the public in small quantities for personal use.

Export The selling of goods and services to other countries.

Warehouse Large building for storing products before they are sold, used or rented out to shops

Dairy A place where milk is collected and stored

Co-operatives A group of people that come together to fulfill their economic and social needs formally.

Middlemen Persons who buy goods from producers to sell them to consumers. They take charges for it.

Pasteurisation It is a process by which milk is preserved through heating at a specific temperature and kills harmful bacteria.

Factory A place or building where goods are produced.

ECONOMIC ACTIVITIES AROUND US

Classification of Economic Sectors

Economic activities can be classified based on similar characteristics.

Primary Activities

- The activities in which people are directly dependent on nature to produce goods are called primary activities.
- For example, Agriculture, fishing, forestry, etc.

Secondary Activities

- Such activities in which people are dependent on ouputs of primary sector and transform them in goods.
- For example, Construction of buildings, flour mills, processing of tea

Tertiary Activities

- All those economic activities that provide support to people involved in primary and secondary activities are called tertiary activities.
- Also called 'Service sector'
- For example, Fruit or vegetable vendors, doctors, teachers, lawyers, etc.

Interdependence Among Sectors

- All three forms of activities play major role in transformation of raw materials into finished goods.
- All three sectors work together in making a final product.
- For example, extracting pulp from the trees to making paper and finally producing the books require all three sectors to work together.

NCERT FOLDER

Detailed Answers of All NCERT Questions

Think About It (Page 199)

Q1. Can you think of any primary activities that you may have seen in the past? What are the natural resources used in these activities? Name two of them and discuss your experiences with your classmates.

Ans. Farming is an example of a primary activity which I have seen in the past. Soil and seeds are two natural resources used in farming. (Students can discuss their own experiences).

Let's Explore (Page 200)

Q2. Now that we have seen some examples of secondary sector activities, can you name two more economic activities in the secondary sector?

Ans. Two examples of secondary sector activities are

- Making jam from fruit pulp.
- Making paper from wood.

Think About It (Page 207)

Q3. Observe the different stages of the process shown in the figure given below and discuss them with your fellow classmates.

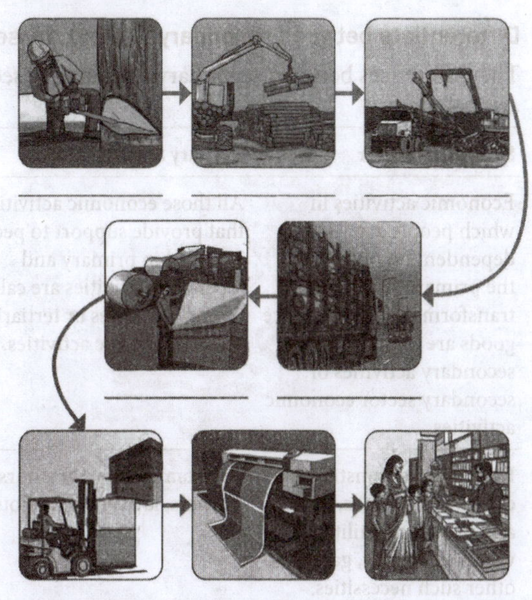

Ans. The image shows different stages of manufacturing a book. This image represents how all three sectors of the economy are dependent on each other.

Let's Explore (Page 208)

Q4. List the economic activities in your neighbourhood and label them appropriately as primary, secondary or tertiary. Draw arrows to show how they are connected to each other. In what ways are they dependent on each other? What would happen if one of the activities ceased to exist?

Ans. Some economic activities in our neighbourhood that we often see are

- Vegetable vendors
- Milk vendors
- Transport services
- Farming
- Teaching
- Medical services
- Bakery

These activities are interdependent on each other. A farmer requires transport services to take his produce to mandis. Then bakery buys flour or grains to make cookies. Again bakery will require transport services to sell their product to market.

If any one of these activities ceases to exist then the working of two other activities will also be disturbed.

Questions, Activities and Projects

Q1. What is the primary sector? How is it different from the secondary sector? Give two examples.

Ans. The economic activities in which people directly extract raw materials from nature are the primary sector of the economy.

The secondary activities deal with the manufacturing of goods from the outputs of primary activities, while in primary activities produce is extracted from nature. Examples of primary sector activities are as follows

- Cultivation of grains is an example of a primary activity while making flour at a mill is a secondary activity.
- Extracting iron from mine is a primary activity while using iron in automobiles is an example of secondary activity.

Q2. How does the secondary sector depend on the tertiary sector? Illustrate with a few examples.

Ans. The secondary sector depends on the tertiary sector in the following ways

- When the goods are produced they are transported to the market, in which tertiary sector services are required to load and transport goods.

- In a factory, some technicians provide services to repair the machines.

Q3. Give an example of interdependence between primary, secondary and tertiary sectors. Show it using a flow diagram.

Ans. Primary, secondary and tertiary sectors are interdependent in the following ways

- **Primary Sector** The process of cultivation, requires tractors, seeds, fertilisers etc. that are produced by the secondary sector activities.
- **Secondary Sector** Secondary sector activities are dependent on primary activities for raw materials and tertiary sector for marketing, research, finances and transportation.
- **Tertiary Sector** The tertiary sector does not produce any goods. It complements the other two sectors, hence dependent on them.

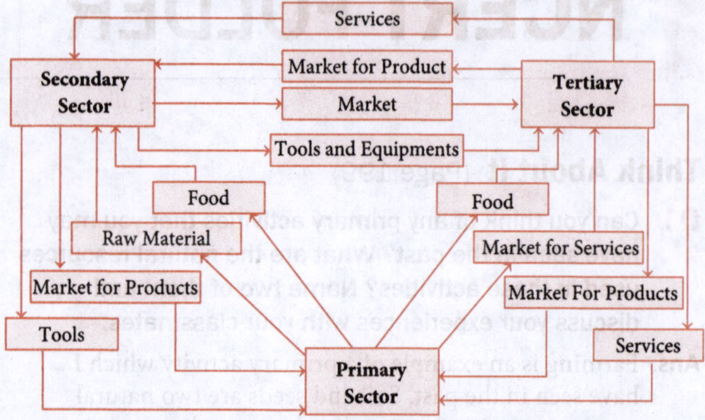

REVIEW EXERCISE

Including Competency Based Questions

PART I

Very Short Answer Type Questions

1. In what ways, the tertiary sector support the growth of primary and secondary sectors?

Ans. The tertiary sector supports the growth of primary and secondary sectors in the following ways

- It supports the primary and secondary sectors by providing services like transportation and warehouses.
- Tertiary sectors provide vendors to sell outputs of primary and secondary sectors.

2. Why do you think the number of economic activities has increased over time?

Ans. Earlier, the majority of the population was involved in activities like agriculture, fishing, mining, etc. but over time with development of technology, other activities like transportation, manufacturing, banking, teaching, etc. developed. This represents that the number of economic activities has increased over time.

3. How might the formation of co-operatives like AMUL impact rural economies?

Ans. The formation of co-operatives like AMUL impacts rural economies in the following ways

- It increases the decision-making power of the group.
- It reduces the dependency on the middlemen.
- It increases the scale of production and profit.

Short Answer Type Question

1. Differentiate between secondary and tertiary sectors.

Ans. The differences between secondary and tertiary sectors are as follows

Secondary Sector	Tertiary Sector
Economic activities in which people are dependent on outputs of the primary sector and transform them to produce goods are known as secondary activities or secondary sector economic activities.	All those economic activities that provide support to people involved in primary and secondary activities are called tertiary activities or tertiary sector economic activities.
For example, construction of buildings, roads, etc., and providing utilities like water, electricity, gas and other such necessities.	For example, doctors, nurses, teachers, lawyers and pilots.

Long Answer Type Questions

1. Explain how the three economic sectors are interconnected, using the example of the milk co-operative.

Ans. The interconnection of economic sectors is demonstrated in milk production and distribution in the following ways

- The production of milk begins in the primary sector with dairy farming, where cows are raised and milk is produced.
- This raw milk then moves to the secondary sector, where it is processed in factories into various dairy products like cheese, butter and packaged milk.
- Finally, the tertiary sector comes into play as these products are transported, marketed, and sold in stores. Additionally, tertiary sector services like veterinary care for the cows, financial services for the dairy farmers and software for managing production all support the primary and secondary activities.

This interconnectedness shows how each sector relies on and supports the others, creating a complex economic web.

2. Give some examples to show that services provided by the tertiary sector make our lives easier.

Ans. Tertiary sector includes economic activities which support people involved in primary and secondary activities. Some examples to show that services provided by the tertiary sector make our lives easier are as follows

- **Transportation** The driver of a truck transports grains and vegetables from the farm to a factory or the market.
- **Trade** The fruit or vegetable vendors sell the farm produce to household consumers.
- **Professional Services** Doctors, nurses, teachers, lawyers and pilots provide their services to those who need them. There are technicians who repair and service electronic items including mobile phones and televisions, mechanics who repair vehicles like cars and tractors, and electricians who ensure regular supply of electricity.
- **Communication** Development of mobile and internet, software development has made communication easier and faster.

PART II

Multiple Choice Questions (MCQs)

1. Primary activities are directly dependent on nature to produce goods. Which of the following can be included as primary activity?

(a) Agriculture (b) Software development
(c) Banking (d) Automobile manufacturing

2. Which sector involves transforming raw materials into finished products?

(a) Primary sector (b) Secondary sector
(c) Tertiary sector (d) Service sector

3. What type of economic activities does the tertiary sector include?

(a) Agriculture and mining
(b) Manufacturing and construction
(c) Healthcare and banking
(d) Fishing and forestry

4. What economic activity is associated with the service sector?

(a) Mining (b) Agriculture
(c) Transportation (c) Construction

5. A milk cooperative in Anand district in 1946 was set up to increase the income of farmers. This cooperative was set up under the leadership of Tribhuvandas Patel and Dr. Varghese Kurien. Which of the following cooperative is it?

(a) Mother Dairy (b) AMUL (c) Vijaya (d) Sudha

6. Consider the following statements.

I. The group of activities that involves the provision of services which complement both primary and secondary sectors are tertiary activities.

II. The group of activities that involve processing of raw materials derived from the primary sector into products for sale or consumption are secondary activities.

III. The group of activities that involve extraction of raw materials indirectly from nature are primary activities.

Which of the statements given above are true?

(a) I and II (b) I and III
(c) II and III (d) All of these

Ans. 1. (a) 2. (b) 3. (c)
4. (c) 5. (b) 6. (a)

Fill in the Blanks

1. Economic activities that create .... value are called economic activities.
2. Activities in which people are directly dependent on .... to produce goods are known as primary activities.
3. The secondary sector includes the construction of buildings and ....

4. The tertiary sector involves the provision of .... that complements both primary and secondary sectors.

5. The cooperative AMUL was set up in 1946 under the leadership of .... and ....

Ans. 1. monetary 2. nature 3. roads 4. services 5. Tribhuvandas Patel, Dr. Varghese Kurien

True or False

1. Economic activities are classified into three main sectors: primary, secondary and tertiary.
2. The secondary sector involves the direct extraction of raw materials from nature.
3. The tertiary sector includes manufacturing goods from raw materials.
4. AMUL was initially set up to eliminate the role of middlemen in the milk trade.
5. The primary sector includes activities like agriculture, mining and fishing.

Ans. 1. True 2. False 3. False 4. True 5. True

Assertion-Reason

1. **Assertion** (A) The primary sector is crucial for economic activities.

   Reason (R) It involves the extraction of raw materials directly from nature.

   Codes

   (a) Both A and R are true and R is the correct explanation of A
   (b) Both A and R are true, but R is not the correct explanation of A
   (c) A is true, but the R is false
   (d) A is false, but the R is true

2. **Assertion** (A) Tertiary sector activities are not important for the economy.

   Reason (R) They provide support to primary and secondary sector.

   Codes

   (a) Both A and R are true and R is the correct explanation of A
   (b) Both A and R are true, but R is not the correct explanation of A
   (c) A is true, but the R is false
   (d) A is false, but the R is true

Ans. 1. (a) 2. (d)

Case Based Questions

1. **Read the following source given below and answer the questions that follow**

   Economic activities in which people are dependent on outputs of the primary sector and transform them to produce goods are known as secondary activities or secondary sector economic activities. The secondary sector includes the construction of buildings, roads, etc. and providing utilities like water, electricity, gas and other such necessities. It also includes the manufacturing of products in factories and production units to process raw material from the primary sector into some other form that can be further sold or consumed. Some examples of secondary sector activities include the processing of grains obtained from agricultural fields to make flour in mills, extraction of oil from groundnuts and processing of tea leaves to derive tea. Similarly, wood from the forest is converted into furniture and paper, cotton is used to make clothes, and steel from iron ore is used to make automobiles like cars, trucks, etc.

   (i) **Under secondary sector activities output of primary activity is converted into final goods. Which of the following can be good example of such activities?**

   (a) Cotton into clothes (b) Fish into fish oil
   (c) Coal into electricity (d) All of these

   (ii) **Which of the following is not the part of secondary activities?**

   (a) Processing raw materials
   (b) Providing direct services
   (c) Manufacturing goods
   (d) Constructing infrastructure

   (iii) **In which sector would the construction of roads and buildings be classified?**

   (a) Primary sector (b) Secondary sector
   (c) Tertiary sector (d) Quaternary sector

   (iv) **Which of the following activities is not a part of the secondary sector?**

   (a) Processing of grains to make flour
   (b) Refining of crude oil to produce gasoline
   (c) Cultivating vegetables in a farm
   (d) Construction of residential buildings

Ans. (i) (d), (ii) (b), (iii) (b), (iv) (c)

2. **Read the following source given below and answer the questions that follow**

   All those economic activities that provide support to people involved in primary and secondary activities are called tertiary activities or tertiary sector economic activities. These include services that we may not be able to see but which still play a very important role.

For example, the driver of a truck transports grains and vegetables from the farm to a factory or the market.

The fruit or vegetable vendors sell the farm produce to household consumers. Similarly, doctors, nurses, teachers, lawyers and pilots provide their services to those who need them. Some technicians repair and service electronic items including mobile phones and televisions, mechanics who repair vehicles like cars and tractors and electricians who ensure regular supply of electricity. Their services make our lives easier. Similarly, communication services through mobile and internet, software development and services at hotels, restaurants, banks, schools, hospitals, airports, shops, warehouses, etc. are all examples of tertiary sector economic activities. This sector is also called the service sector.

(i) What kinds of services are considered part of the tertiary sector, and how do they support primary and secondary activities?

(ii) How do tertiary sector activities contribute to making our lives easier?

(iii) Why is the tertiary sector also referred to as the service sector and what are some examples of services it includes?

Ans. (i) Services in the tertiary sector include transportation, vending, healthcare, education, legal services, repair and maintenance of electronic items, vehicle repair, and ensuring a regular supply of electricity.

These services support primary and secondary activities by facilitating the movement of goods, providing essential services to people, and maintaining the infrastructure required for primary and secondary activities to function smoothly.

(ii) Tertiary sector activities contribute to making our lives easier by providing essential services such as transportation, healthcare, education, legal advice, repair and maintenance of electronics and vehicles and ensuring a regular supply of electricity.

These services support our daily needs and enhance our quality of life.

(iii) The tertiary sector is referred to as the service sector because it primarily involves providing services rather than producing goods. Examples of services included in this sector are transportation, healthcare, education, legal services, communication, software development, hospitality, banking and retail. These services are essential for supporting other economic activities and improving the quality of life for individuals.

Competency Based Question

1. The most common primary activities are agriculture, mining, fishing, raising livestock, forestry, etc. Why?

Ans. The activities in which people are directly dependent on nature to produce goods are the primary activities. Agriculture, mining, fishing, raising livestock, forestry involves processes such as cultivation of grains and vegetables from agricultural farms, collecting wood from the forests, extracting coal from mines, fish from fisheries, eggs from poultry farms, etc.

Here, people are directly dependent on nature to produce output. That is why the given activities are the most common primary activities as in these activities.

Skill Based Questions as per NEP 2020

1. Give an example of how modern economic activities have evolved from traditional ones.

Ans. Traditional economic activities included agriculture, pottery and weaving. Over time, these have evolved into more complex and diverse activities.

For instance, while traditional agriculture focuses on basic crop cultivation, modern economic activities include manufacturing computers and mobile phones, software development and providing services in banks, schools and hotels. This evolution reflects the advancement in technology and the increased specialisation in different fields.

2. There is a bakery in your locality that is dependent on farming for fruits and mills for flour.Based on this example, discuss in class how the economic sectors interact with each other to produce goods and services?

Ans. Economic sectors interact by relying on each other's outputs to function. The primary sector provides raw materials, such as crops or minerals. The secondary sector processes these materials into products, like turning crops into flour or minerals into steel. The tertiary sector supports both by providing services like transportation, banking and retail, which help in distributing the finished products to consumers. This interdependence ensures a smooth flow from raw materials to finished goods and services.

ASSESSMENT EXERCISE

Objective Type Questions

1. Which sector involves activities directly dependent on nature?
(a) Primary sector
(b) Secondary sector
(c) Tertiary sector
(d) Quaternary sector

2. Which of the following is an example of a secondary sector activity?
(a) Fishing (b) Mining
(c) Manufacturing (d) Healthcare

3. What term describes a group of people who voluntarily come together to meet their economic and social needs?
(a) Corporation
(b) Cooperative
(c) Union
(d) Association

4. What process involves heating milk to kill harmful bacteria?
(a) Filtration (b) Fermentation
(c) Pasteurisation (d) Distillation

5. **Assertion** (A) The tertiary sector is also known as the service sector.

Reason (R) It includes activities like manufacturing and construction.

Codes
(a) Both A and R are true and R is the correct explanation of A
(b) Both A and R are true, but R is not the correct explanation of A
(c) A is true, but R is false
(d) A is false, but R is true

6. Activities that create monetary value are called .... activities.

7. The process of preserving milk through heating to a specific temperature is called...............

8. The secondary sector includes activities like banking and transportation. (True/False)

9. Dairy farming is considered as a primary sector activity. (True/False)

Subjective Questions (VSA, SA & LA)

1. What are the three main types of economic sectors?

2. Give two examples of primary sector activities.

3. Differentiate between primary sector and tertiary sector activities.

4. How secondary services are dependent on primary activities.

5. Explain the interdependence among the primary, secondary and tertiary sectors with examples.

Sample Question Paper 1 (Unsolved)
Social Science

Time : 3 hrs	M.M. : 80

General Instructions

1 All questions are compulsory.
2 Marks for each question are indicated against the question.

Multiple Choice Questions (MCQs)

1. Which statement about the Earth's shape is correct? **(1)**

(a) It is a perfect sphere.
(b) It is slightly flattened at the poles.
(c) It is completely flat.
(d) It is shaped like a cube.

2. The International Date Line is located approximately along which longitude? **(1)**

(a) 90°E (b) 0°
(c) 180° (d) 90°W

3. Which ocean lies to the East of India? **(1)**

(a) Atlantic Ocean (b) Pacific Ocean
(c) Arabian Sea (d) Bay of Bengal

4. Which of the following rivers originates from the Vindhya Range? **(1)**

(i) Ganga **(ii) Yamuna**
(iii) Ghagara **(iv) Son**

Codes

(a) Both (i) and (ii) (b) Only (iv)
(c) Both (iii) and (iv) (d) Only (iii)

5. Match the elements in column I with their correct description in column II. **(1)**

Column I	Column II
A. Geologists	1. Study the remains of plants, animals and humans from millions of years ago
B. Palaeontologist s	2. Study the physical features of the Earth
C. Archaeologists	3. Study human societies and cultures
D. Anthropologists	4. Study past remains left by humans, plants and animals

Codes

	A	B	C	D		A	B	C	D
(a)	2	1	4	3	(b)	1	2	3	4
(c)	4	3	2	1	(d)	3	2	1	4

6. Which of the following was an important crop grown by the Harappans? **(1)**

(a) Rice (b) Tea
(c) Coffee (d) Cocoa

7. What is a characteristic of a nuclear family? **(1)**

(a) Includes grandparents, parents and children
(b) Includes only a couple and their children
(c) Includes uncles, aunts and cousins
(d) Includes multiple generations living together

8. What does the term 'grassroots democracy' refer to? **(1)**

(a) Rule by a single leader
(b) Involvement of ordinary citizens in decision-making
(c) Avoiding elections
(d) Eliminating local governments

9. In the context of Indian governance, what does a Municipal Corporation handle? **(1)**

(a) National Defense
(b) City infrastructure and services
(c) International Relations
(d) State Education Policies

10. What is the primary role of the legislature in a government? **(1)**

(a) Implementing laws
(b) Making new laws
(c) Deciding whether laws are fair
(d) Enforcing laws

11. Assertion (A) The Equator is the largest circle that can be drawn on the Earth's surface.

Reason (R) The Equator is located at 90° latitude.

Codes

(a) Both A and R are true and R is the correct explanation of A.

(b) Both A and R are true, but R is not the correct explanation of A.

(c) A is true, but R is false.

(d) A is false, but R is true.

12. What is the name of India's first scientific base station in Antarctica? (1)

(a) Dakshin Bharat (b) Dakshin Gangotri

(c) Northern Star (d) Sagar Mata

13. Which of the following was not a characteristic of Harappan cities? (1)

(a) Wide streets oriented to cardinal directions

(b) Houses with individual bathrooms

(c) Large, open marketplaces

(d) Fortifications around the city

14. What does the term ' atman' refer to in Vedic culture? (1)

(a) The world

(b) The self

(c) The cosmos

(d) The divine essence of nature

Fill in the Blanks

1. Jainism emphasises the idea of ________, which means non-attachment to material possessions. (1)
2. The process of taking decisions, organising society's life with different sets of rules, and ensuring they are followed is called ________. (1)
3. The ________ branch of government implements laws and includes the head of state and ministers. (1)

True or False

1. The Ganga is the largest river originating in the Himalayas. (1)
2. Jambudvipa is derived from a tree native to India. (1)
3. The Harappans were the first in Eurasia to grow cotton. (1)

Very Short Answer Type Questions

1. Which mountain is known as the highest in South India? (2)
2. What is a significant feature of the Harappan reservoir at Dholavira? (2)

   Or

   What was a major feature of Harappan town-planning?
3. Which Indian plain supports a large population and agriculture? (2)
4. Suppose a historian finds conflicting accounts about a historical event in two different sources. How should they proceed? (2)
5. What did the 'People of India' project reveal about the linguistic diversity in India? (2)

   Or

   What is one feature of Indian literature that illustrates unity in diversity?

Short Answer Type Questions

1. Evaluate the importance of Harappan seals and their inscriptions in understanding trade and communication in the Indus-Sarasvati civilisation. (3)

   Or

   Examine the significance of agricultural practices in sustaining Harappan cities.
2. Discuss the reasons for the decline of the Indus-Sarasvati civilisation around 1900 BCE. (3)

   Or

   Describe the types of artifacts found in Harappan cities and what they reveal about daily life and social organisation.
3. Evaluate the role of community support as illustrated by the Bhil community's response to the water crisis and Kamal Parmar's initiative for underprivileged children. (3)
4. Discuss the concept of 'Participatory Democracy' and provide examples of how citizens can engage in governance at the local level. (3)
5. Explain how rivers contribute to the formation of floodplains and how these areas become ideal for agriculture. (3)
6. Discuss the environmental threats oceans facing today. (3)

Long Answer Type Questions

1. Explain the differences between joint and nuclear families, and discuss the advantages and disadvantages of each type. (5)

Or

Discuss the concept of 'dharma' in the context of family life. How does the principle of dharma influence the roles and responsibilities of family members?

2. Discuss the importance of the separation of powers in government. How does this separation prevent abuse of power and ensure fairness in governance? (5)

Or

Describe the roles and responsibilities of the three branches of government: legislature, executive and judiciary, and explain how they interact with each other to maintain governance.

3. Compare and contrast the teachings of Buddhism and Jainism, focusing on their core principles and how they address the concept of suffering and enlightenment. (5)

Or

What are the main features of Vedic society as described in the Rig Veda? How were the different janas or clans organised and governed?

Case Based Questions

1. Any government operates at two levels at the least - local and national. In many countries, including India, it functions at three levels or tiers - local, state or regional and national. Each level deals with different matters. To use a comparison, if a bulb in your home is not lighting up, you will first check the bulb, switch, fuse, etc. If that does not work, you may call an electrician, and if it is found that the problem is not within your home, you may need to go to the Electricity Board and file a complaint. These are also three levels of dealing with a problem.

   (i) Discuss why it is important for a country to have multiple tiers of government?

   (ii) In what ways does the presence of local governments enhance decision-making and problem-solving at the grassroots level? (1)

   (iii) Analyse how the interaction between local, state and national governments in India can lead to more effective governance, particularly in resolving complex problems. (2)

2. Today, there are diverse economic activities such as manufacturing computers, mobile phones and drones; working in banks, schools and hotels; driving various types of vehicles for transportation; making furniture; tailoring clothes using machines; creating software; repairing refrigerators and washing machines; etc. Classifying all these activities helps us to understand how they function and the links they have with each other.

   (i) Discuss how different sectors of the economy, such as manufacturing, services and transportation, contribute to the overall functioning of society. Provide examples. (1)

   (ii) Analyse the interdependence of various economic activities mentioned in the passage, such as manufacturing, transportation and services. (1)

   (iii) How has the rise of technology-based activities, such as creating software and repairing electronic appliances, transformed the traditional economic landscape? (2)

3. **Year after year, the region around the town of Jhabua, in Madhya Pradesh, suffered from an acute water crisis. Following their halma (see facing page) tradition of coming together to support any individual or family in times of crisis, the Bhil community decided to plant thousands of trees in hundreds of villages. The Bhils also dug many trenches to conserve rainwater and created other water harvesting structures. They did not get paid for this work but did it as their duty towards their community and the environment.**

   (i) Analyse the role of community-based initiatives, like the one taken by the Bhil community, in solving environmental challenges such as water scarcity. (1)

   (ii) Why do you think the Bhil community chose not to accept payment for their work in water conservation? What does this reveal about their values? (1)

   (iii). Why is it important for communities to take proactive steps in conserving natural resources? (2)

Map Based Questions

1. Locate the following on a world map. **(3)**

(i) Largest ocean in the world

(ii) The smallest ocean

(iii) Largest island in the world

2. On the given map of India, identify and label the following. **(2)**

(i) Identify and label the continents on the map that are generally considered to be two continents but if seen as a single landmass, they can also be considered as one.

(ii) Island group of India.

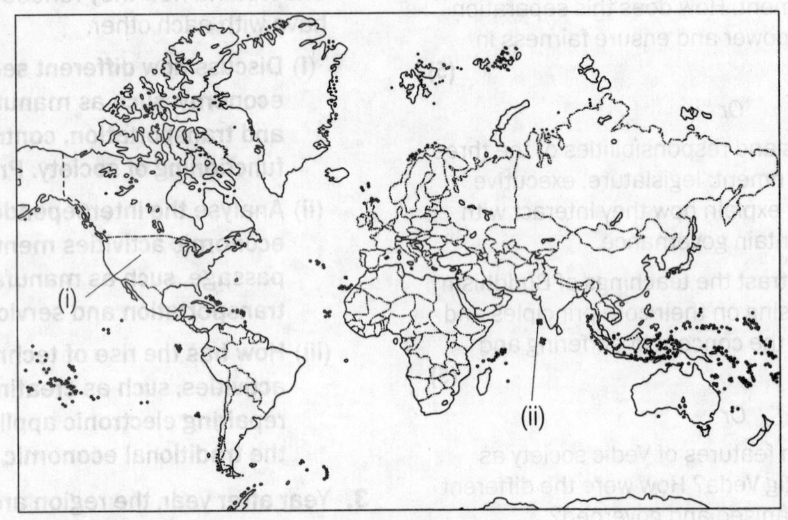

Answers

Multiple Choice Questions (MCQs)

1. (b)	2. (c)	3. (d)	4. (b)	5. (a)
6. (a)	7. (b)	8. (b)	9. (b)	10. (b)
11. (c)	12. (b)	13. (c)	14. (b)	

Fill in the Blanks

1. aparigraha 2. governance 3. executive

True or False

1. True 2. True 3. True

Map Based

2. (i) North America and South America
   (ii) Lakshadweep Islands

Sample Question Paper 2 (Unsolved)

Social Science

Time : 3 hrs	M.M. : 80

General Instructions

1 All questions are compulsory.

2 Marks for each question are indicated against the question.

Multiple Choice Questions (MCQs)

1. India's Standard Time is ahead of Greenwich Mean Time (GMT) by **(1)**

(a) 4 hours (b) 5 hours

(c) 5 hours 30 minutes (d) 6 hours

2. What is the latitude of the Equator? **(1)**

(a) 0° (b) 90°N

(c) 45°S (d) 180°

3. How did ancient Greeks refer to the region we now call India? **(1)**

(a) Hind (b) Yindu

(c) Indoi (d) Sindhu

4. What does 'dharma' represent in the context of family life? **(1)**

(a) Duty and responsibilities.

(b) Entertainment and leisure.

(c) Financial status.

(d) Educational qualifications.

5. What is the main role of a Residents' Welfare Association in urban communities? **(1)**

(a) To manage agricultural practices

(b) To create new job opportunities

(c) To make rules about waste management and cleanliness

(d) To provide financial assistance

6. Which of the following is a key feature of a democracy? **(1)**

(a) Direct rule by all citizens

(b) Representation through elected officials

(c) No laws or rules

(d) Control by a single leader

7. In which sector does transportation of goods fall? **(1)**

(a) Primary (b) Secondary

(c) Tertiary (d) Quaternary

8. Assertion (A) Oceans are vital for the survival of life on Earth. **(1)**

Reason (R) Oceans provide rain and more than half of the oxygen we breathe.

Codes

(a) Both A and R are true and R is the correct explanation of A.

(b) Both A and R are true, but R is not the correct explanation of A.

(c) A is true, but R is false

(d) A is false, but R is true

9. Match the elements in Column I with their correct description in column II. **(1)**

Column I	Column II
A. Common Era (CE)	1. Period of 1000 years
B. Before Common Era (BCE)	2. Years counted forward from Jesus Christ's birth
C. Century	3. Period of 100 years
D. Millennium	4. Years counted backward from Jesus Christ's birth

Codes

	A	B	C	D
(a)	4	1	3	2
(b)	1	2	3	4
(c)	3	4	2	1
(d)	2	4	3	1

10. Which activity would fall under non-economic activities? **(1)**

(a) A person running a small business.

(b) A mother helping her children with schoolwork.

(c) A truck driver transporting goods for a company.

(d) A technician operating machines at a construction site.

11. What type of payment is described as "payment in kind"? (1)

(a) Payment made through money
(b) Payment made through credit
(c) Payment received in the form of goods instead of cash
(d) Payment received for non-economic activities

12. Which of the following is a characteristic of primary sector activities? (1)

(a) They involve service provision
(b) They require the processing of raw materials
(c) They directly depend on nature
(d) They focus on the management of businesses

13. Which of the following activities belongs to the tertiary sector? (1)

(a) Coal mining
(b) Manufacturing of textiles
(c) Software development
(d) Crop cultivation

14. In the context of urban governance, what does a Ward Committee typically do? (1)

(a) Create national policies
(b) Manage city infrastructure
(c) Report local issues like water leaks
(d) Implement foreign policies

Fill in the Blanks

1. Harappan cities often had wide streets oriented to the ________ directions. **(1)**
2. The ancient text Rig Veda first mentions the ________ river. **(1)**
3. The Nohkalikai Falls are located on the ________ plateau. **(1)**

True or False

1. Mountains like the Aravalli Range are relatively younger than the Himalayas. **(1)**
2. The Ujjayini prime meridian was used in ancient Indian astronomy. **(1)**
3. The Equator divides the Earth into the Eastern and Western Hemispheres. **(1)**

Very Short Answer Type Questions

1. What do we call land surrounded by water on all sides? **(2)**
2. List any one feature of Indian literature that illustrates unity in diversity. **(2)**

   Or

   How has the sari been used creatively beyond just a dress?
3. Imagine an archaeologist discovers a set of ancient tools buried under a city. What could this tell us about the civilisation that used them? **(2)**
4. What evidence shows that Harappans engaged in long-distance trade? **(2)**

   Or

   What type of structures were commonly used in Harappan cities for water management?
5. What is the primary economic activity on plateaus due to their mineral deposits? **(2)**

Short Answer Type Questions

1. Describe the three main components of a map and explain why each is important. **(3)**
2. There is a connection between latitude and climate. Explain. **(3)**

   Or

   The Greenwich Meridian is not the first prime meridian. Justify the statement.
3. Compare and contrast young mountains like the Himalayas with order mountain ranges such as the Aravalli range. **(3)**
4. Discuss the importance of oceans in regulating the Earth's climate and how they contribute to life on the planet. **(3)**
5. Describe the secondary sector and its significance in the transformation of raw materials from the primary sector into finished products. **(3)**

   Or

   Examine the role of the tertiary sector in supporting both the primary and secondary sectors.
6. Evaluate the significance of sacred mountains in different cultures. **(3)**

Long Answer Type Questions

1. Explain the classification of economic activities into the primary, secondary and tertiary sectors. How do these sectors interrelate in the process of economic production? **(5)**

Or

Discuss the role of the primary sector in economic development. Provide examples of different primary sector activities and how they contribute to the economy.

2. Describe the evolution of human societies from hunter-gatherers to agricultural communities. How did the shift to settled farming communities influence social structures and the development of villages? **(5)**

Or

Analyse how different sources of history contribute to our knowledge of the past. Why is it important to use multiple sources when studying history?

3. Explain the differences between economic and non-economic activities. Provide examples of each and discuss how these activities impact both individuals and society. **(5)**

Or

What are non-economic activities and why are they considered valuable despite not generating income? Explain with the help of examples.

Case Based Questions

1. Altogether, urban local bodies are responsible for a range of functions - helping take care of the infrastructure, maintaining the burial ground, garbage collection and disposal, checking the implementation of government schemes, collecting local taxes and fines and so on. They also have some role in planning for the area's economic and social development. However, for these bodies to be able to perform their functions efficiently, people living in the city must also perform their duties, which means that they must show care and concern for their area (remember, this is a participatory democracy).

(i) How do urban local bodies ensure the implementation of government schemes and the collection of local taxes? Discuss the significance of these functions for city management. (1)

(ii) Explain the relationship between participatory democracy and the efficient functioning of urban local bodies. How does citizen involvement influence governance? (1)

(iii) How do urban local bodies contribute to grassroots democracy? (2)

2. Over the decades, the number of economic activities has increased tremendously. For example, earlier most people were involved in activities such as agriculture, livestock rearing, production of tools, pottery and weaving cloth. As societies progressed, the number of economic activities through which people earn their livelihoods increased vastly.

(i) Compare the types of economic activities people were traditionally engaged in with the modern economic activities that exist today. (1)

(ii) How do technological advancements contribute to the increase in economic activities over time? (1)

(iii) How do modern economic activities differ from traditional ones in terms of skills and resources required? (2)

3. Around 1900 BCE, this Sindhu-Sarasvati civilisation, despite all its achievements, began to fall apart. The cities were abandoned one by one. If any inhabitants remained, they adopted a rural lifestyle in the changed environment - it appears that the earlier government or administration no longer existed. Gradually the Harappans scattered over hundreds, if not thousands, of small rural settlements.

(i) Discuss the possible reasons for the decline and abandonment of cities in the Sindhu-Sarasvati civilisation around 1900 BCE. (1)

(ii) How did the lifestyle of the Harappans change after the cities were abandoned? (1)

(iii) Discuss how the abandonment of cities in the Sindhu-Sarasvati civilisation might have affected trade, economy and social organisation. (2)

Map Based Questions

1. On the political map of India , locate the following. (3)

(i) State in which the site of Kalibangan is located.

(ii) First site in the Indus Valley Civilisation to be excavated.

(iii) State in which the site of Dholavira is located.

2. On the given map of India, identify and label the following.

(i) Identify the first city of the Indus-Sarasvati civilisation to be discovered.

(ii) The site which is believed to have been an ancient dockyard.

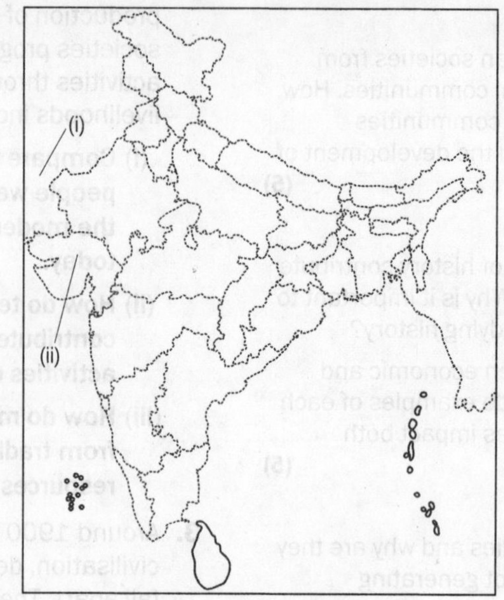

Answers

Multiple Choice Questions (MCQs)

1. (c)	2. (a)	3. (c)	4. (a)	5. (c)
6. (b)	7. (c)	8. (a)	9. (d)	10. (b)
11. (c)	12. (c)	13. (c)	14. (c)	

Fill in the Blanks

1. Cardinal 2. Sarasvati 3. Cherrapunji

True or False

1. False 2. True 3. False

Map Based

2. (i) Mohenjo-daro (ii) Lothal

Sample Question Paper 3 (Unsolved)
Social Science

Time : 3 hrs	M.M. : 80

General Instructions

1 All questions are compulsory.

2 Marks for each question are indicated against the question.

Multiple Choice Questions (MCQs)

1. Which Vedic deity is associated with the oceans in Indian mythology? **(1)**

(a) Indra (b) Agni

(c) Varuna (d) Surya

2. What is the primary source of the world's oxygen production? **(1)**

(a) Forests (b) Oceans

(c) Ponds (d) Deserts

3. Assertion (A) Plateaus are less faovrable to farming than plains. **(1)**

Reason (R) Most plateaus have rocky soil, making them less fertile than plains.

Codes

(a) Both A and R are true and R is the correct explanation of A

(b) Both A and R are true, but R is not the correct explanation of A

(c) A is true, but R is false

(d) A is false, but R is true

4. What term is used to refer to the years before the conventional date of Jesus' birth? **(1)**

(a) AD (b) CE

(c) BCE (d) BC

5. What is the focus of anthropology as a discipline? **(1)**

(a) The study of physical features of the Earth.

(b) The study of human societies and cultures.

(c) The study of fossils and ancient remains.

(d) The study of ancient inscriptions.

6. Which term from the Mahabharata refers to the Indian subcontinent? **(1)**

(a) Bharatavarsha (b) Sapta Sindhava

(c) Jambudvipa (d) Hind

7. Which of the following is not a characteristic of Harappan civilisation? **(1)**

(a) Development of writing systems

(b) Formation of complex government and administration

(c) Development of advanced metallurgy techniques

(d) Exclusive reliance on hunting and gathering

8. What type of objects were commonly exported by the Harappans? **(1)**

(a) Precious stones and metals

(b) Agricultural tools and clothing

(c) Ornaments, beads and possibly cotton

(d) Military weapons and armor

9. Match the Harappan cities from Column I with their corresponding modern states or regions from column II. **(1)**

	Column I		Column II
A.	Harappa	1.	Punjab
B.	Mohenjo-daro	2.	Sindh
C.	Dholavira	3.	Rajasthan
D.	Kalibangan	4.	Gujarat

Codes

	A	B	C	D		A	B	C	D
(a)	1	2	4	3	(b)	2	3	4	1
(c)	4	1	2	4	(d)	1	2	3	4

10. Which organ of government is responsible for enforcing laws? **(1)**

(a) Judiciary (b) Legislature

(c) Executive (d) Parliament

11. What is the main purpose of rules and laws in society? **(1)**

(a) To restrict freedom

(b) To maintain order and harmony

(c) To increase confusion

(d) To eliminate jobs

12. What is the primary role of the Gram Panchayat in the Panchayati Raj system? (1)

(i) Overseeing district-level administrative functions

(ii) Implementing national policies

(iii) Addressing local issues and promoting development

(iv) Conducting state elections

Codes

(a) Only (i) and (iii) (b) Only (iii)
(c) Only (iv) (d) None of these

13. In the context of economic activities, what is 'value addition'? (1)

(a) Adding more time to complete a task.
(b) Transforming something into another form that has monetary value.
(c) Increasing the number of people involved in an activity.
(d) Reducing the cost of production.

14. Which of the following is an example of an economic activity? (1)

(a) Volunteering to teach computer skills
(b) Cooking food for family
(c) Selling furniture made from wood
(d) Taking care of grandparents

Fill in the Blanks

1. The term 'millennium' refers to a period of ____ years. (1)
2. The Mahabharata uses the terms 'Bharatavarsha' and '____' to describe the Indian subcontinent. (1)
3. The word "Veda" comes from the Sanskrit word '________,' which means 'knowledge.' (1)

True or False

1. Pañchangas are still widely used in India to list days of the month and related astronomical data. (1)
2. The term 'Hindustan' was first used by the ancient Greeks to refer to India. (1)
3. The Vedas were originally written down in text form. (1)

Very Short Answer Type Questions

1. A new tourist destination is being developed in a mountainous region. What measures should be taken to protect the fragile mountain environment? (2)
2. Which Indian plateau is known for having huge reserves of iron coal and manganese? (2)

   Or

   What term is used to describe water falling from the sky in solid form?
3. What is the term used in the Rig Veda to describe the North-West region of the Indian subcontinent? (2)

   Or

   What does the term 'Bharatavarsha' mean?
4. Which natural disaster can originate in the ocean and cause widespread damage to coastal areas? (2)
5. Which continents are symbolised by the five rings in the Olympic Games? (2)

Short Answer Type Questions

1. Explain the challenges and opportunities associated with living in mountainous regions. Provide examples. (3)
2. What is the Gregorian calendar, and how is it commonly used today? (3)
3. Describe the agricultural practices of the Harappans and their importance to the civilisation. (3)
4. Using the example of AMUL, describe how a cooperative model can impact economic activities in rural areas. (3)

   Or

   Analyse the interdependence among the primary, secondary and tertiary sectors using a detailed example.
5. Discuss the life and teachings of Siddhartha Gautama. (3)

   Or

   Describe the key principles of Jainism as taught by Mahavira.
6. How do oceans contribute to the cultural, economic, and historical development of human societies? Provide examples of how oceans have shaped human migration, trade and expansion. (3)

Long Answer Questions

1. Describe the three-tier structure of the Panchayati Raj system in India. Discuss the key functions and responsibilities of each tier in the governance and development of rural areas. (5)

Or

Discuss the importance of the Panchayati Raj system in strengthening democracy at the grassroots level. How does it facilitate local participation in decision-making processes?

2. Discuss the various theories proposed to explain the decline of the Indus-Sarasvati civilisation. Which factors are most widely accepted by archaeologists? **(5)**

Or

The term 'civilisation' is used for an advanced stage of human societies.Discuss the essential characteristics of a civilisation.

3. Evaluate the role of textiles and clothing, specifically the sari, in representing the unity and diversity of Indian culture. **(5)**

Or

Analyse the impact of Indian epics, such as the Ramayana and the Mahabharata, on the cultural unity and diversity across different communities in India. How have these epics been adapted and interpreted in various regional and tribal contexts?

Case Based Questions

1. The Harappans were engaged in active trade, not only within their own civilisation (other cities nearby or far away), but with other civilisations and cultures within and outside India. They exported ornaments, timber, and some objects of daily use, probably also gold and cotton, and possibly some food items. The most favoured ornaments were beads of carnelian , a reddish semi precious stone found mostly in Gujarat. Harappan craftspeople developed special techniques to drill them, so a string could pass through them, and to decorate them in various ways. They also worked conch shells into beautiful shell bangles, which requires sophisticated techniques as shell is a hard material.

(i) What was one of the main reasons Harappan craftspeople were able to work with carnelian beads? (1)

(ii) Describe the types of goods that the Harappans likely exported and the possible benefits they derived from this trade. (1)

(iii) What can be inferred about the Harappans' trade practices based on the types of goods they exported and imported? (2)

2. The strength of community participation The Swachh Bharat Abhiyan is based on the collective efforts of all Indian citizens to keep our surroundings clean. Individually, we keep our homes and surroundings clean. People have also come together to clean up streets, roads, parks and other public places or community areas. Together, these efforts lead to a clean home, neighbourhood, society and nation. Another example of collective community participation is the celebration of Van Mahotsav (the festival of forests) in India to promote awareness about the value of trees and the conservation of forests. The initiative brings together members of the community for tree plantation drives.

(i) Describe how non-economic activities, such as volunteering and community service, contribute to societal development. (1)

(ii) Evaluate the impact of the Swachh Bharat Abhiyan on community cleanliness. (1)

(iii) How do these initiatives demonstrate the strength of community involvement in addressing environmental issues? (2)

3. Hiware Bazar, a village in Ahmednagar district of Maharashtra, used to be affected by frequent droughts and poor agricultural yield. After Popatrao Baguji Pawar became its Sarpanch, he started applying Anna Hazare's model of rainwater harvesting, watershed conservation and massive tree planting of lakhs of trees, all of which contributed to the recharge of groundwater. With the collaboration of the villagers, Hiware Bazar became a green and prosperous village in a few years. Shri Popatrao Pawar was awarded the Padma Shri in 2020.

(i) List three key measures taken by Popatrao Pawar to address the problems in Hiware Bazar. (1)

(ii) How did the collective efforts of the villagers contribute to transforming Hiware Bazar into a prosperous village? (1)

(iii) What was the impact of massive tree planting on the village of Hiware Bazar? How did it contribute to its prosperity? (2)

Map Based Questions

1. On the political map of India , locate the following. **(3)**

(i) Highest mountain in South India

(ii) 2 highest peaks of the Himalayan range

(iii) Mountain ranges which are much older and have been rounded by erosion

2. On the given map of India, identify and label the following. **(2)**

(i) Anaimudi is located in this region.

(ii) The largest and highest plateau in the world.

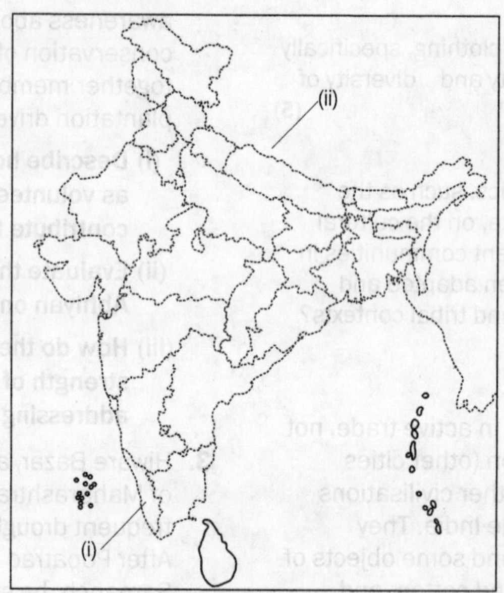

Answers

Multiple Choice Questions (MCQs)

1. (c) 2. (b) 3. (a) 4. (c) 5. (b)
6. (a) 7. (d) 8. (c) 9. (a) 10. (c)
11. (b) 12. (b) 13. (b) 14. (c)

Fill in the Blanks

1. 1,000 2. Jambudvipa 3. Vid

True or False

1. True 2. False 3. False

Map Based

2. (i) Kerala (ii) Tibetan plateau